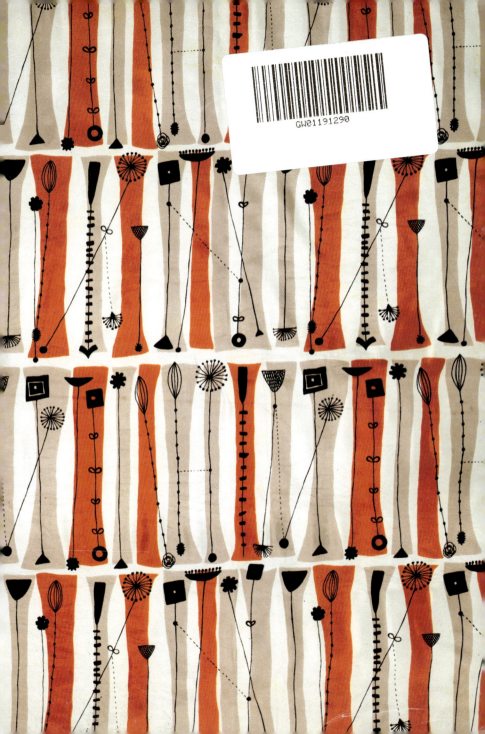

A WOMAN'S PLACE
1910–1975

Persephone Book N°20
Published by Persephone Books Ltd 2000

First published 1975 by Chatto & Windus

© The Estate of Ruth Adam 2000

Preface © Yvonne Roberts 2000

Endpapers taken from 'Palisade', a 1952 screen-printed
acetate rayon furnishing taffeta designed by Lucienne Day
for British Celanese Ltd and marketed by Sanderson's,
reproduced by courtesy of the Trustees of the
Victoria & Albert Museum, London

Typeset in ITC Baskerville by Keystroke,
Jacaranda Lodge, Wolverhampton

Printed and bound by Biddles Ltd,
Guildford and King's Lynn

ISBN 1 903155 096

Persephone Books Ltd
28 Great Sutton Street
London EC1V 0DS
020 7253 5454

www.persephonebooks.co.uk

A WOMAN'S PLACE
1910–1975

by

RUTH ADAM

with a new afterword by

YVONNE ROBERTS

PERSEPHONE BOOKS
LONDON

CONTENTS

1	**A MAN'S WORLD 1910–1914**	1
	1. *The Power and the Glory*	1
	2. *Liberated Wives*	8
	3. *The Superfluous Women*	16
	4. *The Suffragettes*	32
2	**WHEN THE BOYS WERE FAR AWAY 1914–1918**	41
	1. *Men Who March Away*	41
	2. *The Munition-Girls*	54
	3. *The Land-Girls*	65
	4. *The V.A.D.s*	68
	5. *The Unmarried Mothers*	73
3	**THE BOYS COME HOME 1918–1920**	83
	1. *Into Parliament*	83
	2. *Back to the Kitchen*	94
	3. *Case for Unequal Pay*	109
4	**THE SEX REVOLUTION 1920–1930**	113
	1. *The Mutilated Society*	113
	2. *The Amazons*	129
	3. *The Women M.P.s*	148

5 DEPRESSION 1930–1939 — 157
1. *Unemployed Breadwinners* — 157
2. *Pin-money Wives* — 171
3. *Marriage – the Perpetual Honeymoon* — 178
4. *Divorce* — 186
5. *Peace Ballot* — 190

6 WOMEN IN UNIFORM 1939–1945 — 194
1. *Evacuation* — 194
2. *Conscription* — 201
3. *Planning Utopia* — 213
4. *Whose Children?* — 221

7 WIVES AND MOTHERS AGAIN 1945–1960 — 226
1. *Woman's Place in the Home* — 226
2. *Broken Homes* — 239
3. *Failed Marriages* — 245
4. *Affluent Working Wives* — 251

8 EMANCIPATION 1960–1970 — 257
1. *The Teenagers* — 257
2. *Abortion* — 268
3. *The Churches and the Permissive Society* — 270
4. *Equal Education* — 273
5. *Equal Pay* — 279

9	WOMEN ALONE 1970 onwards	282
	1. *The Polygamous Society*	282
	2. *Fatherless Families*	287
	3. *Unrationed Sex*	295
	4. *Women's Lib*	299

References	308
Index	318
Afterword	325

A WOMAN'S PLACE
1910–1975

CHAPTER ONE

A MAN'S WORLD
1910–1914

1. *The Power and the Glory*

There were too many women in Britain, as her great days of power and wealth drew towards their close. At the beginning of the reign of King George V, it was taken for granted that the birth of a daughter must be a disappointment, in any walk of life, because men were in short supply and it was a man's world. All the colour and romance of having an Empire – the beautiful uniforms which made women look as drab as peahens by comparison, the marching processions with their blood-stirring music and throbbing drums, and the great ships riding the storms – belonged to the men. The possession of all those faraway countries, coloured pink on the globe, as every schoolchild knew, depended on the men of the navy, the army and the colonial service. That made them an élite caste, regarded, by the public, with the awed respect which priests got, in more devout countries. (British parsons were not encouraged to put on spiritual airs, but to stick to the conventional public-school image.) It was the men of the forces and the imperial officials who had a special aura, because they were the ordinary stay-at-home citizen's link with his Empire. They came and went between the homeland and that other world beyond the seas, which was preached about, and sung and prayed about, but not seen.

Its existence, however, was proved by certain familiar phenomena; by the retired Indian civil servant with his brass trays and model elephants and his fiery temper, now living in Bexhill; by the sailor-boy on leave from Malta whose collar one touched for luck, as he passed in the street; and by the real-life prototype of Kipling's ex-sergeant, shivering in the English drizzle, dreaming of the China Sea:

> ... Learnin' 'ere in London what the ten-year sodger tells;
> If you've 'eard the East a-callin', why you won't 'eed nothin' else. . . .
> No! you won't 'eed nothin' else
> But them spicy garlic smells
> An' the sunshine and the palm trees an' the tinkly temple bells!
> On the road to Mandalay . . . [1]

Even the humblest British male who held no place in the service of the Empire thought of himself as part of it. The shabby, round-shouldered city clerk, who would never rise any higher than stepping into the dead man's shoes of the next one up, nevertheless had no doubt that he was a member of the ruling race and the natural superior of the 344 million natives who were also the subjects of King George. The unemployed miner, squatting on his haunches at a street corner in Durham, could always tell himself that if things didn't take a turn for the better, he would go out and try his luck in the colonies. The black sheep expelled from his public school had the consolation of knowing there were traditional refuges for his kind, where they could redeem themselves by roughing it, out there in the wide open spaces. The Empire gave men an identity, a silent pride in being British, a patriotism passing the love of women.

The most popular symbol of Britain's power was the Royal Navy. 'All the nice girls love a sailor', sang the seaside pierrots, and Board School pupils in midland cities, who had never seen the sea in their lives, learned more songs about naval battles and the satisfaction of dying that way than about any other single topic. ('There'll be many a grim and gory, there'll be few to tell the story, But we'll all be one in glory on the Fighting Téméraire!') It was quite 'the thing', as the Government's *Annual Report on Sea Fisheries* noted approvingly, for steady young fishermen who were thinking of getting married, to join the Royal Naval Reserve – 'the pay being a much-prized addition to their earnings'.[2] Naval uniform of any kind was the most admired male costume. Any children whose parents could afford Sunday-best clothes for them wore sailor blouses and miniature ratings' caps with an H.M.S. ribbon on them. The upper-class London child's regular Christmas holiday treat was to be taken to *Where the Rainbow Ends*, which told the story of two naval cadets who set out, with their sisters, on a magic carpet, to defeat the forces of evil. Its message was that Britain needed a larger navy than that of Germany. For three Christmas seasons before the war, a boy actor named Noël Coward played in it. (Thirty years later he played the naval-officer hero in the war-time propaganda film *In Which We Serve*. The message was still the same.)

The naval cadet was the ideal son-figure. The mother who could walk down the street with her miniature sailor by her side was the envy of her neighbours. She did not often get the chance of showing him off, because the education system of the period was to take middle- and upper-class boys away from the emasculating influence of their mothers. Naval cadets were finally withdrawn to be licked into shape for the man's world, in their early teens.

'Bartimeus' – a favourite naval propagandist of the period – described the process in *A Man in the Making*. On his last night at home, before he is sent overseas, Euan is given a private talk by his father. '"You know about women, Euan, and all that. This ain't going to be a pi-jaw, but there's only one way to keep a clean mind and that's to sweat good and hearty every day and turn in dog tired. . . . Go on believing in the things your mother taught you. Don't get too jolly manly to say your prayers and write home once a week." He turned and strode to the door, "Come back a man. Good night."'

Next day, when the parents return to their empty house, Euan's mother, for the first time, weakens so far as to give 'a sort of gulp. "*Why* did we do it? Oh why?" Her husband pressed her arm as they retraced their steps. "Because he's all we've got. All we prize and love and value in the world. He's good stuff, Nina, though I say it what shouldn't. He's worthy of the Empire. And now, so are we."'

THE POWER AND THE GLORY

As it turns out, apart from a girl in Malta with a flower in her glossy hair, who 'murmured something in Spanish and kissed him lightly on the cheek', Euan has no woman problem as he 'learns to acquire the standards of tradition and caste by daily experience . . . and not a little of it was the fruit of physical pain.' At night, the Lieutenant of the Watch sends him, with a signet-ring to indicate the reason, to the Sub who is waiting alone in the Mess and whose enviable duty it is to beat the boys.

The officer rose lazily from the only armchair the Mess boasted, put the ring in his pocket and selected a flexible rattan cane from the rack. 'Smell the spot' – and Euan knelt on the settee with his nose flattened against the surface of the table in an attitude undignified but eminently appropriate to the business in hand. The Sub stepped back a pace, measured his surroundings with the rattan to ensure a free hand and passed the tip of his tongue over his thin lips. . . . 'Tighter than that'. . . .

Euan's fellow-cadet grins sympathetically when Euan returns,

rather white and with a queer hiccupy desire to sob somewhere in his throat. 'How many? Six? That's nothing, when I was a wart I had to turn out and take a dozen and a half in my pyjamas from the Sub to amuse one of his guests after dinner.'

This passage could be safely included in a book intended for mothers and sweethearts to read, as well as men, because the pre-1914 woman was kept in comfortable ignorance of the homosexual patterns of the man's world. Since these were woven into the whole grand design of militarist-imperialist culture, from the little boys' preparatory school upwards, it must have been the best-kept secret in British history. Clemence Dane's heroine, Elinor Broome, stumbles on it when her eldest son explains why his younger brother has run away from school to escape the attentions of his seniors.

D'you mean to tell me, Richard, that all over England fathers can know that there's a risk of their own sons, boys of ten and eleven, being frightened as John has been frightened, and that they let it go on? It's not credible! D'you suppose if women knew – d'you suppose that if I'd known, I'd have let it happen?[3]

Mothers of sons, however, although prevented from knowing the truth about what happened to their young sons in the Greek-based educational system of the man's world (a concealment which incidentally had not been considered necessary among the ancient Greeks) did have all the status and the credit owed to them as producers.

Euan himself, patrolling the Empire on which the sun never sets, reflects, with a tightening of the heart-strings, how an empire demands other sacrifices, how, in order that men might die to martial music, women must give an even greater heroism of self-denial. Years of thrift and contrivance, new clothes foresworn, a thousand renunciations, this had been his mother's part, that her son might in time bear his share of the Empire's burden.

Mothers of the period prayed to have a son rather than a daughter. The majority had their prayer answered. An average 1,039 males were born for every 1,000 females, according to the census of 1911. But the boys were not as tough as their sisters, who had a lower death-rate at all ages, particularly from birth to five years old. Therefore the position was reversed, as the boys and girls grew up, so that by the time a young woman reached marriageable age there were not enough bridegrooms to go round.[4] The supply was further reduced by the constant drain of men in their prime to administer the colonies, who were only in the country on 'home leave', at three-yearly intervals, for the period of their working life, and also by an increasing number of eligible bachelors who left home permanently, to start a new life overseas. Between the accession of George V in 1910 and the outbreak of the 1914 War, the number of emigrants of this kind rose from an annual 284,000 to an annual 454,000.[5] Most of them were young, single, working men, who had despaired of ever getting a steady job with an adequate wage in Britain. Their loss was a matter of concern, not only to the generation of girls who might have been their brides, but also to the ruling hierarchy, because they were afraid that the nation would be short of recruits in the anticipated war against the German Emperor. Their only consolation was that at least the young men were no longer emigrating chiefly to the United States but to Britain's loyal colonies, from which they would be more likely to hurry home if called to defend the Mother Country.

2. *Liberated Wives*

The fact that there was a large female majority in the population – 1,327,000 in 1911 – coloured the whole outlook of a girl from early childhood onwards. Her first nursery card-game – in which there was no winner, only a loser left humiliatingly unpartnered – was 'Old Maid'. From then on, she was kept in order by the fear of ultimate rejection by the male. E. M. Delafield (later the famous *Provincial Lady* diarist) says of her pre-1914 girlhood that she 'could never remember a time when she had not known that a woman's failure or success in life depended entirely on whether or not she succeeded in getting a husband. It was not even a question of marrying well, though mothers with pretty and attractive daughters naturally hoped for that. But any husband at all was better than none.' Anxious mothers handed on warning folk-lore on the subject to their daughters. 'A girl who gets herself talked about is done for. She gets left.' 'Men don't propose to "actressy" women.' 'Men like a girl to seem bright and happy and enjoy things.' 'Women who want to get married and can't often turn very queer as they grow older.'[6]

Just over half the female population had a husband, just over a tenth had had one and lost him, through death or divorce. The spinsters were referred to, officially, as 'the superfluous women' though the bachelor majority out in the colonies were never referred to as 'the superfluous men'.

It was particularly unlucky that bridegrooms should be in such short supply at the very time when the institution of marriage was developing into a new and liberal pattern. Since the Married Women's Property Acts, a wife had a legal right to her own earnings and her own capital. Other changes in the law took away a husband's legal right to shut her up in the house, and to arrange for someone else to have control of their children after his death. These changes were important, (although they only affected married couples who were already in dispute with each other) because the history of women's emancipation was to be built on the patient amendment of such laws affecting women. But the really important change at the beginning of the twentieth century, which affected the majority of wives and transformed everyday married life, was the drop in family size.

Victorian marriage had been about raising a large family. The average completed family size was between five and six children. Over 40% of families had seven or more and 16% had ten or more. Since the infant mortality rate stayed steadily at 157 per thousand for the whole of the Victorian era, this meant that the average wife must expect to bury at least one baby, apart from losing children through chronic or epidemic diseases.[7] The larger her family the more children's death-beds she would probably have to remember. Beatrice Webb, whose seven elder sisters all married 'well' – that is, to rich and personable young men on the way up – was depressed by seeing most of them change from joyful, adventurous girls into sickly, grumbling matrons, grimly welcoming miscarriages and haunted by suspicion about what their husbands were up to, while they were tied to sickbed and nursery.[8]

'Painful to me to see her so poorly and painful to be with her', she wrote in her diary, of her favourite sister Maggie now pregnant and 'seedy and miserable, the natural result of the condition of married existence.'[9] When it came to her own turn, Beatrice deliberately chose to make a late, childless union, based on intellectual companionship, with Sidney Webb, and never regretted it. (In fact the 'junta' – of the early Fabian society, who were the intellectual leaders of their own world – set an example of restraint in family size. The Webbs, the Shaws and the Wallases only produced one child among three marriages.)

The change from the large nineteenth-century family to the small twentieth-century one, as a social custom, took place with startling speed, so that mothers could be shocked or envious (probably both) at the difference between the life of their married daughters and their own past. The transformation was brought about – not by a Lysistrata-type political campaign or by a change of heart on the part of the male sex – but, like most of the landmarks in women's emancipation, by a material fact; which in this case was the invention of convenient birth-control equipment.

In 1877, Annie Besant and Charles Bradlaugh had been prosecuted for publishing information about it. By 1886, the entirely respectable *Wife's Handbook* had a note about 'Malthusian appliances'. By 1905 the popular magazine *Myra* had what the *Lancet* scoldingly described as a 'filthy advertisement' which was the picture of a rubber contraceptive sheath and by 1911 the Census showed that the people making most use of it were doctors and their wives. By this time, the birth-rate had dropped from 35.4 per thousand to 26.3. There was a wide difference between that of the well-off and educated, who could get hold of the information and the equipment and that of the ignorant poor, for instance 17.5 in Hampstead as opposed to 30.2 in Shoreditch.[10] But it was clear that the secret was spreading downwards. The Hearts of Oak Friendly Society, which was composed of skilled artisans and small tradesmen, found its claim for 'lying-in benefit' for members' wives reduced to half of what it used to be. By the time George V was crowned, the average family size was down to just under three. Spaced-out pregnancies gave the babies a better chance, both at birth and through undivided attention during their first year. The infant mortality rate ran down to 110 per thousand and continued to shrink.

The release from continual child-bearing and child-rearing was the starting-point of women's emancipation. A wife's time was no longer ear-marked, from the year of the wedding to the change of life, for whole-time duties of motherhood, nor her energy drained by pregnancies in close succession. The early twentieth-century women had the time, and the health – and above all the spirit – to agitate for better conditions for themselves, for education, for careers and for the vote. They *felt* emancipated, themselves. They believed themselves to be happier women than their mothers and grandmothers. And even if the happiness of any generation of wives, compared with any other, is impossible to measure, at least these neo-Georgian ones, who had fewer dead children to mourn than any women before them, had one certain cause of unhappiness the less.

Young couples now aimed at having a higher standard of living for a smaller family, and there was a great building boom of smaller houses with smaller rooms to accommodate them. Public transport had spread further outside the cities and the newly wed couple were able to live in a modern house in a modern suburb, with tree-lined roads and little gardens. Here they could join the tennis-club together or go for a spin on their bicycles into the country on Saturday afternoons. (The bicycle did more to liberate the pre-1914 woman than any other machine, not excepting the typewriter. Not only did it make her completely mobile at minimum cost but enabled her to roam about on her own, without the watchful eyes of either her own household or the neighbours on her. George Gissing's 'odd women' who always got caught out either in secret drinking or secret sex would have had their fortunes transformed by the possession of a bicycle.)

Even a young clerk could probably afford to provide his wife with a living-in maid, at from £10 to £23 a year, and if not, he could at least buy her some of the new labour-saving devices which were advertised in the popular papers, to provide for the new kind of life now led by the middle-class housewife: the 'labour-saving carpet-sweeper' with the promise of a vacuum-cleaner just round the corner and the 'patent washing-machine'. For 2s 3d a quarter the young couple could hire a gas-stove, which, as the maker hinted, was 'very useful where ladies have to do their own work and where actual labour must be reduced to a minimum'.

The new vogue was for a light-hearted jokey comradeship between husband and wife. *Punch* recommended novels of married life which described such couples as 'the Tracy Tubbses, who embraced each other with magnificent heartiness whenever they had a moment to spare from their domestic problems'. More sophisticated couples took their ideas from Bernard Shaw's *Candida* and *Man and Superman*; from H. G. Wells' *Ann Veronica* and James Barrie's *What Every Woman Knows*. All of these mocked the authoritative, know-all husband and made it clear that British men simply make tedious fools of themselves when they try to dictate to their wives and daughters. In any case, all the popular humorists made a practice of caricaturing the pompous German husband, who strutted about in over-elaborate uniform and relegated his wife to Küche, Kirche und Kinder, and no English husband wanted to be anything like him. One of the most popular books of the period was *The Caravanners*, by the Countess Russell, who was already well-known for her ironic sketches of German life in *Elizabeth and Her German Garden*. Now she wrote about the adventures of an arrogant Prussian officer and his meek wife, sharing a caravan holiday with English friends. In the book she describes the easy comradeship of the English married couple, and how it gives the German Frau the spirit to rebel against the way she is treated by her husband. The crestfallen Prussian consoles himself by reflecting that the weak good nature of the British male will make the country easy to conquer in the approaching Anglo-German war.

The new attitude about fairness and equality in married life now stretched to divorce. The case of *Stark v. Stark and Hitchins* in 1910 was a landmark. Up till then, the accepted rule had been that no punishment could possibly be too severe, if a wife actually committed adultery. She could lose her husband's support and have her home and children taken away from her, because, as one judge explained, 'It will probably have a salutary effect on the interests of public morality that it should be known that a woman, if found guilty of adultery, will forfeit, as far as this court is concerned, all rights to the custody of or access to her children.' Mrs Stark had been divorced and eventually married the co-respondent. Her daughter ran away from her father to her mother, who was imprisoned for not sending her back. But the Court of Appeal freed her, and made history by laying down the principle that 'the benefit and interest of the infant is the paramount consideration, and not the punishment of the guilty party'.

Reform of the divorce law was in the air, with 'Ann Veronica' running away with her lover who could not get a divorce, and living happily ever after. (The couple bore a noticeable resemblance to the author and Amber Reeves, the girl with whom he had run away, to the embarrassment of his Fabian friends, whose talk of sexual freedom had not meant quite that.) Bernard Shaw's *Getting Married* made a plea for simplified laws of everything concerning marriage. John Galsworthy's *Justice* described the plight of the heroine who cannot free herself from a violent and dangerous husband because he has not been adulterous as well as brutal. The law was that a wife could be divorced for adultery alone; a husband only for adultery if it was 'aggravated' by another matrimonial offence.

A Royal Commission under Lord Gorell had been appointed to examine Divorce and Matrimonial Causes. It produced a report recommending that the grounds for dissolving marriage should be adultery; wilful desertion for three years and upwards; cruelty; incurable insanity after five years' confinement; habitual drunkenness found incurable after three years from the first order of separation; and imprisonment under commuted death sentence. The Commission also recommended that the law should be amended so as to place the two sexes on an equal footing as regards the grounds on which divorce might be obtained.

The Gorell Report's only fault was that it was ahead of its time. The public was prepared to listen to discussions about easier divorce on the stage; and to read novels about the trials of parted lovers and the hardships of – for example – Thomas Hardy's heroines, unjustly prevented from getting free from men whose touch made them shudder as well as from those who treated them shamefully. But when it came to tampering with the institution of marriage in real life, they were instantly alarmed and hostile to any suggestion of change. The Church, as represented by the Archbishop of York, who was a dissenting member of the Gorell Commission, came out firmly against its recommendations. Various reformers, during the next few years, tried to get various pieces of the Report implemented. Clemence Dane hopefully wrote a play on the subject, *A Bill of Divorcement*, in which she asked the audience to imagine they were living at a future time when the Gorell Report had become law. She put the date as 1933. In fact it was 1937 before the 'Herbert Act', which included the substance of the Gorell Commission's recommendations, was finally accepted.

3. *The Superfluous Women*
On the whole, the man's world which came to an end with the Great War was a pleasant enough one for wives – at least compared with any previous period. But it was a very harsh world indeed in which to be a spinster. Spinsters had to face the fact that they were a nuisance to everybody, because there was no provision for them to be independent of a man's help, in an economy set up by males for males.

A socialist pamphlet, published in Britain in the nineties (*Working Women and the Suffrage,* by Mrs Wilbaut) had already pointed out that women's labour was 'a golden source of profit for the capitalist because girls and women who live in their father's or husband's household can work for smaller wages than men. But woe to the girl, the forsaken wife or the widow who has to earn a living alone! Working as hard as she can, she can seldom really provide for herself.' Ethel Snowden underlined the same fact in *The Feminist Movement* in 1913. 'The plain unvarnished truth is that work open to women is not sufficient in amount or sufficiently well-paid to enable them to live in a condition of ordinary comfort and decency.' Spinsters, therefore, whether they worked or not, still had to rely on a male relative for the roof over their heads. An unmarried daughter would go on living at home, dependent on her father, until he died, and the only possible happy ending for her was that he might leave enough to keep her mother and herself until they both died. Otherwise, she would have to move in with a married brother or brother-in-law who would be morally obliged to do something about her, willingly or unwillingly. As the dependent old maid in the home, she would be expected to put herself second to the wife and wait on her at all times as a matter of course.

Middle-class spinsters were always hoping to find some job in which they were not obliged to 'live in' as they usually were, as governess or 'lady companion'. But only the minority trained for and practising a profession earned enough to be really self-supporting; and of these, doctors were the only women who could support themselves on anything like a masculine standard. *The Woman's Book* (1911) which was a household encyclopaedia of information aimed at the progressive middle-class housewife advised that:

The prospects for a qualified woman practitioner are becoming greatly extended now that a great deal of the old-fashioned prejudice against her has been removed. In the first place, there is none of that 'undercutting of fees' which has to be adopted by women in most other professions. The Medical Council has decreed that emoluments must be on the same basis as those for men and this rule is always kept.

Male hierarchies like that of the doctors, who insisted from the first on equal pay, were not inspired by enlightened views on sex equality, but by enlightened self-interest. The main threat from women is always the fact of their coming cheaper. Men doctors, therefore, from then until now have never suffered from any real competition from the women.

The Woman's Book added encouragingly that 'several women doctors who have settled in practice for themselves are now making incomes of from £800 to £1,000 a year'. But there were, in 1912, only 553 women physicians in Britain (of whom, incidentally, 518 were suffragists or suffragettes).

It was the unmarried, untrained and unprovided woman who was a drug on the labour market. And she was not encouraged by her family to struggle too hard to be independent because the fact that they were not looking after her might reflect unfavourably on them. When 'Ann Veronica' first runs away, simply in order to get free from her father's tyranny and be independent, her elder brother is sent to coax her back home.

I'd chuck this lark if I were you. It's all very well starting out on your own but it's too damned hard. There's nothing a girl can do that isn't sweated to the bone. You got to take the world as it is, and the only possible trade that isn't sweated is to get hold of a man and make him do it for you. You go home and live on the Guvnor and get some other man to live on as soon as possible. It isn't sentiment, but it's horse-sense. All this woman-who-diddery is no damn good.

The typewriter, which had first come into use in the eighteen-seventies, had been hailed as a possible liberator for dependent spinsters. George Gissing's heroine, Rhoda, who supports the Woman's Movement, starts a typewriting school in order to give them a chance of making themselves independent.[11] In Barrie's play, *The Twelve-Pound Look*, the wealthy Lady Sims, who is under the thumb of a tyrannical husband, gazes 'with a little envy perhaps' at the woman typist who comes in to do her husband's letters and who is carrying her typewriter (according to one of Barrie's impossibly whimsical stage directions) 'in a friendly way rather than as a badge of servitude'. She confides to Lady Sims that she can earn 36s a week by typing letters at ten shillings the hundred. Lady Sims watches her typing and 'sighs, she could not tell why'. The 'twelve-pound look' turns out to be the dreamy expression of every woman wondering where she can get the money to buy a typewriter and become independent of a man's support. Though John Galsworthy's heroine, in *The Fugitive*, a wife who has run away to live with a penniless lover in the belief that she will be able to keep herself by typing cannot get enough free-lance work and is obliged to take up prostitution instead.

All the same, by the beginning of the 1914 War, women had taken over the typewriter as their own machine, the only one (apart from the sewing-machine) on which they were admitted to be the better skilled workers. By that time, the number of women clerks in business and the Civil Service was twenty times larger than before the typewriter. Or, to put it another way, the typewriter had taken over white-collar women workers and doomed them to be second-class employees in business for generations to come. The shorthand typists of 1911, who had broken into a man's world and now had one in five of office clerk jobs, felt triumphant about their victory. They might not have been so pleased with themselves if they could have known that their great-grand-daughters would still be anchored to the limitations and profound boredom of their cherished machine, still shouldered out of the interesting and stimulating jobs in the business world because typing had been established as a woman's rôle. The very noun had become feminine, so that one has to specify 'male typist' like 'male nurse'.

The unfortunate fact was that the typewriter took over the office and became a feminine preserve just at the time when women were humbly insinuating themselves into it by taking a lower salary than a man or boy doing the same work. *The Woman's Book* warned them that 'there is a deplorable tendency to make women work longer and at lesser salaries than men in clerical positions . . . for this many girls have themselves been responsible, working for pocket-money only', and Ethel Snowden pointed out tartly that 'only well-paid jobs are ever designated as "unfeminine"'.

At the very bottom of the work-ladder were the 'home-workers' doing sweated labour. Ethel Snowden reported on one who was charged by the magistrates with trying to commit suicide and told them that 'by working nearly eleven hours a day she received eightpence for making a pair of territorial riding-breeches and she found it utterly impossible to make two pairs in a day'. Just above this were the factory-hands, comprising the largest category of women workers.[12] Female wages in industry were lower than male, which were themselves barely enough to live on, particularly since the fall in value of the pound. When Mary Macarthur, of the National Federation of Women Workers, organised a strike for the Bermondsey women factory-hands, their average wage was 7s to 9s a week and 3s for girls, compared with the average male workers' £75 a year.

Mary Macarthur, who dedicated herself until her early death in 1921 to making a place for women in the fiercely masculine world of Trades Unionism,[13] had got over 300,000 of them organised out of a total of 5,000,000 by the time the war gave them their first chance of a real breakthrough. The men were as appalled at the idea of having to admit the women as if their wives had threatened to invade their favourite bar in the local pub. Also, as Ethel Snowden summed up,

Trade Unionism without political power is of very little use these days. A prominent trade-unionist, asked why he did not favour the admission of women to his Union but insisted on their forming a Union of their own, is known to have replied that the status of his Union would suffer in the eyes of politicians if it were known that it contained a large percentage of non-political, non-voting members and that as women could not be voters they had better form Unions of their own.

They needed them, because girls working in – for example – the small jam-factories of Bermondsey lived and laboured in worse conditions than the average male industrial worker, partly because the whole operation, being designed for women, was set up on the cheap and also because of that fatal weakness in any effort to reform women's work – nobody thought of the job as permanent. Although there were not enough available husbands in Bermondsey, or anywhere else, to go round the female factory staff, the girls, in their own minds, were only working until they got married. The only work-setting in which this hampering day-dream did not prevail was in industries with a tradition of married women keeping on their job – for instance in the textile factories of Lancashire.

Factory-girls might be excused for dreaming of escape, as D. L. Woolmer explained in *Living London*:

> When the monotonous day's work is done, many get half drunk and some often make the evening hideous with wild play or rough street fights before herding together for a few hours of darkness in close sleeping-places. These are girls whose pay at the small factories of the east-end never exceeds 4s 6d a week and is usually claimed by their parents. Their highest matrimonial ambition is to marry a coster and share his open-air life. What though the barrow is out early and late in fair and foul weather! It presents emancipation from dull routine.

The second-largest number of occupied women were in Domestic Service.[14] It has had a lot of emotion expended on its memory, in the years since its pre-1914 heyday. Conservative romantics are lyrical about the personal relationships it created; radical romantics work themselves into a lather of generous indignation on behalf of the exploited slavey of 1912. But the fact is that maidservants have not died out. They have simply moved from the home into the office, where the scrubwomen get up before dawn, according to the hallowed tradition that the later-rising ruling class must not be inconvenienced, and where the secretaries relieve the master of all the tedious jobs which he is too important to do for himself. And just as, in 1912, the poor but genteel housewife denied herself even necessities in order to have a little maid to answer the door, so the small businessman of today has to afford a girl to answer his telephone, or lose caste. But in 1910 domestic service was the softest job a working-class girl could get, and much sought after, though not quite as much as it had been ten years before. There were places in which a girl was not much better off than a slave and also places in which she really did have a warm, mutually respecting relationship with the family. But what mattered was that 'good service', unlike most women's jobs, was a craft job, in which skill and experience could earn more money and promotion, and in which the skilled craftswoman could pick her job, if she knew the ropes of bettering herself in the field of her own employment. Her working conditions were (in spite of the horror-stories) better, on the whole, than in industry. Enlightened middle-class wives now concerned themselves with the maids' hours of work and accommodation. 'A certain amount of leisure must be granted to the servant and then strictly adhered to', says *The Woman's Book*. 'She must have a comfortable place to sit, with a few books and magazines. She must have her own bed with a good mattress and sufficient covering and the room itself should be light and airy with washable distemper of a nice colour.'

Board and lodging were free, because the necessary supporting male to supplement a women's wage was in this case the employer, who supplied accommodation, food, laundry and sometimes uniform, as part of the work-bargain. This meant that the domestic servant, alone among working girls, could afford to put part of her wages aside to save up for marriage or for unsupported old age. She was also included in Lloyd George's Insurance Act.

A scullery maid, who was the equivalent of a craft apprentice, might start, as a school-leaver, at only £8 a year; but if she rose to housemaid or parlourmaid she could get up to £25, and as lady's maid or cook, up to £40.[15] A girl could bargain for the usual wage because registry-offices and advertisements in the papers kept the rates known; and there were always jobs going as 'general', though the competition for upper-class establishments was keen. The housekeeper in one of these could expect to earn £80 a year, that is, more than the average industrial worker got on which to support his family, but to her it was pocket-money. In fact a working-class spinster who reached the top of the domestic-service tree could live better than most middle-class wives, with only administrative work to do and a maid to wait on her.

Higher up on the social ladder, the most important of all working spinsters were the teachers. They were the largest category of professional women, 180,000 strong in 1911, and still the largest group twenty years later. They were one of the only two professions in which women were actually welcomed, instead of being merely tolerated. (Nursing was the other.) They mattered most, of all women in the story of women's emancipation, because they sowed the seeds of progress in the next generation.

The aristocracy of the profession, at this time, consisted of young women graduates teaching in the new high-schools which had been established in most large towns. They could get £100 to £250 a year as assistant mistresses, and live in lodgings, thus independent of their fathers' authority. The high-school also offered one of the sweets of girls' new freedom – the chance of outdoor sports and organised games which the boys had always enjoyed. This gave these schools a special glamour of progressiveness and triumphant feminism – apart from the girls' sheer physical pleasure in being allowed to wear short tunics and sports shoes and run about in the open air without any restraint – a pleasure which had been deliberately denied to their mothers at their age by cumbersome clothing designed to hamper and restrict movement. Young schoolmistresses who could coach the girls in games, gym and athletics were much in demand.

Probably the most important contribution which the young high-school teacher made to the women's movement was to show the girls a new model woman: herself, a woman with a work-identity instead of only a family one – for instance as daughter, wife, mother, aunt – or a class one. The graduate teacher in a plum job was important, not because of what she was, but because of what she could do. The mothers of the pupils could not despise her, as they could despise all other spinsters, for being second-class citizens. They might call the teachers 'schoolma'ams' and titter at their severe blouses and wisps of hair escaping from the 'bun'. But they could not get away from the fact that their daughter's form-mistress was better educated, more independent and quite possibly better off than they were with husbands to support them but children to rear.

The schoolmistress of the period gave the girls a new concept of themselves, as scholars, potential leaders, or even as athletes, instead of the old limited concept of being a young lady, a well-behaved and affectionate daughter and a future happy wife or frustrated old maid. She encouraged her pupils to plan what they wanted to do with their own lives, instead of waiting for the tide to carry them on to the next step and to wash Mr Right up at the appropriate time. She started a new kind of élite conformism in progressive girls' schools, which insisted that being ostentatiously 'feminine' (liking frills and curls and giggling about boys and weeping when upset) was 'silly'. Being sensible was keeping your mind on your Latin exercise and the hockey team and becoming a prefect. Parents – particularly fathers – were often uneasy at what seemed a perversely unnatural ideal to put before a girl. But there was nothing much they could do about it, since the women teachers were formidable to tackle in argument, and, by now, depriving a daughter of her education was 'not the thing'. Headmistresses would get a gifted girl her chance of higher education by persuading conservative fathers that it would be a good investment. As *The Times Educational Supplement* put it, 'Business to-day is uncertain; investments uncertain. The careful father would rather secure a provision against disaster in the girl's own capacity to provide for herself . . . the best preparation is to go to college or take a thorough course of sound technical training after a good education at school.'

Vera Brittain, whose *Testament of Youth* tells the story of her own struggle to break free from the mould, describes how difficult it was for the progressive headmistress to convince not only the girl's mother, but probably the girl herself, that higher education was worth the effort of achieving it, because most girls' ambition, on leaving school, was 'to return to impress their schoolfellows with the glory of a grown-up toilette and to get engaged before anyone else'.

Elementary education was one of the very few ways in which an enterprising girl could actually pull herself up into the social class above that of her parents, through her own effort. Usually, her only hope was to marry her social superior and be raised to his level. But the clever working-class daughter whose family was willing to forego her wages for five years after they had a right to expect them, could become a schoolmistress, which made her a member of the middle class. For sixty years, the way in had been through the pupil-teacher system, with a maintenance grant. (It was the only way to freedom which Hardy's *Jude the Obscure* could think of for his intelligent, penniless 'Sue'.) But in 1907 this convenient system was stopped; and the recruit to training had to stay on at school until 17 or 18 and then go on to college, helped by Bursar grants. The immediate effect was a startling decrease in entrants, because this meant not earning real wages until about the age of 21. The *Manchester Sunday Chronicle*, under the indignant headline 'A Stolen Profession', pointed out that now 'a barrier has been set up against the entrance of working-class children into the profession'. It did far more damage to working-class girls than boys, because parents who might be willing to make this considerable sacrifice for a boy felt differently about making it for a daughter, who would be marriageable age by the time she qualified and so might well only have a year or two in the profession to compensate for their effort. In fact this extra obstacle put the girl's chances back again into the old sex-discrimination rut. Parents fell back on the old excuse that a girl's career was temporary and not a very serious matter, since she would probably get married. The result was that this, the largest section of teaching, was flooded by uncertificated teachers, and the great majority of them were female, 37,000 compared with 4,000 uncertificated men.[16] Even at this very humble level, untrained men got more than untrained women, and a (trained) Assistant Master got £4 a year more than a fully qualified Headmistress, as a prize for belonging to the right sex. Elementary school-teaching now settled into the familiar division of jobs in which both sexes were employed; that is, the trained, first-class, better-paid workers were predominantly male, while the untrained, underpaid, second-class workers were predominantly female.

But the women teachers were not prepared to sit down under this indefinitely. Since the beginning of the century they had been moving towards forming their own professional organisations. Now that their standing inside their profession was threatened by the new recruitment scheme, some of them broke away from the mixed National Union of Teachers and formed the National Union of Women Teachers. Those who stayed in the N.U.T. were given a little influence inside it, just to keep them sweet, but not encouraged to agitate for equal pay. They were not really valuable as union members because of not having a vote, so there was no point in their brother trade-unionists overdoing the professional-solidarity line. Every single year they tried to get

Equal Pay added to the N.U.T. aims as drawn up by the annual conference. Since this was the happy ending most dreaded by men teachers it was not listed as an aim until 1919, and then only because the Women's Suffrage Act and also the Sex Disqualification (Removal) Act had been passed. At that time, when male citadels were crumbling right and left, unions were more welcoming towards women members. The N.U.W.T., however, continued as a separate union until Equal Pay was actually achieved.

The second-largest professional women's group was that of the nurses, who were 78,000 strong in 1911.[17] Their record in the women's struggle for work-status was less single-minded and less successful than that of the teachers. One reason was that, since Florence Nightingale, they had been brainwashed about making sacrifices for their vocation, such as putting up with long hours, low pay and dismal working conditions, which was extremely convenient for their employers. The other, less creditable, reason was because the leaders of the profession wasted a lot of time and energy on in-fighting, mostly on the subject of class distinctions, when they should have been united against an all-male government which refused to give them even the standing of a recognised profession until it came to the point where they dared not refuse.

The internal argument was between two kinds of nurse – working-class girls who had gone into the profession because they had ambitions above 'good service' and young ladies who had taken up nursing because they were bored at home. The working-class girls trained on the job for two to four years, depending on the habits of the individual hospital, received a certificate, and were expected to stay on as staff nurse, at an average of £25 a year above board and lodging, rising to a possible £40. The other grade, the lady-pupils, paid £1 a week to learn and were given a certificate at the end of a year.

What the profession needed, to give it official status, was to have a Register for nurses who had acquired a definite standard of training, instead of hospitals issuing their own certificates, which had no standard. But the men doctors and hospital governors were against registration, because they were very happy with the situation as it was, with authority firmly in the hands of the male, and the nurses overworked and underpaid but going meekly on because they had an image of themselves as something between a dedicated nun and an upper servant. As Sidney Holland (later Lord Knutsford) of the London Hospital put it, with disarming honesty, when giving evidence to a Select Committee on Registration: 'We want to stop nurses thinking themselves anything more than they are, namely the faithful carriers out of the doctors' orders . . . the other side are always talking about nursing being a profession and about "graduates" in nursing, just as they do in America.'[18] Another witness, a country doctor, had a nightmare vision of nurses 'flourishing their certificates in front of patients and patients might send for the nurse when they might otherwise send for the doctor because you can get a nurse for very little and the doctor's fee is higher'. But the Select Committee was unmoved, and recommended a Register of Nurses kept by a central body appointed by the State, to ensure that only properly trained women from an approved training-school should have the right to be registered nurses.

For ten years before the war, a Registration Bill lay before Parliament and each year the Government refused to give it facilities. It could have transformed the hospital system and provided Britain with a complete organisation of qualified nurses. The politicians were openly awaiting a war with Germany. In July 1911 (at the time of the Agadir incident) it was expected to start any moment. But it apparently did not occur to them that in a war soldiers get hurt and need nurses, although the crisis in the Crimea was still within living memory. Nevertheless, an all-male parliament allowed their sex prejudice to triumph over their sense of justice and their common-sense and over their enlightened self-interest as well. By refusing the nurses professional status – for fear it might detract from that of men – they prevented the country from reaping the benefits of over sixty years of professional growth and development in the skills of hospital nursing. The direct result was that when the wounded and mutilated and dying young men were brought back from the Marne and Ypres and Neuve-Chapelle, there were neither enough hospitals nor enough trained nurses to save those who might have been saved.

The Nurses' Registration Act was not passed until 1919. As Lord Russell said in the House of Lords debate on the subject: 'The nurses have the vote now, and so have to be considered more than they used to be.'

4. *The Suffragettes*

The nemesis which followed the rejection of the nurses' claim can help later generations to understand the ruthlessness of the suffragettes. It was born of the frustration of women being prevented from doing what they could do, and what they longed to do. It was the final breaking-down of patience, waiting for the men to agree to do what was clearly going to be done sometime, but not now.

The first women's suffrage committee had been set up in 1866, and for the next forty years its image was worthy, but dull. When Beatrice Webb was asked by the best-selling woman novelist, Mrs Humphry Ward, to sign an anti-suffrage manifesto, she did so, excusing herself afterwards by saying that she found women suffragists 'so narrow' and adding that an American one who asked her to lunch had not even offered her a cigarette.

Until the Pankhursts came into the picture, the figurehead of the movement was Millicent Fawcett, president of the National Union of (sixteen) Women's Suffrage Societies. Ray Strachey described their work as 'strong and of old standing, but quiet and uninteresting . . . decorous public meetings, unnoticed in the press, petitions from women (which M.P.s consigned, without a glance, to their waste-paper baskets) and private letters to candidates at election times. . . .'[19]

The Pankhursts changed all that. They were the widow and daughters of a Manchester barrister who had stood as Parliamentary candidate for the Independent Labour Party. It was his idealism about equality which started the Pankhursts on their campaign and his friends who helped them. The history of woman's emancipation is peppered with men of his kind. The suffragette movement had more than its quota of them, unappreciated, unthanked and their help barely remembered.

His daughter Christabel was a brilliant careerist, who came to see the Suffragettes as an élite group, a kind of female Samurai. Her sister Sylvia saw the movement as a means of getting social justice for women at the bottom of the social scale. Mrs Pankhurst saw it as a Joan of Arc operation for overturning male supremacy and all the evils (such as sexual licence) which it involved. She accepted martyrdom as a natural consequence of what she had been inspired to do.

The Pankhursts started their new suffrage society – the Women's Social and Political Union – in 1903 and agreed to use nuisance-value as a weapon to prick the government into interest. In 1905 Christabel, with an adoring factory-girl follower, Annie Kenney, was thrown out of the Free Trade Hall in Manchester for asking questions about Women's Suffrage at a Liberal meeting. They held a protest meeting on the pavement outside, were arrested for causing a disturbance and chose to go to prison rather than pay a fine. The plan succeeded. Next day, the papers were full of Women's Suffrage and it became an angry talking-point all over the country.

From then on the militants (now christened 'Suffragettes') pursued a regular policy of harassment against the politicians; asking unwelcome questions, going on unwelcome deputations and presenting unwelcome petitions. When Mr Asquith – known to be anti-suffragist and backed up by his fashionable Society wife – became Prime Minister, they decided to step up their militancy, using what Mrs Pankhurst called 'the argument of the broken window-pane'. But Mr Asquith's counter-policy of 'Wait and See' was just as effective. A routine developed by which suffragettes demonstrated, were arrested, went to prison, went on hunger-strike and were forcibly fed. When this aroused too much public concern, Mr Asquith went through the motions of getting a suffrage bill drafted, which quietened the women down for a time; until it dawned on them, all over again, that he had no intention of actually letting it get passed, at which they resumed demonstrating. The Conciliation Committee which he appointed to draft the bills was an all-party one. But female suffrage was an embarrassingly unwanted baby on any party's doorstep. Conservatives disliked it because it would upset the *status quo*; Liberals, because they had other schemes for political reform; and Labour members (apart from their two resident idealists, Keir Hardie and George Lansbury) because they anticipated that votes for women would start with upper- and middle-class ones, who would certainly not use them for the benefit of the Labour party. They guessed correctly. The first Conciliation Bill offered to enfranchise some million-odd female householders and owners of business premises. It passed its first and second reading in the House and then, by a parliamentary sleight-of-hand which – for a moment – deceived even his own supporters, Mr Asquith consigned it to cold storage. At this even the patient and diplomatic Mrs Fawcett was enraged, and the suffragettes prepared to march on the Houses of Parliament.

THE SUFFRAGETTES

That was Black Friday, November 18, 1910. Churchill, who was Home Secretary at the time, instructed the police to avoid arresting the women but to keep them away from Parliament somehow. The police felt free, therefore, to pummel and pinch, grip breasts and twist arms, force back thumbs and knock down. This was the first time that police controlling suffragettes reverted to the traditional methods of the bullying husband showing his wife who was boss. Judging from the grins on male faces, in photographs of the scene, it was being found highly enjoyable.

Twice more a Conciliation Bill was introduced and then dropped. Finally, Mr Asquith announced that the Government would bring in their own bill, to extend the franchise to 'all citizens of full age and competent understanding'. At the last moment the Speaker announced, in answer to a question from Mr Asquith, that this wording did not imply women's suffrage. Mr Asquith replied regretfully that in that case the government had perhaps better withdraw it. The suffragettes' reaction to being outwitted this time was so militant and the destruction so widespread that public sympathy for their rough treatment cooled off and Mr Asquith felt safe enough to tell the National League for Opposing Women's Suffrage that to grant votes for women would, in his opinion, be 'a political mistake of a very disastrous kind.'[20] From then on, the suffragettes settled down to militancy as a way of life. Annie Kenney explained that 'Infuriated at what we considered foul play, we all felt we did not care what happened to us, provided that we would force Parliament to give way.' The effect of their long terrorist campaign was to frighten the public into a hysterical hatred of violent women which allowed normally civilised and kind-hearted people to decide that, harsh as forcible feeding might be, it was all they deserved.

But before the bitterness against the suffragettes had become really dark and deep, there was a period of exhilaration and revolutionary enthusiasm in which they were able to fulfil all the frustrated dreams and longings of their childhood and youth as girls in a man's world. At last, they could do what their brothers had always been allowed to do while they looked on enviously. Now they had the mischief and the fun; they could cock a snook at authority; they could kick over the traces. For the first time, *they* had the pageantry and the processions and the marching music; instead of always being limited to watching the men from an upstairs window. On the eve of King George V's coronation they borrowed the decorated route for their own procession.

Ahead rode Joan of Arc in silver armour, followed by a symbolic group of New Crusaders, wearing purple mantles . . . the Prisoners' Pageant, seven hundred women, all in white, carrying silver-tipped arrows. . . . Then was heard the skirling of the pipes of the Scottish contingent. . . . Wales sent her singers dressed in old costumes, Ireland her women wearing Colleen Bawn cloaks . . . New Zealand with their emblematic fern trees and the Australians with their kangaroo . . . the phalanx of nurses . . . the stately band of university women . . . the numerous Fabian group, the ethical societies, the gymnastic teachers (who looked ready at once to wrestle for the vote. . . .)[21]

Now they could take their turn to have the kind of 'rag' which their brothers were always permitted, during the years of exuberant youth. The suffragette rags had tremendous style and panache.[22] They met their released comrades at the prison gates, with a carriage drawn by a team of white horses, on which girls sat as outriders. (One bonus of having so many upper-class young women in the movement was that you could always find enough accomplished horsewomen for any show.) They sailed up the river to the Houses of Parliament in a steam-launch and harangued members and their guests having tea on the terrace. They smuggled themselves into halls where political meetings were to be held, the night before, so that they could disrupt them. At Kinnaird Hall in Glasgow a young woman in a gym-slip climbed on to the roof and lay in wait for seventeen hours till the meeting began and then, attaching a rope to the roof, swung herself down through a skylight.

But later in the campaign, when Authority versus Suffragettes settled down to a grim routine of defiance with destruction, countered by imprisonment with ill-treatment, all the exuberance and gaiety went out of it. It became only a question of how long one could endure martyrdom, not to let one's comrades down. Forcible feeding meant being held down by wardresses, having one's mouth forced open by a gag, and nourishment pumped in through a tube, by a male doctor. The process involved agonising vomiting, torn and bleeding gums and, when it was applied through the nose, damage to the membrane which often lasted for life. When the victims were fainting too often (or trying to kill themselves rather than choose between betraying the Cause and facing the torture again) they were turned out to get back some strength among their friends before being collected by the police again to resume the punishment. Keir Hardie's misery that his continual protests were not backed up by his Labour colleagues is said to have hastened his death. George Lansbury rushed across the House of Commons to shake his fist in Mr Asquith's face,shouting, 'You'll go down to history as the man who tortured innocent women!'

The suffragettes pushed paraffin-soaked flaming rags into pillarboxes to set fire to the mail, burned down empty houses and churches, slashed irreplaceable paintings in art galleries and went on smashing-up exhibitions that would have awed the Luddites.[23] A casual group of fashionably dressed ladies would drift towards Bond Street or Piccadilly in ones and twos, their elegant shopping-bags on their arms. At an exact moment they would all whip out a hammer and break all the shop windows within reach so that the street would be a mass of shattered glass.

Mrs Pankhurst went to prison and on hunger-strike so often that the time came when the prison authorities were so nervous of her dying on their hands that they took to releasing her, under the 'Cat and Mouse Act', after the first day or two, and allowing an increasing interval for her to regain strength before re-arresting her, so that when she was condemned to three years' penal servitude after a bomb had wrecked Lloyd George's house, she had still only served a total of three weeks, nine months later.

Christabel fled to France after a police raid on W.S.P.U. headquarters and continued to direct the campaign from

Paris where she lived in some elegance and comfort. Sylvia, who, as a pacifist, had never been happy about the policy of arson, and who resented Christabel's contemptuous treatment of her two loyal comrades, Keir Hardie and George Lansbury, had formed a break-away suffrage group, the East London Federation of Working Women, for which her mother and sister never forgave her.

But it was Sylvia's supporters who were invited, after so many years of deadlock, to meet the Prime Minister, who announced that his Government was now prepared to support a woman's suffrage bill. (Sylvia could not go with the deputation because she was thought to be dying, after a combined thirst and hunger strike.) No one will ever know whether Mr Asquith was in earnest this time, because the war saved him from having to prove it.

The episode of the suffragettes left a permanent scar on British society. Before it, the public had complete faith in the integrity of the British system of justice. It was over a hundred years since a British Imperial official in the West Indies had been prosecuted for even permitting a woman to be tortured there, under Spanish law. But now it was accepted as quite natural and inevitable that British women political prisoners should come tottering out of jail and that lacerations and bruises and abrasions were one of the ordinary hazards of a few days in Holloway. It was also taken for granted, with a certain amount of lip-licking, that male police should treat demonstrating women with sexual brutality.

It was the suffragettes themselves who had introduced a provocative fierce sexuality into the suffrage movement which had not been part of it when the more sober suffragists had been in charge. Mrs Pankhurst had, from the first, claimed that votes for women were urgently necessary in order to reform the 'double standard' of sexual morality for men as opposed to that for women, and was fond of citing real-life examples of it, such as the eminent judge who had been found dead one morning in a brothel and little girls in Manchester slums who had babies by their fathers. Christabel liked to write articles in *The Suffragette*,[24] claiming that 75% of men had gonorrhoea and 25% syphilis and that women's only resort was to get hold of, and administer, the medicine which the government was said to give male prisoners in order to damp down their sexual desires. Mrs Fawcett and her suffragists had kept their campaigns cool and political. Mrs Pankhurst and Christabel whipped up theirs into a frenzy of sexual hostility. As Ray Strachey said, they 'read into the Cause all the discontents which they as women were suffering and a multitude of trifles which made them hate being women and long to have been men'. And because their emotional commitment was not really limited to the vote, the sex-war became an end in itself. 'The militants will rejoice when victory comes', Christabel wrote.[25] 'And yet, mixed with their joy, will be regret that the most glorious chapter in women's history is closed, and the militant fight over – over when so many have not yet known the exaltation, the rapture of battle . . .' However, a benevolent fate was about to provide her with a new enemy and a new exaltation and rapture in rousing her followers against him.

CHAPTER TWO

WHEN THE BOYS WERE FAR AWAY
1914–1918

1. Men Who March Away
On the evening of August 4, 1914, Mrs Fawcett presided over an anti-war meeting in the Kingsway Hall, hurriedly got up by three women's labour organisations and two suffrage ones. When she came out of the meeting, into the summer night, the crowds were already waving Union Jacks and singing patriotic songs and the paper-boys were calling the war news.

She always remembered that day, 'when we knew we were actually at war with the greatest military nation on earth'[1] as the most miserable one of her life. She never thought, for a moment, that Britain could be defeated; but she was just as certain that side-issues, such as giving women the vote, would be swept right out of the way and would not be reconsidered in the foreseeable future. She felt that her life-work had been destroyed. Only the age-old obligation of women, to be self-effacing and self-sacrificing, to give up their own less important interests when a men's crisis arose, still remained. Next day, she put out a message to all the suffrage societies.

'Women, your country needs you... we have another duty now. Let us show ourselves worthy of citizenship, whether our claim to it be recognised or not.'[2] They obediently turned their national organisation over to war welfare work, forthwith, and the London Society for Women's Suffrage changed its identity to the London Society for Women's Service, a free bureau to advise women and girls as to how they could most usefully help the war effort.

Within hours, the suffragettes declared that their own aims were entirely shelved and that they would instantly convert their organisation to the nation's service. 'Militants will fight for their country as they have fought for the vote.'

Christabel pointed out sombrely, in *The Suffragette* of August 7, that 'This great war is God's vengeance upon the people who held women in subjection', but later went on a tour of the United States making pro-Allied speeches, starting with a mass meeting in New York's Carnegie Hall. 'A pink-cheeked slip of a girl', said the *New York Tribune*, 'with fluffy yellow hair, in a gown of white satin and pale green chiffon, she looked so dainty and appealing that more than one in the audience was moved to say she didn't see how Asquith could have done it.'

At the beginning of the war, the Home Secretary announced that all suffragette sentences would be remitted, since 'His Majesty is confident that they can be trusted not to stain the cause they have at heart by any further crime or disorder.'

So ended the only women's terrorist campaign in British history and not so much as another window-pane was ever broken for it.

Sylvia, however, was not moved either from her suffragism, her socialism or her pacifism. She continued to agitate, in her own weekly paper, *The Woman's Dreadnought*, as well as in the Fabian *New Statesman*, for justice for poor women, and suggested that the government should take over the nation's food supply and distribute it fairly. She also urged her followers to have a 'no-vote, no-rent' strike. They accordingly slung a home-made calico banner across the street, announcing,

> Please landlord, don't be offended,
> Don't come for the rent till the War is ended.[3]

Meanwhile, husbands, sweethearts, sons and brothers hardly noticed what the women were doing, as they gave themselves up to the old, heady, male rituals of preparing to fight for the tribe. 'As I marched through the cheering crowds I felt like a king among men', said eighteen-year-old Lieutenant Brian Horrocks.[4] 'When I left Chatham, I had ninety-five men under command, but on arrival at Southampton there were ninety-eight – three men hidden under the seats, so as not to miss the battle.'

'It was a challenge to what we felt was our untested manhood', said one of Kitchener's recruits, J. B. Priestley.[5] 'In centuries gone by, other men who had not lived as easily as we had, had drilled and marched and borne guns – couldn't we? Yes, we too could leave home and soft beds and the girls to soldier for a spell if there was some excuse for it, something at least to be defended. And here it was. In those first months, we believed that war still held movement, colour, adventure, drama.'

This extraordinary emotional experience, this feeling of being possessed, for an intoxicated moment, by a passion which outweighed everything else overflowed into a sudden outburst of poetry, a brief golden age, with poems written, not by the imperialist Kiplings and Newbolts, but by men of the intelligentsia who, in the ordinary way, were merely amused at the fire-eaters and jingoists. To these men, the experience of being carried away by the war-fever of 1914 was like falling unexpectedly and helplessly in love. Professor Gilbert Murray, who had signed a plea for British neutrality on the first day of the war, underwent an agonising change of heart afterwards: 'I think again of the expressions on faces that I have seen or read about, something alert and glad and self-respecting in the eyes of those who are going to the Front.... To have something before you, clearly seen, which you know you must do and can do and will spend your utmost strength and perhaps your life in doing is one form at least of very high happiness...'[6]

And Rupert Brooke, an earnest young Fabian who had written poems mocking German militarism, now greeted the outbreak of war with an outburst of religious ecstasy:

> Now God be thanked, Who has matched us with His hour
> And caught our youth, and wakened us from sleeping....[7]

And the Prime Minister's son wrote a requiem for 'The Volunteer' whose 'waiting dreams were satisfied' at last.

> Here lies a clerk, who half his life had spent
> Toiling at ledgers in a city grey,

Thinking that so his days would drift away
With no lance broken in life's tournament.
Yet ever 'twixt the books and his bright eyes
The gleaming eagles of the legions came
And horsemen, charging under phantom skies,
Went thundering past beneath the oriflame.[8]

And even that sombre critic of God and the System, Thomas Hardy, wrote a 'Song of the Soldiers'.

What of the faith and fire within us,
Men who march away?[9]

Only the women were out of it. There was nothing for them to do while the men queued outside the recruiting offices and drilled in the square and marched about the countryside singing ribald men-only versions of patriotic songs. There was no exhilaration, no sense of starting a new and adventurous life for women. They were as untouched by it as a teetotaller at a champagne party, as they glumly considered what the war would do to their home and family. 'We can visit the small houses about us and talk hopefully to those poor wives and mothers whose anxiety equals our own', was *The Lady*'s suggestion for harmless diversion, and *The Times* said kindly that there was no need for women to give up every luxury and pleasure since 'too strict a parsimony would throw wage-earners out of employment'. It already had. After the initial Stock Exchange Panic, on the declaration of war (only softened by the fact that the weekend of the ultimatum to Germany was also Bank Holiday), most of those people who lived on unearned income expected to be ruined, any time. Therefore their first defensive idea was to cut down on luxuries and this resulted, with startling speed, in a great many factories having to dismiss staff.

The situation was not exactly improved by Lloyd George really letting himself go, in his best Welsh-chapel, hell-fire oratory, on the moral purpose of the war. 'The great flood of luxury and sloth which had submerged the land is receding and a new Britain is appearing', he thundered, to an eagerly applauding audience at the Queen's Hall. After that it became a point of patriotic honour among 'ladies' not to buy, for instance, their usual new dresses.[10] This fashion for instant economy threw a quarter of a million women industrial workers out of a job. In many families, this happened at the moment when the breadwinner had departed from the scene, with undisguised eagerness according to *The Times* correspondent. 'I heard only one grumble from the troops; they don't mind so much not being able to get beer and papers; only one thing they cannot stand and that is any delay in going to the Front.'[11] The allowance for their families had been arranged according to War Office custom of always preparing for the last war; that is, it was the sum which had been judged sufficient for dependants in the Boer War: 11s 1d per week, with 1s 9d for each child.

People with money were quite certain that the war would bring unemployment and poverty to the working-class on a scale not experienced within living memory. ('And there may be hard times in store even for the rich', added *The Lady*, sombrely.) Accordingly, they began to set up charitable funds to be distributed among the starving poor when the time came, notably the Prince of Wales Fund for the Relief of the Unemployed. But none of the ruling class's conscientious good intentions seemed to work out at this time.[12] Long before the proceeds could be handed out to grateful recipients, the poor had become so over-employed and affluent that the Fund was never needed at all.

Meanwhile, women's life seemed to have ground to a standstill, since their skills were not needed, during this great apotheosis of the fighting man. A distinguished Scottish woman doctor, Elsie Inglis, offered a ready-made Medical Unit, staffed by qualified women, ready to go anywhere, to the Royal Army Medical Corps. She was told, 'Dear lady, go home and keep quiet.'[13] (She took it to Serbia, instead, where it was much appreciated. 'No wonder England is a great country if the women are like that,' said the Prefect of Constanza.)

There was a great outbreak of knitting mittens and comforters for the men at the Front.[14] It was said that such a stock of knitted goods flooded into the trenches that men cleaned their rifles and wiped their cups and plates with their surplus socks and scarves.

Rose Macaulay, in her poem 'Many Sisters to Many Brothers', summed up the anguished frustration of all the girls who had tasted emancipation in their schooldays, and now found themselves back again in the bored idleness of the old British middle-class purdah.

> Oh, it's you that have the luck, out there in blood and muck;
> You were born beneath a kindly star;

All we dreamed, I and you, you can really go and do,
And I can't, the way things are.
In a trench you are sitting, while I am knitting
A hopeless sock that never gets done.
Well here's luck to you, my dear – and you've got it, no fear;
But for me – a war is poor fun.[15]

Meanwhile, the Man's world of British society settled contentedly down into the military manoeuvres which had been the beginning and were the logical end of ruling an empire.

At first, the military arrangements seemed to be properly in hand, at least to the watching public. Lord Kitchener, who was appointed Secretary of State for War, was the perfect imperial father-figure: stern, strong, authoritative and apparently infallible. Before the war was a week old, his face and pointing finger ('Kitchener Wants You!') was the best known poster in the country. He appealed for 100,000 volunteers to add to the regular army and got them in less than a fortnight; and then called for another 100,000. By the middle of September half a million of the country's bravest and most idealistic young men were committed; a doomed group whose massacre left gaps in British life for a whole generation.

Meanwhile, the British Expeditionary Force had landed in France, only a fortnight after the declaration of war, without the loss of a single man, and had deployed themselves, as arranged, in the path of the German army. Lord Kitchener told the House of Lords as much, in his first speech, in the brief, barking style expected of the man of action, calculated to reassure a public to whom the image was real.

But a few days later came the first of the disturbing omens. Refugees from Belgium came fleeing to England, with stories of a relentless German advance. Suddenly the news leaked out that the whole French and British forces were in retreat across France and the Germans advancing towards Paris. The government was angrily attacked for keeping the news quiet until it was blurted out by the Americans. Kitchener's defence was that it was thought the shock would have a good effect on the recruiting figures. By now the casualty lists were such that it was clear more men were going to be needed quite soon. As an old Etonian with the B.E.F. had put it, in a letter home: 'If we are all wiped out, just pour in another army and keep on till we win', which was, in fact, a précis of Kitchener's thinking.

When the first wild enthusiasm to volunteer died down, inevitably, as the supply of male military-romantics of the right age was used up by the War Office, the authorities began to get worried about where their next million was to come from. So far, their best propagandists had been the enemy: the Kaiser's reference to the B.E.F. as 'this contemptible little army' (if indeed it was ever really made); the officially approved ruthlessness of the German top-speed advance tactics (which provided material for atrocity-stories); the German shelling of British east-coast towns and Zeppelin raids; all designed to terrify the civilians into pacifism, all having the exact reverse effect.

But it now occurred to recruiting propagandists – both

amateur and professional – to persuade the women to coax or coerce or nag their men into joining up. Probably the most famous women's recruiting campaign of all was a small amateur one launched by Admiral Penrose Fitzgerald of Folkstone, who called a patriotic meeting which he addressed from the bandstand and then assembled a squad of young women whose job it was to patrol the beach presenting white feathers of cowardice to all young men not in uniform.[16] This plan spread like wildfire through the country. It was said that suffragettes were the most zealous of all, in confronting their late enemy males. The people who suffered from the campaign most were the armaments firms, who had enough difficulty keeping their skilled personnel at work as it was; and who suggested that the government should issue badges certifying that the wearer was on work of national importance and not just your ordinary cowardly shirker.

The women's amateur recruiting-sergeant job was as easy as possible, because all the sanctions against physical cowardice which had been a necessary part of the militarist-imperialist culture were still in full force. They claimed that a man who suffered from – or anyway gave way to – fear was not merely an outsider, but a kind of monstrosity, a eunuch, a masquerader in a man's body. Later on in the war, this strict male morality was relaxed as shell-shocked victims had to be accepted, if only because so many of them were officers with a previous good record.

Meanwhile the letter-columns of newspapers were full of recruiting propaganda. ('After Lord Kitchener's speech about our recent losses, I saw every lawn-tennis court near me with able-bodied young men and girls. Girls should refuse to consider non-recruits.')[17] The women's magazines joined in. *Home Notes* had an approving story of a girl telephoning the homes of complete strangers, asking if there was a man in the house and when one came to the telephone saying, 'I have a message for you from Kitchener.'[18] *Answers to Correspondents* pressed the point home, 'Believe me, dear "Soldier's Lassie", you who have bravely allowed your lover to go into the very firing line are showing your love for him far far better than those girls who, confusing love with selfishness, hold their dear ones back.' The *Daily Mirror* laid down that 'every woman in England who has trained herself to do a woman's work should nag every man she has influence over to enlist',[19] but the *Daily Herald* stipulated that class barriers should be respected.

A trend which is the popular prerogative of the middle-class women [who] . . . accost hypothetically eligible men in the streets and by taunting, insulting and presenting them with white feathers strive to thrust them willy-nilly into the trenches . . . but an intelligent and spirited bricklayer would reply, 'If I enlist it will be for my own reasons and not for your safety, not to protect you against an invasion, the thought of which terrifies you so much that you will get as many men between it and you as you possibly can.'[20]

At the beginning of 1915, the Parliamentary Recruiting Committee commissioned a set of posters, aimed directly at women, inciting them to do the required nagging. Since married men were not enlisting as eagerly as needed, if

Kitchener's requirements were to be met, one was specially directed at young wives, and its caption was: Women of Britain say – 'Go!' It showed two beautiful young women, in stylish déshabillé (presumably to suggest what a wonderful night in bed the one before the parting would be), watching their men in khaki march away. Another poster of this time was: 'Go! It's your duty lad. Join to-day', which showed an ideal (middle-class) white-haired mother with her hand on her young civilian son's shoulder. This poster was the starting-point of Barrie's lachrymose play *The Old Lady Shows Her Medals*. It was about a poor old charwoman who pretends that she has a son at the Front, because 'It was everybody's war except mine. I wanted it to be my war, too. The neighbours looked down on me. Even the posters on the walls of the women saying "Go, my boy" leered at me.'

This orgy of military romanticism lasted for almost the first nine months of the war. After that, two of the old certainties began to crumble. One was the pre-1914 belief that war was a business for professionals to manage by themselves, while the rest of the nation looked on encouragingly and paid the bills. The other was the belief that a great and famous soldier, who looked and talked exactly like a story-book hero (and not unlike a nicer English prototype of the Kaiser himself) must also be victorious and infallible in real life. The dawn of doubt was the Battle of Neuve-Chapelle, in March 1915.

Frances Stevenson, a highly educated, self-supporting spinster who at that time was Lloyd George's secretary and mistress, was present when he was discussing the battle with Lord Balfour and Lord Kitchener, and recorded the conversation in her diary:

Kitchener said, 'I told French he has wasted his ammunition. He told me he would want 5,000 shells and he used 10,000. He is far too extravagant.'

'But think of the casualties,' said Balfour, 'There must have been nearly 10,000 men lost in these engagements.'

'Eight thousand seven hundred at Neuve-Chapelle,' said Kitchener. 'But it isn't the men I mind. I can replace the men at once. But I can't replace the shells so easily.'[21]

First, the public had been told that 'the capture of Neuve-Chapelle' was a splendid victory. A week later the casualty lists were announced. The British had not had enough shells to knock out the enemy batteries, or even to cut his barbed wire properly before the infantry attacked the trenches hand-to-hand, so that the British soldiers had died hung up on it 'like washing' as the newspapers now reported.

Kitchener's colleagues now began to face up to the fact that the Prime Minister had put the whole military operation, including the problem of supplies, in the hands of a Boer War veteran who was out of his depth but too arrogant to admit it. Lord Haldane told the Webbs privately that 'K' was autocratic and ill-informed and Asquith indolent and that 'things had been allowed to drift'.[22] Arnold Bennett, dining with the Home Secretary, heard that 'Nobody *could* be worse at the War Office than Kitchener.' It was all brought to a head by a press campaign, which both Bernard Shaw and

General French afterwards claimed to have set in motion. On May 21, the *Daily Mail* headlined, 'The Shells Scandal. Lord Kitchener's Tragic Blunder', and five days later the Prime Minister created a new department, the Ministry of Munitions, and put Lloyd George in charge of it. He did not dare remove Kitchener altogether because of his public image, the face that had launched a million recruits. The following year, however, to his colleagues' secret relief, Kitchener was drowned at sea, on a secret errand to the Russian government. For a long time afterwards there was a persistent rumour throughout the country that he was not really dead, but would come back some day. It was perhaps another way of pretending that the great days of Britain's military might were not really finished.

It was a profound shock to the British to realise that they were not by God's grace invincible (as they had believed ever since Shakespeare first put the story about), but were quite likely to be defeated by the Kaiser, quite soon. The incredulous dismay, which spread through civilian life, that summer of 1915, and which no one who shared it will ever forget, marked the end of a world, the military-romantic man's world of the power and the glory. It was the beginning of a new and much less glamorous one, in which women were required to play quite a different rôle. A similar quick change of character has been demanded of them every ten years or so of this century. Men are not required to be flexible in the same way.

2. *The Munition-Girls*

The appointment of Lloyd George to Munitions at this moment was a turning-point in the history of women in industry. He was too committed a politician, himself, to be emotionally involved, one way or another, about sex discrimination. He simply needed to use the only large untapped source of labour, in order to get the munitions made without robbing the army of men. And he knew that, because of the tension in the country, he could now break through union taboos and class taboos and social taboos which were usually immovable. Through him, the girls got their first chance since the Industrial Revolution of getting hold of some of the more skilled and interesting jobs which had up till now been strictly men's jobs, although there was often no physiological reason why one sex should perform them rather than the other. But since they had been established as men's jobs they had automatically become superior and better-paid. The women's problem was to be allowed to do them without their being automatically reduced to a female level of status and pay. The men were even more afraid of this because they foresaw that employers might well prefer to keep on the stand-ins, not only because they could arrange for them to be cheaper, but also because they would not be so respectful of trade-union practices built up painstakingly since Tolpuddle.

Women's war-work developed in four stages. First, their own customary callings (food, textiles, clothing), which had been cut down at the beginning of the war, picked up again and normal production intensified to meet war-time demands – such as the threatened food shortage and the insatiable need for more uniforms. The only cloud over this brightening prospect was that because these had always been female occupations, the pay was not enough to live on in ordinary times, and now the cost of living had gone up.

The second stage was the 'substitution' of women for men, to release the men to the forces; that is, their acceptance into jobs which were traditionally a male rôle, so that it seemed unnatural to see a female in the part. Lord Northcliffe produced a *Handbook of Employment* which listed 'New Occupations for Women', such as tramway conductors, lift attendants, shopwalkers, bookstall clerks, ticket collectors, motor-van drivers, van guards, milk-deliverers, police. Most of these, because they were classified as men's work, offered the girls more than they were used to getting. For instance, bus conductresses ('between 20 and 35 years, 5' to 5' 10" with a week's training on a bus with a conductor') could straight away get £2 5s a week. Before the war, the average woman's wage was 11s 7d a week. The bus conductresses were the first girls to get 'real' money early in the war; that is, money which would support an individual, if not a family, entirely, instead of the customary female wage which assumed the existence of a backing-up male. They could pay their own way. Consequently there was a sudden shortage of domestic servants as girls realised they could do as well in the outside world, and have more personal freedom into the bargain. The London bus conductresses were one of the only two groups of women workers who were given equal pay for equal work at once, without question. The others were the women welders, who had been trained by an organisation set up by the one-time London Society for Women's Suffrage.

The third stage in women's war-work was their entry into munitions. This was the most important in the long term, not only because it prevented our losing the war but because of the barriers it broke down.

During the months of singing and marching about and cheering, with women distributing white feathers, 'the most vital industries had suffered losses which no subsequent effort could altogether repair', Lloyd George reported. 'When once a man had joined the Colours no power could make him return to civil work against his will and the influence of his military superiors was exerted to keep him in the army. . . . But great as were the difficulties of . . . getting skilled workers back from the Colours, the difficulties of introducing dilution of labour were far greater, though the ultimate results of this policy were more fruitful.'[23] 'Dilution' was a plan for making the most of skilled craftsmen's particular skills. It consisted of introducing a set of semi-skilled or unskilled assistants, in this case women, into the process he performed, so that he could (so to speak) sub-contract that part of his operation which could be done by less-trained persons. It was very difficult to get the craft unions to consider this scheme, because, as Lloyd George realised:

Through long years they had built up as a protection against the dangers of cut wages, unemployment and blackleg labour an elaborate set of rules and customs designed to control the rate of output and narrow the doorway into industry. . . . It was not a fear of falling wages during the War which troubled them. I had guaranteed this would not occur. It was rather a dread of losing the tradition of mystery and technical difficulty which they had built up to protect their craft . . . and the apprehension of unemployment, lower wage rates and a reduced standard of craftmanship and of living in the years to come.[24]

He went on a round of speech-making, to get some kind of agreement, however grudging, from the unions. In Glasgow he was shouted down.

On rising to speak Mr Lloyd George was received with loud and continued booing and hissing.... Owing to the incessant interruption and the numerous altercations it was quite impossible to catch every word of his speech. 'Let me put this to you, friends, there are hundreds of thousands of our fellow-countrymen, some of them our sons, some of them our brothers, in the trenches, facing death' ... (Interruption, 'No sentiment; you're here to talk about the dilution of labour').[25]

But the customary trade-union retort to this appeal was also emotionally loaded, claiming they had just had a letter from a fellow-member in the trenches entreating them not to give way about dilution even though it would mean the shells would arrive too late to save him.

At the works of Lang and Sons, Johnstone, the workers' committee declared 'That no women shall be put to work on a lathe and if this is done the men will know how to protect their rights.' The arguing continued all through the rest of 1915, with Lloyd George getting agreements and concessions where he could until by December he had enough of them to draw up a Munitions of War (Amendment) Bill to give them statutory force. The Amalgamated Society of Engineers held out longest, perhaps because, as one munition girl working in an engineering shop explained:

Engineering mankind is possessed of the unshakeable opinion that no woman can have the mechanical sense. If one of us asks humbly why such and such an alteration is not made to prevent this or that drawback to a machine she is told with a superior smile that a man has worked the machine before her for years and that therefore if there were any improvement possible it would have been made. As long as we do exactly what we are told and do not attempt to use our brains we give entire satisfaction and are treated as nice good children. Any swerving from the path prepared for us by our males arouses the most scathing contempt... they have to be managed with the utmost caution lest they should actually imagine it was being suggested that women could do their work equally well, given equal conditions of training – at least where muscle is not the driving force.[26]

The fourth stage of women's war-work was not reached until the increasingly desperate days of 1917–18 when they had to substitute for men, not only in process work likely to be suitable for them, but also in processes and manual work heavier than anything women workers had yet attempted – for instance in forging bullet-proof plates and driving overhead cranes. Systems were worked out whereby the muscular strength of three women could do a job which was usually done by two men. At this period there was a large crop of fatal accidents to women workers.

Lloyd George said afterwards that 'the history of women's work in the production of munitions was one of the brightest chapters in the story of the war',[27] and that although the agreements were only temporary, 'yet a standard was set up which could not easily be set aside afterwards'. In fact the standard was not exactly lavish, since equal pay only applied to piece-work and the vast majority of women were on time-work, and Mary Macarthur, who organised the National Federation of Women Workers, had a long hard struggle to get them a minimum standard wage of £1 a week. The other snag was that, come what might, the dilutees had got to be 'first out' at the end of the war. That had been one of the conditions laid down by the various Crafts Unions, for agreeing to dilution at all. And it was not only the craftsmen who were insuring their monopoly of the good jobs with the good money against having to share them with women permanently. As Helena Swanwick remarked bitterly, 'It is unfortunate that at the Trades Union Congress of September 1916, the solitary expression of policy towards women's war-time work should have been one calling for a revocation, after the war, of all licences to women to act as conductors on trains or omnibuses.'[28] This kind of reminder to women cut both ways. The women were in any case unfamiliar with trade-union wariness over stepping up the speed of any operation; and had not much interest in the long-term effects of doing so, since they were to be ousted as soon as possible. They did quite often work much faster than the men. As William Beardmore, one large employer reported, 'The actual output by girls with the same machines and working under exactly the same conditions and for an equal number of hours is quite double that of the trained mechanics.' Such an announcement was like a death-knell to men left in a factory when the 'comb-out' began, which meant that where the girls were managing the one-time men's processes well enough, the men were taken out and sent off to the underpaid miseries of the Front.

In the National Shell Factories, the flat rate for male workers was £2 19s 3d a week, and, with a bonus, £4 6s 6d, whereas the flat rate for women was £1 12s 8d and £2 2s 4d with bonus. In the National Filling Factories, the ratio of female to male was 28,000 women operatives to 2,500 men. The men's rate was £2 a week and total earnings £3 7s 0d; the women's £1 12s 7d and £2 2s 4d. A foreman took home £5 1s 10d; a forewoman £3 8s 0d. As Beatrice Webb pointed out tartly, 'The treasury agreement of 19th March 1915 embodied a pledge that the women employed in war-work in substitution of men should receive the same pay as the men they replaced. The pledge has been wholly ignored by some government departments and only fulfilled by others tardily and partially, to the great loss of the women concerned.'[29]

In spite of the cheese-paring and the cheating and the rising cost of living, this was still a heady experience for women workers. For the first time, women in industry were getting breadwinners' wages – enough money to support themselves wholly, and enough for someone else. They could hardly believe it was true. The projectile girls, for instance, could earn £3 4s 2d a week. It was not only five times as much as the wage they were used to, but despite war-time prices it would buy a really comfortable quantity of good food, which was a thing they did not expect, even in peace-time. In their canteens, 'two Zepps in a cloud' (sausages and mash) cost 2½d, mince and mash 2d and beans 1d. A woman worker, giving evidence to an official inspector of factories,[30] told him that she worked from 7 a.m. to 8.30 p.m. and on Sundays from 8 to 5; that she spent two hours daily travelling to and from work and was supporting an invalid husband and six children under twelve, but that she felt better than she ever had done in her life because with her wages they could all have as much as they wanted to eat every day. Sickness among women workers diminished sharply at this time and they experienced, in spite of everything, a new sense of well-being. When under-nourishment and hunger has been a regular part of your home life as long as you can remember, it takes a long time to exhaust the pleasure of there being enough to go round all the time.

All sorts of stories went the rounds about the munition-girls' affluence. 'Fur coats have come to be known as "munition overalls"', *The Times* reported sourly:

Take a visit to a typical industrial district of London . . . the bakers will tell you that many of their customers are buying more bread than they did before the war . . . consider how it comes that seven butchers' shops can exist and do a flourishing trade in a space of less than a hundred yards . . . watch the business going on in shops of every kind, provision dealers, furnishers, drapers . . . it is not without significance that pears are displayed in a fruiterer's shop in Walworth Road at 3d apiece and grapes at 5s a pound . . . every picture palace is crowded, night after night. . . .[31]

Another novel experience for the munition-girls, who had been brought up to believe that their natural function was to be the underpaid drudges of industry, was the continual chorus of praise for their skill as workers. The Parliamentary Secretary to the Ministry of Munitions told Parliament that 'Our armies have been saved and victory assured by the women in munition factories who are now doing some 500 different processes, two-thirds of which were never performed by a woman before.'[32] Lloyd George was fond of boasting (particularly on Clydeside) that his girls could do skilled engineers' tasks after a few days instruction, 'successfully, swiftly'. Even the trade journal, *Engineer*, acknowledged that 'the women's work turned out has reached a high pitch of excellence'. And Professor Cathcart, sent by the Royal Institution of Great Britain to investigate weight-lifting, was as enchanted by the factory-girls as eighteenth-century poets used to be by shepherdesses and dairymaids.

The girls employed are literally remarkable for their physique and the grace of their carriage ... all worked barefoot ... the astonishing thing is that these young, perfect women – no girl employed is under sixteen – were born and bred in one of the worst districts in Glasgow.[33]

Also, he added, remembering what he had been sent to find out, one girl could shovel 20–25 tons of raw material, lifting it to a height of 2' 5" per day.

The third new experience for the munition-girls was to find themselves so much valued, as workers, that their health and welfare became the anxious concern of the authorities. A committee appointed by Lloyd George recommended that

It is important that they should be allowed an hour for dinner and for the principal meal during the night. Ten minutes are easily spent in reaching the mess-room and returning to work, certainly another five are occupied in the washing of hands and in the service of the dinner, and so but fifteen remain for the meal. The effect upon the health and energy of women and girls which results from clean, bright and airy workrooms, well warmed in winter, can hardly be exaggerated . . . the refreshing effect of washing and its influence on self-respect . . . has been dwelt on by many witnesses. Lavatories should be kept scrupulously clean; clean towels supplied before every meal.[34]

Even the unmarried mother, who was in the ordinary way – at best – turned over to a Moral Welfare Home, was cherished in the munitions factory for the skilled work she had done and would be able to do again.

Provided that the work is not injurious to her, she is retained as long as possible. Friends are found for her and she has a weekly grant from the Hospital and Benevolent Fund; also help in putting her in the way of receiving maintenance from the father of the child. . . . I have at different times brought in a girl to work as cleaner in the Canteen . . . the baby comes with its mother and lies in a cot on the verandah and thrives and is a source of interest and joy to the factory girls.[35]

As Lloyd George said,[36] in one of the rare understatements of his political career, it was a strange irony that the making of weapons of destruction should afford the occasion to humanise industry.

3. The Land-Girls

As factory-girls had been the underpaid drudges of industry, before 1915, so had the rural wives and daughters been the drudges of agriculture.

Agricultural labourers were the second-class citizens of pre-war Britain, because as long as there had been an unfailing supply of cheap food from the Empire, successive governments had been content to leave them to rot. Farm workers' wages were low; both farms and cottages were dilapidated and without the amenities taken for granted by town-dwellers, and village life was mean and narrow, with the women's outlook bounded by the struggle of bringing up large families on too little money in primitive homes.

At the beginning of the century, the Agricultural Organisation Society, a rather unconvincing effort to make farmers and small-holders co-operate, had conceived the idea of putting some sparks of life into this apathetic group of the population, by starting some Women's Institutes in Britain, that is, groups of country women who would combine to restore traditional skills and crafts, to educate themselves in hygiene and housekeeping and to improve the life of their own village community. These Institutes had been a great success in Belgium and Poland, Canada and the U.S.A. But in Britain they had never even got off the ground, and the reason was that British rural wives had such a low opinion of themselves that they would not take part in any women's conferences, discussions or meetings, 'for fear of being made fun of by the men'.[37]

But in 1914, the countryside began to stir, because the production of food at home now mattered again, for the first time since 1880 and the start of refrigerated shipping of food from the colonies. When war was declared and imports were cut down – and also sunk by the German U-boats – everyone began to look at our own farm produce with more interest, and the sense of emergency spread to the villages, and the Agricultural Organisation tried again and this time it was more successful. By the autumn of 1916, in twenty-four localities, the country wives had formed Women's Institute groups to help the war effort, by organising backyard poultry-keeping, fruit-preserving, haybox cookery and vegetable-raising. By 1918 there were 760 of them; and over the next fifty years they were to become so powerful a national pressure-group that Ministers of Agriculture trod warily when confronted by any demands they decided to make.

But although this organised saving and conserving mattered, we needed to grow much more of our own food, if we were not to be starved out, as the Germans hopefully predicted. The male landworkers, like the skilled men in industry, had been encouraged to join up in far too large numbers. Therefore, by 1917, there was far less than the normal labour force on the land to carry out cultivation on an ambitiously large scale.

As early as 1915, the Board of Agriculture had tried to

induce the farmers to employ female labour, or 'the lilac sunbonnet brigade' as some rustic wit christened them, but the idea that women could do the men's work of a farm, as they did the women's work of milking, butter-making, poultry-keeping and giving a hand with the hay-making, 'called forth bucolic guffaws' as Lloyd George put it. But by 1916 when households were having regular meatless days and home gardeners grew vegetables instead of flowers, he tried again. His first speech to Parliament was about the food problem and early in 1917 the Board of Agriculture began to recruit a Land Army of women and girls; some to do part-time work near their homes, others to go full-time wherever they were sent.

The farmers instantly refused this 'substitution' as anxiously as the industrial trade unions had, earlier on, though they were not moved by pure anti-feminism so much as the fact that they were making do with schoolchildren, who came much cheaper than land-girls. However, after the Minister of Agriculture had admitted, at last, that 'England is like a beleaguered city' with only three weeks' food supply left, the government passed regulations compelling farmers to cultivate land in the way they were told, in spite of protests from the country-gentleman class who saw their own position threatened by such measures. The Board, in addition, now launched the land-girls as an official part of the labour force.

'Lloyd George's Land-girls' raised the status of rural women as his munition-girls had for women in industry. 'Breeched, booted and cropped, she broke with startling effect upon the sleepy traditionalism of the English countryside.'[38] She was trained at a government training-centre; she had to be accommodated by the farmer (and at a reasonable standard or the government inspector would want to know why) and she got free railway passes, a free outfit and minimum pay of 18s a week. The average pay for a male agricultural worker before the war had been 14s.

From the first, the press treated land-girls kindly, with a little mild teasing about their breeches. ('Is this the way to Wareham?' 'Well, they look all right to me, missy.') Newspapers were enthusiastic about any sex-warfare stories in which they came off best, and loved to organise competitions in which land-girls challenged some die-hard male who had been denigrating them to a ploughing match or a muck-spreading one, and which the girls somehow always won. At one of these gatherings, Walter Long, Minister of Local Government and a notorious anti-suffragist, made a public recantation on the subject, lamenting that an unfortunate idea had been impeding the progress of village women to the effect that a woman's place was in the home. 'That idea must be met and combated.'[39] Mrs Fawcett, who was at his meeting, reported 'a broad grin on the faces of all the suffragists round me'.

4. *The V.A.D.s*
The V.A.D.s were the young-lady heroines of the war. You could hardly open one of the Royal gift-books without coming on a picture of a titled one, in her becoming uniform, or go to a concert for war charities without the tenor getting up,

THE V.A.D.s

sooner or later to sing of 'The Rose That Grows In No-Man's-Land'.

> It's the one red rose,
> The soldier knows;
> It's the work of the Master's hand.
> In the war's great curse
> Stood the Red Cross Nurse,
> She's the rose in No-Man's-Land!

The Voluntary Aid Detachments scheme had been set up, with an eye to the anticipated war, in 1909, by a joint committee of the Red Cross and the Order of St John. Idle and bored middle-class and upper-class girls, detained at home until Mr Right should come along, had attended first-aid classes for something to do. They had been a stand-by joke for *Punch* in pre-war years, with humorous drawings of a terrified male who has sprained his ankle keeping them off with a stick. By the time the wounded men began to be shipped back in crowded boats and trains, to be looked after in Britain, the V.A.D.s were not a joke any more. Largely because the nurses had not been permitted Registration, there was neither enough hospital accommodation nor enough trained staff to cope with the casualties. The immense overflow had to make do with borrowed private houses for hospitals and with the V.A.D.s as nurses.

'The golden drawing-room became a ward for ten patients,' remembers Lady Diana Cooper.[40] 'The ballroom held another twelve. The centre skylit saloon was the dining and club room. The walls were hung with glazed linen; the floor was covered by linoleum. Lady Diana, as a V.A.D., found herself within a few weeks of starting to nurse 'giving injections, intravenous and saline, preparing for operation, cutting abscesses, and saying prayers in the Sister's absence'.

'These ignorant amateurs,' stormed the *Nursing Times*, 'these young women with their express training are assuming full nurses' uniforms with the addition of a large red cross and being called and treated as trained nurses by medical men and society people connected with the Red Cross Society.'[41] A trained Sister of ten years' standing wrote to the *British Journal of Nursing* to complain that in the Red Cross Hospital where she was working, 'the untrained commandant – a girl young enough to be my daughter – insists upon all the volunteers being called 'Sister', whether titled dames or domestics'.[42]

The V.A.D.s were accused of coming into the hospitals expecting to hold the patients' hands and smooth their pillows, while the regular nurses attended to everything that looked or smelled disagreeable. But according to Vera Brittain, whose autobiography *Testament of Youth* made her the most famous V.A.D. in history, professional nurses took their revenge on hapless girls who got trapped in a real hospital.

We went on duty at 7.30 a.m. and came off at 8 p.m; we were never allowed to sit down in the wards and our off-duty time was seldom allocated before the actual day, making it impossible to plan how to

THE V.A.D.s

spend it. . . . Every task, from the dressing of a dangerous wound to the scrubbing of a bed-mackintosh had for us in those early days a sacred glamour which redeemed it equally from tedium and disgust. Our one fear was to be found wanting in the smallest respect; no conceivable fate seemed more humiliating than that of being returned as 'unsuitable' after a month's probation. The temptation to exploit our young wartime enthusiasm . . . was not fiercely resisted by the military authorities. . . .[43]

Eventually, she was sent to nurse at a field hospital in France. (One of the many grievances against V.A.D.s was that they were said to get the exciting overseas assignments because they had influential friends, while the run-of-the-mill nurses had not.) At the time of the German 'Big Push' she remembers:

Gazing half-hypnotised at the dishevelled beds, the stretchers on the floor, the scattered books and piles of muddy khaki, the brown blankets turned back from smashed limbs bound to splints by filthy blood-stained bandages . . . beneath each stinking wad of sodden wool and gauze an obscene horror waited for me, and all the equipment I had for attacking it was one pair of forceps standing in a potted-meat glass half-full of methylated spirit . . . the enemy within shelling distance, refugee sisters crowding in with nerves all awry . . . gassed men on stretchers, clawing the air – dying men reeking with mud and foul green-stained bandages, shrieking and writhing in a grotesque travesty of manhood . . . dead men with fixed empty eyes and shiny yellow faces. . . .

Vera Brittain had given up her much-longed for university education in order to become a V.A.D. and had written to a friend that 'Nothing would induce me to stop what I am doing now, and I should never respect myself again if I allowed a few slight physical hardships to make me give up what is the finest work any girl can do now. . . .' But while she was still engaged in – quite literally – saving soldiers' lives by her hurriedly acquired nursing technique and her courage and endurance, her father wrote to her, telling her that her mother had 'cracked up' and had been obliged, owing to the inefficiency of the domestic help then available, to go into a nursing-home. 'My father had temporarily moved into a hotel, but he did not, he told me, wish to remain there. "As your mother and I can no longer manage without you, it is now your duty to leave France immediately, and return to Kensington."'

Unmarried daughters' first duty was to look after their ageing parents. Unmarried women owed final obedience to their father, the supporting male, until they married their second supporting male. 'I knew that no-one in France would believe a domestic difficulty to be so insoluble . . . if I were dead, or a male, it would have to be settled without me . . . half-frantic with the misery of conflicting obligations I envied my brother his complete powerlessness to leave the Army whatever happened at home. . . . I felt a cowardly deserter.'

Yet she went back to Kensington, obediently. The taboo against treating her father's orders with indifference was too strong, even for Vera Brittain who had all the advantages of education and had proved herself as enduring and brave as her brother. She had all the tools of emancipation, but she did not feel free. Her conditioning in an ordinary, amiable middle-class home had been too permanent.

5. *The Unmarried Mothers*
The field in which women took over most jobs from men, over the whole length of the war, was in transport, where they held some 18,000 in 1914, but 117,000 by 1918. But here, most of the increase was a matter of simple 'substitution'. The women railway porters and van drivers and bus conductors and chauffeurs looked on it as work 'for the duration' only. They were standing in for the rightful holder of what was naturally a man's job, and when he came back from the war, he would want it back again. Whereas in commerce, administration and banking, where there was the second-largest increase, the invaders did not by any means intend to move out when peace came. Many of the posts they filled had not even existed before. There were hundreds of new government committees which all needed clerks, and there were no men available. Now the shorthand typist, from copy-girl to confidential secretary, really came into her own. Even by the middle of 1915, she was enough in demand for wages to be almost double their pre-war figure of £1 a week, and by the next year she was earning enough to have the kind of freedom which only young bachelors had before the war.

'The wartime business girl is to be seen any night dining out alone or with a friend in the moderate-priced restaurants in London. Formerly, she would never have had her evening meal in town unless in the company of a man friend. But now, with money and without men, she is more and more beginning to dine out.'[44] Many of these 'flappers' were earning more each week than their fathers had brought home before the war. They were no longer compelled to live under the roof for which he paid, and therefore under his authority. His traditional final sanction to a defiant daughter, that he would 'turn her out of doors' unless she came to heel, was no longer valid. In any case, girls all over the country and from every social class – munition workers, land-girls, nurses and the women's sections of the Forces – were now living away from home, in hostels, lodgings and camps. They might be under official discipline, but they had at least escaped from that of their parents.

The result of this break in the tradition of young virgins being kept at home for safety's sake was exactly what had always been feared. An entirely self-supporting girl, physically removed from her parents' jurisdiction, could make up her mind about whether to keep or give up her virginity as never before. And for the first time there was a thawing of public opinion on the subject. The conventional attitude had been that it was a venial sin for a man to have a liaison before marriage, but a mortal one for a girl.

But now, a terrible cloud of grief hung over the nation, all the time as the casualty list of the great battles came in, and the telegraph boy became dreaded as a messenger of death.

In daily batches of ten thousand they struck at the endless little villas in suburban roads which had, so short a while before, been warm with pride in the trim young officer or the budding sergeant with his stripes fresh on his sleeve; at the schools which junior masters had so lately been visiting in their new Sam Browne belts; at the universities – terribly heavy there – where name after name on the lists meant that some undergraduate would chatter no more in the college lodge or cross the quad in shorts and sweater; some young don would look no more from his windows upon the gardens; at the country houses which, growing still and stricken, remembered in their fine tradition the cottages in the village which would have grown still too.[45]

Part of the nation's mourning was that so many of the dead had been so young that they had not even tasted adult experiences. Sheila Kaye-Smith wrote a war-time novel of country life in which she suggested, comfortingly, that the boys who made a hurried war marriage at least must have died happy, because they were 'fulfilled'.

To-morrow he could be back where the earth was torn and gutted, scabbed and leprous as if diseased with the putrefaction of its million dead . . . and yet he could put the feel of it out of his mind and smile contentedly and blink his eyes in the sun. . . . From the lumbering unawakened lad of two years ago he had come to perfect manhood, to be husband and father, fulfilling himself in a simple natural way with a quickness and a richness which could never have been if the war had not seized him and forced him out of his old groove into its adventurous paths. If he died the war would have taken away what it had given – a man, for through it he had in a short time fulfilled a long time and at 22 could die in the old age of a complete unspotted life.[46]

In this emotional climate of snatching at straws of comfort in an otherwise unbearable bereavement, it became excusable for a girl to 'give all' to a man on the last night before he went back to the Front. The heroine of *Sometimes Even Now*, a play about war-time love affairs, explains how it used to happen.

During the war, everything women did was swayed by feeling; intense emotion that can never come back into our lives again. But it was wonderful while it lasted; wonderful to be able to give so much without caring about the cost. . . . Noel and I sat talking by the fire . . . he was lonely, he was going back . . . he didn't plead for my body, I gave it to him of my own free will.[47]

In any case, as one strictly-brought-up girl of the period wrote afterwards:

The religious teaching that the body was the temple of the Holy Ghost could mean little or nothing to those who saw it mutilated and destroyed in millions by Christian nations engaged in war. . . . Little wonder that the old ideals of chastity and self-control in sex were, for many, also lost.[48]

Patriotism covered a multitude of sins. Even public figures, pillars of morality, demonstrated their own love of country by hinting that young bachelors on whom everyone's safety now depended must be allowed a little indulgence before marching away. In 1915, after the massacre at Neuve-Chapelle, a Conservative M.P. wrote to the *Morning Post* remarking that there were large numbers of pregnant girls in the village round about army training-camps who ought to be treated gently.[49] (His heart may have been in the right place but his figures were, in fact, premature. This was the time of hasty war marriages, 19.5 for every thousand inhabitants. The phenomenal rise in the rate of illegitimate births came later.) His conclusion was that no shame ought to attach to these 'war babies' when they were born and very little indeed to their mothers. Mrs Pankhurst announced that the suffragettes intended to adopt fifty (female) war babies and bring them up to be superwomen. The project turned out so expensive that only four were adopted and were looked after by Sister C. E. Pine, one of the heroines of militant days, who had used her nursing-home as a refuge for those weakened by prison treatment and wanted by the police.

As early as 1914, the authorities had faced up to the question as to whether the illegitimate children of fighting men should get allowances to keep them going in their fathers' absence or death as the legitimate children did. 'The question of giving relief to unmarried women who have lived with soldiers meets with a good deal of opposition', Frances Stevenson reported. 'The Archbishop of Canterbury signified to the Cabinet his disapproval that these should receive allowances on the same basis as married women. It appears that the Archbishop does not want them to starve, but he does not wish them to be openly treated as deserving of relief – which is a piece of blatant hypocrisy.' She added that Lloyd George had spoken 'very strongly' to two distinguished Nonconformist ministers and told them that 'it is not right to take the lives of the men for their country and after you have accepted the sacrifice to say that you do not approve of their morals and are afraid you cannot make decent provision for the women they have treated as their wives.'

The 1914 War created a new and more merciful attitude towards the unmarried mother. All the pleading of individual reformers had never achieved for her what the massacre of young men did. Before it, society had stuck to the simple principle of deterrence. Having an illegitimate child was deliberately made so painful and humiliating that (so the theory ran) girls would avoid it at all costs. No one ever questioned whether this theory worked. It was assumed that it obviously *must* deter potential sinners. In some periods of British history, the principles of deterring virgins from temptation (and unmarried mothers from a second child) was applied more severely than at others. For instance, before the dissolution of the religious houses, which had always cared for foundlings, having a bastard was not regarded as quite so antisocial as it was afterwards, when the parish rate-payers had to subscribe to its keep. Then the deterrent measures became so intolerable that women used to risk infanticide, which carried a death penalty, rather than face them. Even at the end of the nineteenth century, the law was concerned with protecting society against the unmarried mother and her child. Josephine Butler's campaign for 'helping an illegitimate child by helping his mother' made sufficient headway for the Church of England to found Moral Welfare Homes, but these only solved the problem temporarily, by allowing the mother to stay in a hostel with her baby for a limited time. The last resort was still the workhouse, which meant being parted from the baby at three months, but being compelled to stay on to support it, by scrubbing. Sometimes an unmarried mother would be compelled to remain 'literally in bondage' as a social worker of the period described it, until the child was old enough to earn its own living.[50] Very few young women, before the war, could earn enough to put the child out to a foster-mother at their own expense. In any case, if the unmarried mother got behind in her fostering payments, she was liable to have the baby promptly returned, or perhaps to be told that it had died of feeding difficulties.

It was correct for a respectable family to turn a pregnant unmarried daughter out of doors. This proved to the neighbours that they strongly disapproved of her behaviour; also, of course, it avoided their having to foot the bill. Fathers had been legally liable for maintenance, but difficult to catch up with, since the middle of the nineteenth century. Even if the unmarried mother successfully took one to law, he only had to pay at the most 5s a week towards the child's maintenance.

From 1915 onwards, as the rules of society which aimed at preserving the potential bride's virginity were relaxed and the emotional climate became more feverish, as the death-roll of young men lengthened, so the illegitimacy rate began to climb. By the end of the war it was 54 per thousand live births as compared with the pre-war 43. This meant that there were up to 42,000 new babies, without an official home, born every year, at a time when there were many more profitable jobs for women than looking after unwanted infants.[51] Foster-mothers, in consequence, almost ceased to exist, and the illegitimate baby's chances of survival – which had always been shaky – were still further reduced.

But in 1916 an entirely unexpected knight-errant came to the rescue in the person of the Registrar-General. 'The rate of illegitimate to legitimate mortality in the first week of life has increased from 170% in 1907 to 201% in 1916', he reported. 'The mortality of the illegitimates has increased from 23% in 1911 to 25% in 1915. These facts suggest that the infant welfare organisations might well devote special attention to the first few days of the life of illegitimate children.'[52]

This official invitation to voluntary societies and to local authorities to guard and cherish the soldiers' bastard children came at a time when reform was in the air. The first Reconstruction Committee, to plan for a better country after the war, had just been appointed. The Commission on Venereal Diseases had just published a report which dealt so frankly with the consequences of consorting with professional prostitutes that it made the fault of the unmarried mothers look more excusable than anyone had ventured to suggest up till now. All these influences on public opinion made it possible to set up a new organisation for the unmarried mother and her child which had the sole object of helping with their desperate practical problems and leaving their immortal souls alone. It was the first-ever helping hand of the kind without a deterrent in it. Even the Church Moral Welfare homes, which set out to forgive rather than punish, assumed that the girls were official penitents and – even if they did not make conversion a condition of board and lodging – at least insisted that they attended Church.

The new organisation, the National Council for the Unmarried Mother and Her Child, was the product of a

THE UNMARRIED MOTHERS

Special Committee set up by the Child Welfare Council. It was officially launched in February 1918. In its first report it said:

> It is clear that there is still much prejudice against anything but a purely 'deterrent' policy in dealing with the unmarried mother and her child. 'Will you not encourage immorality?' is a question not unfrequently asked. But it is promising to find the sympathy evoked by constructive proposals to save the child, to restore the mother to good citizenship and to make effective the responsibilities of the father. Public opinion is stirring and this is a time when social reform finds a ready acceptance.[53]

The Council's objectives were to get the laws dealing with bastardy and affiliation reformed; to get accommodation for the mother and child together, all over the country; and to be there when the mother asked for advice and help.

There was complete agreement that the separation of any mother from her baby should be regarded as an exceptional and deplorable necessity, not as the normal and natural procedure temporarily interrupted by the lack of foster-mothers. And to quote the Special Committee's own words, the natural sequence to this was that 'the responsibility of fatherhood must be recognised and that any scheme for the welfare of unmarried mothers must include means for bringing home that responsibility more effectively.'[54]

Within a few months they got the amount payable under an affiliation order doubled; and increased again later, though the Council's contention that it ought to be 'in proportion to the circumstances of both parents' was not accepted until half a century later. A suggestion presented to the Reconstruction Committee for organising a better world after the war was that there should be pensions for mothers. Mrs Vaughan Nash, who was the wife of the committee's secretary proposed that they should be granted to all 'mothers in need – widows, deserted, divorced and separated wives, wives of men in prisons, asylums etc and unmarried mothers'.[55] Her suggestion was taken up again in 1974 by the Finer Report.

CHAPTER THREE

THE BOYS COME HOME
1918–1920

Keep the Home Fires Burning,
Till the Boys Come Home.

1. *Into Parliament*
Since the middle of 1916, the women of Britain had been treated with the anxious consideration and flattery offered to an invaluable servant who might otherwise give notice and leave one helpless. Politicians and newspaper editors gave regular eulogies of each type of woman worker. Public figures who had been noted anti-suffragists recanted publicly, one by one; Garvin of the *Observer*, Northcliffe and finally Asquith himself. As early as August 1916, when he was still Prime Minister, he said, in introducing one of the abortive Special Register Bills about the franchise: 'I have received a great many representations from those who are authorised to speak for the women, and I am bound to say that they have presented to me – not only a reasonable, but I think from their own point of view an unanswerable case.'[1] In the autumn a

Speaker's Conference was called to discuss franchise reform. It was in session until the beginning of 1917, by which time Lloyd George had become Prime Minister. Its recommendations included, by a majority, a compromise proposal to give votes to women householders and the wives of men householders who were over the ages of thirty or thirty–five.

Mrs Fawcett, who was conducting negotiations with the government, was in favour of accepting the compromise as the thin end of the wedge, provided it was made effective at once. When one member of the Cabinet suggested that it could not and perhaps should not be put through in wartime, she briefly replied that renewed women's militancy would be more inconvenient still, and he promptly subsided.

Asquith now made a dramatic public retraction of his previous views, by calling for an early Bill to implement the proposals. 'Some of my friends may think that . . . my eyes, which for years in this matter have been clouded by fallacies and sealed by illusions, at last have been opened to the truth.'[2]

The final debate in January 1918 was wound up by Lord Curzon, the president of the Anti-suffrage League. Mrs Humphry Ward, the leader of the anti-suffragists (who had previously attempted to hedge her bets by offering Mrs Fawcett a bargain by which they would both ask for a special referendum on Women's Suffrage, however the debate turned out) sat next to her arch-enemy waiting for Curzon to speak.[3] Once he had started, word went out to the suffragists waiting in the precincts and was delivered to them by a policeman perhaps anxious to establish that the past was the past. 'Lord

Curzon is up, ladies, but he won't do you ladies no harm.'[4] Curzon did no breast-beating; but he did say that much as he deplored women's suffrage it was now inevitable; and those who could not bring themselves to accept it should abstain from voting on the motion altogether. The Bill was passed with a majority of 63.

Many suffragists were disappointed that it was, after all, only partial female suffrage. Sylvia Pankhurst remarked bitterly:

Some women have been given the vote, for the new measure enfranchises 6 million out of a total of more than 13 million and by its University and business franchise the Act still upholds the old class prejudices, the old checks and balances designed to prevent the will of the majority, who are the workers, from being registered without handicap.[5]

But the salient fact that the Speaker's Conference had realised, even if the women had not, was that the majority of women ('the superfluous women' of the pre-war world) had increased as every battle on the Western Front wiped out more men. If they were given universal suffrage and if they should all choose to vote, it would be their Parliament that was elected. Even with the limited franchise, many dedicated party politicians were getting nervous. Beatrice Webb, never an enthusiastic supporter of women's suffrage – admittedly because she was content with her own position as an outstanding female in a chiefly male field – prophesied that it would push the working men further left than they needed to be pushed. 'Parliament will become the organ of the feminine, or be thought to be so. Soldiers' and workers' councils will seem not only the alternative to communal representative assemblies, but also the alternative to the rule of women.'[6]

The Parliament (Qualification of Women) Act, which was passed ten days after the Armistice, and just as the war-time Parliament was to be dissolved, came as a surprise to the people most involved – that is, to the women who intended to stand for membership when the time came. 'Even those who had fought for women's suffrage had not believed that the vote would be quickly followed by the right to stand for Parliament, and they had often attempted to calm public fears by forecasting an interval of as long as ten years after the franchise was granted.'[7] But now the Bill slipped by almost unnoticed because everyone was taken up with Lloyd George's wire-pulling to get the Coalition back, which was to give his special blessing to five hundred reliable candidates who were known as 'coupon' holders. He also started a hate campaign, promising voters the satisfaction of revenge. 'I feel physically sick when I read the frenzied appeals of the Coalition leaders – the Prime Minister, Winston Churchill and Geddes – to hang the Kaiser, ruin and humiliate the German people – even to deprive Germany of her art treasures and libraries', Beatrice Webb angrily noted in her diary.[8] In this hysterical atmosphere, the first-ever women candidates found their campaigns something of an anti-climax.

Mary Macarthur, of the women's trade-union movement,

had been adopted as prospective candidate by the Labour party four months before, and the I.L.P. had Margaret Bondfield and Ethel Snowden ready in case of need. But the others had to be selected hurriedly because the election was timed for mid-December. There were seventeen in all, one Conservative, four Labour, four Liberal and eight Independent. One of these was Christabel Pankhurst who was expected by everyone to be the first woman M.P. as automatically as an heiress-apparent to become queen. She was the only woman candidate to have a 'coupon' bestowed on her. Also the Coalition organisation persuaded their own man contesting Smethwick to stand down for her. She announced that she was representing the Women's Party, just as the die-hard opponents of women's suffrage had always warned the country that enfranchised females would. But Christabel, who had a straight fight against the Labour candidate at Smethwick, had now less to say about women's rights than about nationalism, and the wickedness of internationalists, pacifists, trades-unionists and 'Bolsheviks' generally. She extended her anti-trades-union campaign against the efforts of Mary Macarthur, in the neighbouring constituency of Stourbridge, who was stressing the need for a just peace. Christabel's slogans were 'Make Germany Pay', and 'Union Jack versus Red Flag'. She kept her supporters busy, as she always had done in the suffrage campaign.

'Poor Mr Lloyd George, poor Lord Northcliffe!' wrote faithful Annie Kenney, still running errands for the adored leader. 'I was never off their doorsteps. By the time they had answered one question, Christabel thought of another. . .

Mr Lloyd George used to be very cross, then he would relax when he saw that I was really sorry to have to disturb him. . . .

'I had another interview with Lord Northcliffe at the *Times* office. The question I had to put was: would he give us his Press support? He promised to send one of his best lady journalists and to devote part of a column of the *Daily Mail* to news of Smethwick. I can honestly say that he never once failed in his promise, though at times we must have been very trying.'[9]

Christabel's election campaign was in fact the only attempt to create a political party especially for women. It never had the whole-hearted support either of the suffragists or the suffragettes. Ray Strachey, Mrs Fawcett's chief lieutenant, standing as Independent candidate for Brentford and Chiswick, said in her election address:

I believe with profound conviction that men and women should work together for the progress and good government of the nation, as they must for that of their homes. I hold that the interests of men and women are so closely bound together that they cannot be divided and that what is for the good of one sex must certainly be for the good of the other.[10]

Sylvia's reaction to the inauguration of the Women's Party was: 'Here is obviously a Tariff Reform, Tory, Imperial jingoist organisation and we who are Socialist and Internationalist have other ideas.'[11]

Christabel lost by 775 votes. She demanded a recount, but her trade-union opponent was still the winner. Mary

Macarthur was also only narrowly defeated, though she had not had the benefit of the 'coupon' and although the returning officer had insisted she should appear on the ballot-paper by her married name, while her trade-union supporters knew her only by her maiden one. Ray Strachey, in spite of having been praised by the press for asking the electors to support her, not because she was a woman, but because she was a candidate who would represent them well, nevertheless lost her deposit, as did three other women candidates.

The first woman ever to be elected to the British Parliament was all the anti-suffragists' nightmare vision of 'that menace to sanity . . . the Woman M.P.' made flesh at last. She was an accomplished terrorist, a militant suffragette and a political romantic. She was Countess Markievicz, born Constance Gore-Booth, sister of the first person to interest Christabel in women's suffrage, long ago in Manchester, the poetess Eva Gore-Booth. Their father was a landowner in the West of Ireland. Both of them had been brought up 'in the strange, split-minded routine of Anglo-Irish society, Protestants in a sea of Roman Catholicism,'[12] dividing their time between the big house in County Sligo and the 'season' in London.

Constance married a Polish count and went to live in Dublin. She joined the militant suffragettes and the Irish nationalists. She was herself a crack shot and formed a troop of Boy Scouts who really shot to kill. She was condemned to death for her part in the Easter Rising, but the sentence was commuted to penal servitude for life 'solely and simply on account of her sex'. She was released during a government attempt at reconciliation and became one of the Sinn Fein leaders and was arrested for inciting Irishmen to resist being conscripted by the British government to fight the Germans. (The suffragette union, meanwhile, was urging the reverse.) She was adopted as Sinn Fein candidate for the General Election while she was serving her sentence in Holloway. From there, where so many of the suffragettes had stood up to starvation, man-handling and forcible feeding, because they thought political equality was worth it, she was writing contemptuously to her sister that 'The English election is like Alice in Wonderland or a Gilbert and Sullivan opera.'[13]

When she was elected, the official summons to her, to take her seat, was forwarded to Holloway Gaol. She never set foot in the House of Commons publicly, though she is said to have slipped in incognito, once, to look at her name below a coat-peg, the first-ever female one to be so inscribed.

A mocking fate seemed to bedevil the victory of the original suffragettes, not only because none of their leaders ever did inherit the political powers for which they had all hoped and worked; but also because the women who did so were ludicrously unlike the feminist image. The Countess who never even bothered to take the seat which had been made possible by so much effort and so much suffering was followed into Parliament by an American Southern belle turned English society hostess, who appeared to 'the embattled women who had suffered and sacrificed so much to make it possible ... a wholly unsuitable representative of the Cause, for which they had been prepared to die and which she, who was not even British by birth, had never seriously supported'.[14]

Nancy Astor had been one of the Langhorne sisters who were Charles Dana Gibson's original inspiration for his drawings of the 'Gibson girl'. She married Waldorf Astor, who was M.P. for the Sutton division of Plymouth, and when his father died and he had to go to the House of Lords instead, he suggested that she would take advantage of the new Parliament (Qualification of Women) Act and stand for election in his place.

It certainly helped the first real heiress of the suffrage struggle that from the beginning of her campaign she had male support behind her. She had a constituency machine in good working order, the Conservative party organisation, the powerful press lords and her wealthy husband with all his staff.

The American papers described the scene approvingly. 'Lady Astor has voters gasping by the peppiness of her campaign. This brilliant woman, dressed in black, driving through the streets behind a dashing team of sorrels, with silk-hatted coachman, his whip and the bridles of his horses adorned with red, white and blue ribands. . . .' The *Evening Standard* said, 'Lady Astor is laughing her way into Parliament'; and *The Times* said, 'To judge by some newspaper reports, she is treating the whole affair as a huge joke.'

Bernard Shaw, who became her close friend and remained so all his life, referred to her election campaign in *The Apple-Cart*. The irrepressible 'merry lady' in the Cabinet, Amanda, although she is based mainly on Ellen Wilkinson, has Lady Astor's particular talent for puncturing male dignity and making her supporters laugh. ('I didn't argue. I mimicked him. I took all the high-falutin' passages in his speech and repeated them in his best manner until I had the whole five thousand laughing at him. Then I asked them would they like me to sing and their Yes nearly lifted the roof off.') Lady Astor had, in fact, got the better of a hostile group of hecklers by starting the whole meeting singing 'Keep the Home Fires Burning'.

She made the suffragists and the suffragettes feel faded and battle-scarred, and no longer the 'new woman' of the period. Her biographer Maurice Collis says

There was but one poignant reminder of past struggles, when the train bearing the newly-elected member drew into Paddington station. There, among the crowd on the platform to meet her was a small band of veteran suffragettes, some of whom had known imprisonment and forcible-feeding. Lady Astor, small, elegant, light-hearted and rich must have been quite unlike the woman they had envisaged as their first M.P. Yet one came forward to present her with a badge, saying, 'It is the beginning of a new era. I am glad to have suffered for this.' Lady Astor was deeply moved. The tension was relieved by an ugly-looking chap in the crowd bawling, '*I* never voted for you.' 'Thank heaven for that', she retorted.[15]

Even Frances Stevenson, who feared and disliked Lady Astor personally ('She is treacherous and not to be trusted'), found herself deeply moved by the occasion.

INTO PARLIAMENT

1 December 1919. Went to see the first lady M.P. take her place in the House. It really was a thrilling moment, not from the personal point of view but from the fact that after all these hundreds of years this was the very first time a woman had set foot upon the floor to represent the people – or a certain number of people. I had a lump in my throat as I saw her come in at the far end – a very graceful, neat figure – and wait for her turn to walk up the floor.

The advent of Lady Astor was the beginning of a new phase in the woman's movement. The battle for suffrage was as good as won. Once the post-war panic about the shortage of men voters subsided, as more schoolboys reached voting age, equal suffrage would be conceded.

The Pankhursts were out of date, figures of even slightly Blimpish fun to a new generation of emancipators. Now that the war was over, the door of No. 10 Downing Street was no longer open to them. They were shuffled from the centre of the stage. Defeat in the election was, for them, final. The Women's Party, with its impossible programme and its impossible expense, was dissolved.[16]

In Lady Astor's second speech in the House, when she was supporting an amendment to the Representation of the People Act which would give women the vote at 21, she was careful to assure the House that this would not mean that future women Members would combine into a sex party. 'We could not do it. We women disagree just as much as the men.'

2. *Back to the Kitchen*
It was obvious that there was going to be trouble when the long-dreamed-of day arrived at last and the boys came home.

What they wanted was quite simple. It was the 'restoration of pre-war practices' which had been promised in return for trade-union concessions made when the need for production was most desperate. To the women, this would simply mean a return to the customs of the pre-war Man's World, in which women were by nature second-class labour, only fit for unskilled monotony jobs paid at a second-class rate.

Mary Macarthur, of the Women's Trade Union League, with Susan Lawrence, her devoted disciple and herself a leading Fabian, had served on the Reconstruction Committee set up in 1916, and had advised the government about the conditions of women's employment after the war. In 1919, the Reconstruction Committee's Report came out, and – thanks to these two – recommended that women should have a properly paid and organised training for industry; a minimum wage; a forty-four-hour week and a fortnight's annual holiday; that women should be represented on workshop committees, and should have an efficient welfare service. The War Committee on Women in Industry, which had been appointed two months before the end of the war because of a strike of transport workers in London in which the men supported the women's claim to an equal war-time bonus, also recommended equal pay for equal work.

Meanwhile, a new branch at the War Office had been established in order to help men to have a better chance when they returned to civil life; by giving them educational and

BACK TO THE KITCHEN

technical classes which would increase their qualifications. The government had also planned a systematic demobilisation programme, to prevent a sudden flooding of the labour market and the consequent discovery of the returned hero that there was no place for him in it. The plan was that men should be released from the forces when they were certain of getting jobs. But this practical and far-sighted scheme infuriated the men, who preferred to stick to the schoolboy code of its being 'fair play' to be let out of the army strictly in accordance with how long you had put up with it, that is, a first-in, first-out scheme. When it came to the point of an actual mutiny, with troops refusing to go back to France when ordered, and demonstrating in Whitehall ('We won the war! We want civvy suits!') Churchill – who in any case appreciated the 'fair' and 'unfair' simplicities of the masculine code – promptly gave way and ordered a fast demobilisation instead of the orderly, planned one. Consequently, there was a discharge rate of 10,000 men a day for six months; and the only reasons why they were able to find enough jobs to go round, for a time, was that there was an unforeseen post-war boom in industry and because the women meekly stepped down. Employers did not want to let them go. They had done what was wanted and had done it well; they had been easy to manage, docile and cheap. But the government was pledged under the Pre-War Practices Act and the employers under various agreements, and the women made no fight. The working world slid back into the old conventions of female jobs and male jobs.

Only where there was a new process or a new trade, the

women could not be sacked as easily as in the old-established ones. Bakers and woodworkers and watchmakers got rid of them without much trouble. But in the electrical trades – or in any callings where new semi-skilled processes had come in – employers were able to claim and keep the women involved. Their wages slipped back to women's level. But at least the range of jobs in which women were employed had widened permanently.

Nevertheless, unemployment hit women long before the men had finished basking in the post-war trade boom. The Central Committee on Women's Training and Employment reported 'a new problem of distress among women affected by the transition from war to peace conditions . . . the shrinking of opportunity due to the desire not to trespass upon occupations specially suited to disabled men and the depression in trade which restricts the development of new branches of work which had given promise of employment for women.'

The women's saga was over. One by one, the jobs in which they had been respected and rewarded vanished.

The Waacs, the Wrafs, the Wrens, the Women's Legion, the military masseuses, the munition workers and their welfare workers ceased to exist. Conductors stepped down for the last time from their buses . . . out of banks and insurance offices the women gradually faded . . . the landwoman was no longer to be seen . . . there was a slump in women . . .[17]

Since the middle of 1915 they had been gallant workers, for whom no praise could be too fulsome; admired, with affectionate amusement for 'playing the man' like Shakespeare's Rosalind. But now the masquerade was over; it was time to hang up the doublet and hose behind the kitchen door and get back to skirts and aprons, to keep an eye on the clock so that the breadwinner's hot tea could be slapped down in front of him the second he got in. The newspapers began to refer to women who did not go back voluntarily to their personal-relationship rôles (domesticated wife, stay-at-home mother and dutiful daughter) as 'limpets' who would not be prised off their war-time job even when the rightful owner came back to resume it.

In February 1919, Lady Rhondda of the Women's Industrial League, (journalist, peeress in her own right and distinguished feminist) wrote to the *Daily News*:

Sir, There are over half a million women workers who are at present receiving unemployment allowance and there are probably an additional million of industrial women at present out of employment... what are the Government doing to find employment for the great army of efficient women in peace-time occupations? Then, instructions have been issued to controlled firms by government departments to discharge women workers in a wholesale manner. The rights of women seem to have been totally disregarded. Women are willing to stand aside and give place to certain classes of skilled men discharged from the Forces, but why should women have been thrown out and male dilutees retained? Why should women who previous to the war were employed on certain processes be discharged as they have been, on the instructions of a government department?[18]

But Mary Macarthur, whose allegiance to trade-union solidarity was at least as pressing as her allegiance to feminism, replied irritably that Lady Rhonddha's letter was 'a gross exaggeration' and that in any case 'it would be small solace to an unemployed woman to know that her father or her brother was to be dismissed to make way for her'.

This split in feminist ranks stood for the difference between the attitude of the middle-class career women and the working-class wage-earning ones, when the men reclaimed their pre-war place in the national life. It was the middle-class rebels who had led the struggle for the vote, and now it was the teachers and the lawyers and the businesswomen who went on fighting to keep at least some part of the ground they had won from the men during the war. At trade-union level, traditional rôles were still binding. In spite of the fact that during the war they had seen through the men's lofty claim that a man's job was so skilled and difficult that no woman could possibly attempt it, they did not attach a great deal of importance to that. Ray Strachey explained that their failure to fight for their right to the work was due to the fact that:

The theory of a man's work and woman's work was quite firmly entrenched in their minds and they did not try to upset it. All this novelty and change was a war thing. When the men came back they must have their work again and everything must be as it had been before. They were not men, but women and so of course they must go back to their proper place. . . . They would have the vote and a lot of new knowledge, but back of course they would go. It was only right. And to use the time when men were fighting to steal their work from them would be a shabby trick indeed. They were not going to be parties to that. And so when the war was over and the period of demobilisation began, women fell out without complaint. Hundreds of thousands fell into unemployment, misery and the loss of their means of life . . . but the men must have their places back whatever came of it and the women went quietly. It had to be.[19]

By the autumn of 1919, ladies were beginning to complain that although so many munition-girls were being laid off all the time, and so many were unemployed, nevertheless they still could not get their maid-servants back. The Central Committee reported that

Reluctance to take up residential work is a feature of post-war employment which characterises all types of women workers. Because of the widening of the scope of employment during the war and the consequent ease with which women were able to find employment, the necessity of seeking anything but daily posts did not arise for the generation of workers growing up from 1914. Now they will not accept the separation from home ties and interests, or the loss of fellowship of factory or workshop.

There was a rather despairing government-backed drive to get the women's unemployment problem settled by forgetting all about the brave new world and the first castle-in-the-air ideas of the Ministry of Reconstruction, and get the girls back to their old stand-by job in married women's homes. The newspapers coaxed them. 'Mistresses are now much more considerate than they used to be – they or their daughters have washed up in canteens and scrubbed in hospitals during the war.' 'A soldier's widow may be allowed to keep her child with her.' 'Mistresses often restrict the number of their fires so that their servants may enjoy the full benefit of the coal ration.' 'The comforts of a refined home will appeal to many superior girls after the necessarily rough life in a munition factory or the Women's Army.'[20] In fact, in spite of the employer's new sense of guilt, it was a less attractive job than it had been before the war, because it no longer offered good prospects (rising from kitchen-maid or nursery-maid to be cook or nannie) and the employer's kitchen was no longer the cosy refuge from the empty streets which it used to be, because now the picture-palace and the palais-de-danse were part of the working-class girl's world, and being free in the evenings mattered a great deal.

However, the Committee attempted to raise the status of the job by setting up training centres for what was now to be called 'Homecraft'. Sixty-five per cent of the trainees were ex-factory workers, many of them down-and-out before they would try this last resort. ('Many who had been unemployed for a long time were obliged to buy the necessary clothes and footwear to enable them to attend the centre.' The Committee had to help them out.) The Queen and Princess Mary visited the training centres to make the girls feel that their work was worth while. But when they finally went out into jobs, the Committee was obliged to record that 'a perusal of many hundreds of their letters made it clear that the loneliness which especially in small households is apparently inseparable from this calling is the difficulty which women find it hardest to overcome'.

The only successful effort to give domestic service a new image was the emergence of the 'Lady Help'. She was, in fact, that original drug on the labour market, the untrained genteel spinster. Once, her only resort had been a job in someone else's house as governess or companion which meant that she was neither family nor below stairs. Being a Lady Help was a continuation of this status but with the advantage that she had a (mild, but still indubitable) scarcity value and therefore was able to stand out for better conditions than before 1914. A typical advertisement for this kind of post would mention that some of the traditional drudgery had been eliminated for her benefit. 'Clergyman's Daughter or ex-V.A.D., lady by birth essential, for house-parlour work in vicarage. Must be capable, methodical and early riser. Live with family (four). Salary, starting £30 and laundry. Age 24–30 years. No brass or silver.'[21]

The little post-war trade boom which had started in 1919, in the belief that Britain would now resume her place among the wealthy nations, lasted for a year and then began to fade. It became more difficult even for men to find work. By January 1921, there were over a million unemployed. At that, the women surrendered and decided to make the best of it and to go back, after all, to their traditional jobs, that is, those which the men had always left to women, and so were lower-paid. According to the 1921 census, the greater number of women were again in only a very few occupations, just as they had been before the war: 33% were in domestic service; 12%

in the textile industries; 11% in the clothing trade; and 4% in teaching. The woman teachers, at least, were still hopeful that some of their improvement in status during the war years might be sustained.

During the war, the teaching profession had had almost complete 'substitution', that is, women had taken over the position of every fit man of fighting age. Elementary education – in particular – had been very far from a reserved occupation. (In fact it was thought of so little importance that children were allowed to flout regulations about part-time or even school-time work during their school years to work in munitions, on the grounds that even if it was bad for their book-learning it was good for their characters to 'do their bit'. H. A. L. Fisher, Minister for Education, admitted it.) In this climate of opinion, boys had to forget their discomfiture about being taught by a woman, and women substituting for men did exactly a man's work, without any formula of the heavy-industries' pattern that three women could perform the workload of two men.

Therefore, towards the end of the war, the women teachers began to feel that their claim for equal pay for equal work, still being raised monotonously every year, might be fruitfully pressed a little harder. But although it was clear enough to them what their claim meant, as they stood in the schoolmaster's shoes, teaching the class he had left to go to the Front, male authority, represented by the editor of *The Times Educational Supplement*, owned himself completely baffled by the concept.

The principle seems to us, when analysed, to convey so little meaning that it is difficult to take it as a serious contribution to the subject of salaries. The question at once arises, 'What is Equal Work?' No two teachers do equal work. It is probably true that some women, as teachers, are better than most men, that some men are less capable than most women. But it is also arguable that the average woman is less capable than the average man in any grade of work in which men and women compete. . . . If this is true, one reason may well be that a substantial proportion of women do not regard their work as a calling for life. The teachers who have secured entrance to the profession are not paid by merit. If they were, we should see many women teachers securing high salaries and many men who now have high salaries paid very little. . . . But that is no reason for raising an uneconomic cry as to equal salaries for equal work, when there is no test possible. Nor indeed is it in the interests of the women teachers. If the concession demanded is granted, the results may be that Local Authorities and Managers will for the most part select men, as soon as men become available, and the women may find that they will either have to offer themselves at lower salaries or be crowded out of the profession.[22]

In 1919, the government took a trick out of Mr Asquith's old repertoire for dealing with contentious women; that is, it lulled the agitation for equality by announcing that they were about to examine the whole question of teachers' salaries with a view to standardising them, and this would naturally include the question of women teachers as well as those of men. The women teachers apparently forgetting the lesson of history, took the promise at its face value, just as the suffragettes had, and subsided for the moment.

The Burnham Committee on Teachers' Pay made its first report on November 27, 1919. It recommended, as anticipated, standard salaries for the country. On the question of equal pay it recommended a differential of 20% between a man teacher's salary and that of a woman teacher.

The women doctors did even worse than the women teachers when the men came home; and the fact they had, in principle, equal pay (that is, they were not allowed to undercut fees) probably worked to their disadvantage. They lost their training opportunities, which was the most serious set-back that any group of women trying to establish themselves in a profession could have. In 1914, there had been an appeal from the leaders of the medical profession for women to train as doctors to replace the men serving in the forces. St Mary's accepted a limited number as clinical students; Charing Cross took some on the same terms as men. St George's, Westminster, St Bartholomew's, King's College, the London Hospital and University College Hospital all opened their doors to women. At the end of the war, when the surviving men doctors returned, and young men could start their careers instead of being conscripted, the teaching hospitals gladly went back to refusing women. The Senior Physician at Westminster summed up the attitude of hospital authorities when he assured the disappointed girls that there was absolutely nothing against them except their sex. He appreciated the devoted and excellent war services rendered by women doctors during a time of national emergency. His staff, who had taught mixed classes during the transient boom in women doctors, had no fault to find with them except that they were occupying places which would be more usefully filled by men, since 100% of the men who qualified would remain in the profession, while about 50% of the women would leave it after a short time to get married. He was sure that there was now ample accommodation for women doctors in their own special teaching hospitals. This meant that the Royal Free was their only hope. The famous teaching hospitals, in any case, were very conscious of their students' image, as healthy ex-public-schoolboys, and this was bolstered by the prestige of their football teams. They were said to be influenced by this in selecting medical students.

The women lawyers, who had started much later, did better than the doctors after the war. Their prospect of being allowed to exist had looked fairly bright in 1914 and now the Sex Disqualification (Removal) Act of December 1919 gave them the right to ask admission to the Inns of Court. The first woman was accepted by the Middle Temple within a few hours of the Act being passed. The very limited number of women trying to win the right to practise law had never run up against the crude hostility which male medical students had shown to the first female ones. Now, apart from the press finding the term 'Portias' irresistible every time a woman barrister was mentioned, and one pettish exhibition of anti-feminism from the Benchers the first time they dined in Middle Temple, the girls had quite an easy passage into this previously closed world. The reason was a melancholy one. Between 5,000 and 6,000 young barristers and solicitors and articled clerks had been in the services. Many were dead and some – as in all walks of life – had come back unfit to practise any profession.

Lawyers, even more than doctors, tended to keep a practice in the family, and their sons to go in for law because it was the family business. The country solicitor in Somerset Maugham's play about the post-war world – *For Services Rendered* – has no one to inherit the firm because his son has come back blind. 'You've had a lot to put up with, Sidney, I know that. But don't think you're the only one. It's been a great blow to me that you haven't been able to follow me in the business as I followed my father. Three generations that would have been. But it wasn't to be.' Those solicitors who had a daughter sufficiently clever to take over for her missing brother thanked heaven for it. The *Daily News* of April 5, 1921, reporting on the Portias, added that 'About 40 women are now in training as solicitors, the majority of them from the enterprising north or from Wales. Many of them are the daughters of country solicitors who have no sons or else have lost them in the war, and who have articled their girls instead, so as to keep the practice in the family.'

In December 1919, nursing was officially recognised as a profession. 'It had been granted what the law and the church had never felt it necessary to seek: a statutory register. It had followed the path of the doctors, the teachers and the midwives, and achieved its objective two years before the dentists.'[23]

In the spring of that year, some 3,700 army nurses had been demobilised, but some 20,000, including the Red Cross nurses, still remained. The two warring nurses' organisations – the Royal British Nurses Association and the College of Nursing – combined, for once, in a shared fear that when the Register came into force the various authorities who administered the profession would somehow contrive to smuggle the V.A.D.s on to it. There had been plenty of hints that Sir Arthur Stanley, who was chairman of the College of Nursing and also actively working for the British Red Cross Society, wanted to use the opportunity to benefit all those gallant young Red Cross volunteers who had been the darlings of the public during the war, but were now something of an embarrassment. This was exactly what the women of the nursing hierarchy did not want. Nurses, from now on, were to have a new status, and a new image and acknowledged qualifications. Amateurs (as they firmly classed the V.A.D.s) were out.

A statutory General Nursing Council, consisting of sixteen nursing members and nine lay ones, was appointed in 1920, to start the Register. Some of them – an articulate minority – wanted the Register to be so select, and entrance to the profession so difficult, that only the best type of young woman would face up to the idea of getting in at all. The Council felt free to make entrance selective because at the moment there were many more nurses than there were jobs for them. There was so much wrangling about qualifications that the Minister of Health had to intervene. In the end it was agreed that three different categories should be admitted to the Register – 'existing nurses' who had been engaged in *bona fide* practice' before the Registration Act; nurses who had completed their training after the Act, but before the new entrance system was introduced; and the nurses of the future, who were to achieve qualification only through professional examinations (and difficult and demanding ones at that). In fact by 1925, when the first exams were set, there was already a shortage of recruits to the profession.

The Marquis of Dufferin and Ava had raised a last, unhopeful objection to the Registration of Nurses, in the House of Lords debate on the subject, by pointing out with great frankness that 'if nurses had standard qualifications it would reduce the great amount of competition from unskilled nursing workers, which would tend to raise salaries not only outside the hospitals, but in the hospitals themselves. Registration really meant the abolition of cheap labour.'[24] He need not have worried. The pay of a probationer in a voluntary hospital was on average about £20 in the first year, £25 in the second and £30 in the third; that is to say that at the end of a gruelling apprenticeship, the girl was getting as much as the 'Lady Help' required for housework in the vicarage ('No brass or silver') was offered as starting salary.

The bitter truth was that in the only profession run by women almost entirely for women, the girl beginners were exploited in a way which would have provided wonderful ammunition for the Women's Movement if only it had been arranged by men. Probationers were the underpaid, overworked, unskilled labourers of the hospitals – scrubbing, cleaning brass, serving meals – in return for their training. Without them, the 'voluntary' hospitals could not have balanced their budgets. Probably the only reason why this cynical exploitation of the girls' willingness lasted on until the next war was in sight was because there was no yardstick of a male breadwinner wage against which to measure the nurse's pay. If there had been, their 'unequal pay' – even with a differential like that of the teachers – would at least have been better than the pittance for which they worked a 59-hour week.

3. *Case for Unequal Pay*
In September 1918, the government appointed a committee to study the relation between men's and women's wages. Beatrice Webb was a member of it. She was no feminist, and the subject bored her. So did her fellow members, all of whom had conventional and utterly predictable views on equal pay for women. When she could not tolerate the way the Committee was moving, she produced a brisk and impatient Minority Report of her own (later published by the Fabian Society under the title, *The Wages of Men and Women; Should They Be Equal?*) which demolished the traditional aphorisms on which unequal pay was based.

The main argument was always that a man's pay has a concealed subsidy for wife and children's support. In that case, Beatrice demanded, why is a bachelor teacher doing the same work as a widow teacher with dependent children paid more than she is? And why does not a childless man get less than the father of a large family? As a carpenter, giving evidence to the Committee, put it, if he was offered a job in London they did not ask him, before settling the rate, whether he had ten children or none. Only 50% of males over 18 working in industry really had any children at all dependent on their wages, and yet the whole wage structure was fixed assuming they all had, whereas a good 25% of adult women had someone to maintain on theirs.

Beatrice accused employers of inventing situations in which men earned more than women doing the same job, in order to avoid having to pay up; such as that a woman conductor on a tram would not be so useful if the tram broke down or ran away or if there was a drunken brawl among passengers. And she accused the trade unions of putting their masculine solidarity before their trade-union solidarity by getting unequal pay embodied in war-time agreements between them and employers' associations, coupled with a solemn bargain that, after the war, women should be excluded from men's jobs. She ended by putting forward the Webbs' favourite universal panacea – the National Minimum Wage, and one that did not differentiate between the sexes.

But by the beginning of 1920, the talk of equal pay for equal work began to die away, as the ominous black cloud of mass unemployment, which was to hang over the whole working world until they started to make munitions for the next war, had begun to hover. The women began to realise that they were going to be lucky to keep any kind of a job which a male worker could do, and in fact to reflect secretly that it might be wise to undercut him if necessary. The little post-war boom was over, and jobs were not there for the returned heroes' asking, any more.

Employers in city offices received the personal applications of young ex-officers somewhat coldly. 'What do you know?' they asked of young men who had left their public schools to join the New Armies, who had been very fine machine-gunners or pilots of aircraft or tank officers with the PBI, which was the Poor Bloody Infantry. They had not been trained for anything except war, which was now at an end. Some of them bought little farms and lost their money. Some of them became agents for vacuum cleaners or cosmetics or women's underwear, and hated ringing the doorbells to ask for the lady of the house and could not make a go of it.[25]

Somerset Maugham's ex-naval-officer, who tries to set up as a garage-owner and fails and is to be imprisoned for debt, but is driven to shoot himself instead, states the case for his kind. 'I suppose it doesn't occur to you that when a fellow has served his country . . . in a job that's unfitted him for anything else, it's rather disgraceful that he should be shoved out into the world with no means of earning his living and nothing between him and starvation but a bonus of a thousand pounds or so?'[26]

It was now the turn of the middle-class women workers to be reproached for their greed and selfishness in sticking to their jobs. The women in industry had been taking them away from their 'fathers and brothers', but the appeal to the career woman was that she was depriving a whole group of men of her own class of the salaries due to them. Lord Haig started a great campaign in the newspapers for work for ex-officers, saying that 'the case of the discharged officer was worst of all the treatment of all the indomitable heroes of the Great War'.[27] The *Lady* had already drawn attention to 'the claims on the public of ex-officers who voluntarily sacrificed their future careers to join up',[28] and launched a scheme of their own, whereby 'woman patronesses' would 'adopt' an ex-officer by personally introducing him to friends whose influence might prove of assistance to him.

Sir George Barnes, M.P., summed up the growing resentment against women workers in general, which was to last for twenty years after they had been thanked for saving Britain from defeat by their efforts.

There are still a good many young women who, but for the war, would have stayed at home, and who are now at work only for 'pin-money'. They should be replaced by the ex-soldier in all cases where he could do the work, and I believe that to be the case in many places, especially government offices. If I were an employer just now, I would have every enquiry made as to the condition in life of my women workers, and I would weed out all those not dependent on their own work for means of living.[29]

CHAPTER FOUR

THE SEX REVOLUTION
1920–1929

1. *The Mutilated Society*
The key to the sex revolution of the nineteen-twenties is to be found in the Roll of Honour in any little country church. There, in villages so small that there is only a single memorial tablet to the dead of the Boer War, probably the subaltern son of the Squire, and perhaps some half-dozen killed – of both sexes – between 1939 and 1945, a single campaign of the Great War may account for that number of young men, all within the same age-group, all living within a mile or two of each other, all wiped out in the same few days, on the Somme or the Maine, at Ypres or Neuve-Chapelle or Verdun. Such villages were left, frozen with grief, with the usual number of women and girls, of old men and boys, but with yawning gaps where the husbands and fathers and sweethearts should have been. And this mutilated society, on a larger scale, was reproduced in every town and city; from Highland fishing ports (out of which the young men had vanished earliest of all, because unemployment drove them to volunteer) to

London, with its half-empty West End clubs and East End pubs where the old and the maimed men now had plenty of space in the Tap Room just for themselves.

The balance of sexes in the population, which had been uneven enough to create much unhappiness and frustration before the war, was now more overweighted by women than ever before. The balance of females over fourteen rose from 595 per thousand persons to 638; there were more spinsters than ever and now more widows – 43 per thousand.[1] The war years, which had yielded such a rich harvest to the women struggling for sex equality, had cost them too much. All the gains in status and freedom and independence were, in the end, arid and tasteless without their men there to witness them. It meant that young women and girls had to face the prospect of forced virginity, and parents the long boredom of waiting for death without grandchildren to give any meaning to their old age.

In the early Twenties, when grief for the dead was still fresh, there was a great revival of Spiritualism, which had been allowed to go out of fashion since its mid-Victorian heyday. Now it caught on again, in neighbourhood associations of the bereaved, meeting regularly at each other's homes for table rapping and planchette; in spontaneous occult experiments at cocktail parties and as a business enterprise. Professional mediums found it profitable to set up in most cities and to charge admission to seances at which participants hoped, each time, that their own dead husband or son would be called up. These mostly took place in the medium's own house, in order (said the sceptics) that she might have the equipment ready to make ectoplasm materialise (by being expelled from her mouth) or perhaps to lower a dangling dummy, in the semi-darkness, to represent the soldier come back in response to a properly presented summons from a professional Spiritualist. Kipling wrote, of this 'craze':

> The road to Endor is easy to tread,
> For mother or yearning wife. . . .
> Whispers shall comfort us out of the dark –
> Hands – ah God! – that we knew!
> Visions and voices – look and hark!
> Shall prove that the tale is true,
> And that those who have passed to the further shore
> May be hailed – at a price – on the road to Endor.[2]

'Poor human beings,' wrote Beatrice Webb, on learning that her sister, Maggie Hobhouse, was trying to get into contact with her youngest and favourite son, killed at Ypres. 'How deep is the craving for extended personality beyond the limits of a mere lifetime on earth!' Maggie wrote, when she visited the battleground,

> As I stood there, I almost felt his spirit by me, telling me how little the mortal remains should mean to us . . . I do not take your view of the entire futility of the psychical phenomena – it may be that no proof can be had. But it is curious that most people who look into it are more or less converted to the spiritualist hypothesis.[3]

This cult, which was reflected in films such as *Earthbound!* and novels like H. A. Vachell's *The Other Side* and Philip Gibbs'

Darkened Rooms, and in plays such as James Barrie's *A Well-Remembered Voice*, all assumed that in spite of the charlatans there must be something in the belief. No one cared to be too damning about the cult, with so many bereaved women whose lives were now so empty, using it for a brief and unsatisfying escape.

The girls who were still young and unmarried when the war ended also suffered from living in a mutilated society. Even if they had not personally lost a fiancé, their chances of getting a husband were the lowest of any British women since records were kept. The men of their age-group had been decimated and the ones left available were quite likely to have been so maimed as to be ineligible. Vera Brittain[4] recalls an advertisement in the Personal column of *The Times* from a woman whose fiancé had been killed, offering to marry any blinded serviceman who needed a wife to look after him.

It was a strange arid social life, with such a shortage of whole men. If a girl was asked to a private dance, she was requested to bring her own partner, and if she could not muster one she had to refuse the invitation. In the new palais-de-danse halls, which mushroomed in provincial cities to accommodate the ballroom-dancing craze, it was quite usual and acceptable for two girls to dance together. Male taxi-dancers could be hired, for one fox-trot or waltz at a time, from a pen at the end of the dancing-floor. There were the original 'gigolos'. As unemployment spread, so did they. Being hired for one's maleness now became a full-time occupation. Rich divorcees and widows would take up a presentable young man and support him, giving him lavish presents, on the condition that he fulfilled at least some of the duties of the missing man in their lives. Some gigolos were merely escorts, others sold sexual intercourse as well. They were an object of angry contempt, not only to other men, but to girls of the same age-group and the same social class, whose mates they should have been.

It was an era of men in bad shape not only physically but mentally. Even if they had not a cork leg or lungs damaged by gas, ex-soldiers who had survived were liable to have been shell-shocked or to relapse into black moods for which they would give no explanation, like the tormented soldier in Siegfried Sassoon's poem:

> No no, not that; it's bad to think of war
> When thoughts you've gagged all day come back to haunt
>   you...
> And it's been proved that soldiers don't go mad,
> Unless they lose control of ugly thoughts
> Which drive them out to gibber among the trees.[5]

Women of all ages now began to put an exaggerated value on masculine strength and virility. Louis Golding, in *Store of Ladies*, told the story of the passion of a middle-aged Society widow for a young boxer from the East End whom she met at one of those

> organised exhibitions of brute force . . . the display of animal force in its crudest or finest forms which swept over every section of society . . . cowboy strength and steers in the Rodeo, bull-fighting, Cossacks disporting themselves into brawny pyramids. . . . Society adapting

its reception-rooms, its studios into roped rings for boxers from Bermondsey.

In 1921, a new romantic writer, Edith Maude Hull, had a runaway success and caused a considerable scandal with her novel, *The Sheik*. Genteel suburban matrons got it out of Boots' library, typists read it under the desk, schoolma'ams kept it discreetly in their lodgings. It was about the pleasure of being raped by a handsome, brutal Arab, in glowing health and not suffering from his nerves. Mrs Hull dodged the most controversial issue before the end of the book by having her hero admit to being, after all, the son of an Anglo-Saxon landowner, gone native after a quarrel with his father. But Bernard Shaw in *Back to Methuselah* stated baldly that women were looking elsewhere because the men of their own race were so limp. 'Our women and their favourite writers begin to talk about men with golden complexions.' In London Society there was a craze for black supermen, satirised by Evelyn Waugh in *Decline and Fall* when his fashionable heroine turns up at her son's prep-school Sports Day with her black gigolo.

The subject of women's need for complete sexual satisfaction had been under discussion for almost twenty years, but until now it had been dealt with discreetly, in books limited to medical libraries. Havelock Ellis's seven volumes on *The Psychology of Sex* which came out between 1897 and 1927 were now openly debated at avant-garde parties, particularly his defence of 'the erotic rights of women'. The other medical man advising the girls to enjoy themselves, at this time, was Freud. He had first come to the attention of the

British lay public when psychologists in special hospitals for shell-shocked men, such as Maghull, near Liverpool, had used his theory of dream imagery to find out what suppressed fear or anxiety, intensified by overstrain, was playing on the patient's mind. But his post-war appeal to the rebels of the Twenties was his (supposed) recommendation that they should get rid of unhealthy 'inhibitions' and 'repressions' by abandoning self-restraint.

All this encouragement to women to help themselves generously to free sexual pleasure left one fact of life out of account, that customs and conventions which ration it, to protect the young female from the male, also protect the male from too urgent demands on him. As long as young men had been subject to a network of social rules and customs, which provided that they were never left alone for long with a girl of their own class (from whom they would eventually choose a bride), the supply of sexual desire was sufficient to satisfy the demand. But in the post-war release from all such rules, the minority of nubile men found themselves threatened by a new anxiety. Havelock Ellis stated it with clinical frankness.

One of the many things necessary for a woman to know which it is unreasonable to expect a husband to explain . . . is the exhausting effect of coitus on a man as compared with a woman. . . . The inexperienced bride cannot know beforehand that the frequently repeated orgasms which render her vigorous and radiant may exert a depressing effect on her husband and his masculine pride induces him to conceal the fact.

A man who had been brought up in a society which assumed that the male had to be kept in check because he was insatiable found the idea of being sexually inadequate as humiliating as the woman who was not sexually attractive enough to get married had found her position before the war.

This male anxiety about impotence was a perpetual undercurrent in the sex revolution. Among the liberated young, a whole set of jokes about 'cavemen' was built up, suggesting that what the girls really wanted was to be dragged away by the hair. But there was a sting in them. When a rich and handsome peer was divorced by a seductive musical-comedy star, on the grounds that the marriage had not been consummated, a cruel jingle went the rounds, not only among their circle, but wherever the popular papers – which had revelled in the case – were read.

> Breathes there the man with soul so dead
> Could lie alongside June in bed
> And let her go, untouched, untried?
> There is a man – Lord Inverclyde.

Havelock Ellis had set up a masculine prototype who was to worry the men of the sexually permissive society for the next fifty years, just as much as the prototype irresistible courtesan (or, as she had been christened since 1918, the 'vamp') had worried the virtuous sweethearts and wives of the sexually regulated society. This was the super-virile lover who is inexhaustible. 'The rare men who possess a genital potency which they can exert to the gratification of women without injury to themselves have been by Benedt termed "sexual athletes". Such men easily dominate women.'

The decade which had started with *The Sheik* ended with another sexual-athlete hero, written about for a more intellectual readership, in the form of D. H. Lawrence's *Lady Chatterley's Lover*. Since it was banned in Britain, its circulation was limited to people who could get a copy from abroad. But it was so much discussed, by the progressive young, that one did not have to read it in order to join in the conversation. It was the story of Constance Chatterley, whose husband has come back from the war paralysed from the waist downward. She tries to get sexual satisfaction from a young man of her own class, but his potency is mediocre and because he cannot satisfy her he rails against her as a domineering harpy. She is bitterly unhappy, frustrated and desperate until she achieves complete sexual satisfaction with her husband's game-keeper, Mellors. He was Lawrence's version of the virile man of another race coming to the rescue. Mellors was from the working-class, Lady Chatterley from the gentry. Lawrence believed that industrial civilisation (as represented by the boss-class impotent husband) was arid and false, and that redemption lay in returning to primitive nature as represented by the game-keeper. 'He preached the Sun as a protective deity and urged women that happiness for them lay only in yielding submissively to the dark sexual urge of strong-loined men.'[6]

This attitude to sex was one of the deviations from pure feminism which most worried the old guard who had fought for women's equality and dignity. Maude Royden, one of the most distinguished suffragists, a scholar and a preacher in her own right despite her sex, who had always given the movement a strong religious and ethical basis, said that: 'The demand for imperfect development in women and the abandonment of self-control in the intoxicating sense of being mastered belong alike to the pathological side of sex.'[7]

But to the girls who had been in Junior School at the time when the suffragettes were being 'mastered' by a prison doctor forcing a feeding-tube into them, Maude Royden's protest sounded prim and old-fashioned and fuddy-duddy. The correct attitude to sex, in their circles, was cool and mocking, like Noël Coward's lyric in which a girl laments that she cannot be the real-life victim of her favourite film villain:

> The way that he uses
> Ingenues is
> Really a sight to see;
> He binds them across his saddle tight,
> Regardless of all their shrieks of fright,
> And carries them upside down all night,
> He never did that to me.[8]

The élite group of the fashionably frivolous young was the Bright Young Things, who conducted a long, original and colourful social rebellion in London Society. They had their imitators in every provincial town, wherever a gang of young people took to going to dance-halls or pub-crawling in motor-cars. Their revolutionary creed included sexual promiscuity. Parents had next to no control over them, because chaperones were an extinct species, and most of these young men and girls had their own money, so were immune to the old sanction of threatening to cut off supplies. Also, it was not socially acceptable, in post-war society, to try to make your children conform to pre-war conventions. Parents anxiously strove to keep up with their children's progressive views. Most middle-class parents calmed their own uneasy fears about what was happening to their 'dancing daughters' who let themselves in at home in the small hours, having spent the time since the Palais closed alone in a car with a young man, by maintaining stoutly that in these days young people were to be 'trusted' and that the girls had too much sense and self-control to go 'too far'. In fact this was much nearer the truth than was the cynical belief that very few brides were virgins these days. The dancing daughters of the Twenties had been brought up in homes and educated in schools where the pre-war ethos about sex was still doctrine. They had the heady experience of throwing the rules of their childhood over, which made the nineteen-twenties such an exhilarating period in which to be young. But their inhibitions about virginity still clung. There was more boasting and more talking about 'going the whole hog' than doing it, as illustrated by the illegitimacy rate, which had been 54 per thousand live births during the war and just after but which then dropped to 43 and stayed round about it until the next war. One of Noël Coward's revue sketches, *Mild Oats*, made fun of the nice girl who thinks she ought to have promiscuous sexual intercourse, but cannot bring herself to do so.

I'm a perfectly ordinary girl. I live in Rutland Gate with my aunt, I go to matinees and dances and walk in the Park and help to get up Tableaux Vivants for charity. . . . I read an awful lot; all the modern writers . . . vehement feminist articles and pamphlets. I've worked myself up into a state of burning indignation at the injustice of sex relationships . . . why shouldn't women have the same chances as men . . . lead the same lives as men . . . I've been thinking myself a clever emancipated modernist with a cool, clear sense of values, and now look at me . . . look at me . . . I should like to go into a convent, right away, this minute. . . .[9]

Among the young intelligentsia the breaking-up of sex conventions was conducted as a conscientious social experiment. In *Autumn Crocus*, a social comedy about the new fashion for Continental holidays, a young unmarried couple staying at a small Austrian inn give a moral lecture to a middle-aged Anglican vicar, also staying there, about the 'trial marriage' in which they are engaged.

Alaric: Oh, my dear man, really you mustn't talk about 'liaisons'; one must try to keep one's mind above the level of French farce.

Audrey: Of course, your generation's always so flippant about sex. Look how you behave – rushing lightly into matrimony, peopling the world with unwanted children, thronging the divorce courts. . . .

Alaric: The duty of every healthy male is to find a suitable mate – who, by bringing the necessary feminine attributes naturally omitted from his ego will complete that ego, enabling it and its female counterpart to vibrate in plastic rhythm – united yet individual – in dual unity with the harmonic cosmos. . . . I am of the opinion that Audrey and I are rather well suited. But we are just at a most important psychological stage and it is absolutely imperative that no-one should confuse our reactions.[10]

None of this kind of experimenting with new sexual mores would have been possible without Marie Stopes, who spread the information about birth-control and the equipment for practising it among a much wider public than had ever had access to either before the war. But she did not embark on her mission of contraception for the convenience of the promiscuous, but for the sake of virtuous wives and mothers worn out by child-bearing.

She was the daughter of an earnestly intellectual couple who had met and fallen in love at a meeting for the British Association for the Advancement of Science. They combined unconventional ideas about freedom in education, rather strangely, with stern old-fashioned Scottish presbyterianism – no playing on the Sabbath and a sense of guilt all round. The combination made Marie into a hardworking scholar who got double honours at London University and a doctorate of philosophy at Munich and after that an appointment as the first woman instructor on the scientific staff of Manchester University. She married a Canadian botanist, Reginald Gates, and embarked on three years of scenes and recriminations and dissatisfaction for which neither of them seems to have realised the reason. In the end she went to the British Museum and read every sex book she could find which was applicable to her own case. She verified that her husband must be impotent and her marriage never consummated, obtained a medical certificate to that effect and eventually an annulment.

This was the study on which she based her famous book of instructions for sexual intercourse, *Married Love*. Two publishers nervously turned it down, one of them giving, as reason, that 'There are few enough men for girls to marry and I think this book would frighten off the few.' A third asked her to share the financial risk. Early in 1918 she met and married Humphrey Roe, a young officer on leave from the Front. He lent her £100 so that her book could be published at once. It was an instant best-seller. Marie had an avalanche of grateful letters from women, most of them asking for more advice about birth-control. She quickly wrote and published another text-book, *Wise Parenthood*, which was equally successful. In 1921 she and her husband were able to open the first birth-control clinic in the British Empire. They chose modest premises in Marlborough Road, Holloway, because they wanted to reach the working-class wives whose only remedy against an unwanted pregnancy was a do-it-yourself abortion. Marie herself charted the maternal histories of the first 10,000 cases and established the link between maternal mortality and too many pregnancies. (The death-rate almost doubled after five babies.) But she was emphatic that she stood for 'constructive' birth-control, that is, for 'freedom, sexual satisfaction and joyful motherhood'. Birth-control as a principle was accepted, except by die-hards and Roman Catholics. Lord Dawson of Penn, the King's physician, supported the principle of family planning and advised the

Church of England authorities to approve it. But there was also a vicious campaign against Marie Stopes personally, which lasted for over ten years. She was abused in the papers and lost her case when she sued; demonstrated against and peppered with anonymous letters threatening her life. It was not simply because she spread contraception among working-class women, when it had already been practised among middle-class ones for twenty years. It was because of her insistence that wives should get the maximum pleasure out of sexual intercourse and above all her detailed instructions as to how this was to be arranged which made those doctors who opposed her say that she wrote 'handbooks of prostitution'. It was this that set off the witch-hunt. The Malthusian League, which also had a birth-control clinic on the bleak principle that 'overpopulation is the cause of poverty', never aroused the fanatical opposition that she did. It came from the older generation which believed that sexual intercourse in the standard position was for wives, and that men who wanted variations on the theme were in honour bound to go to prostitutes for them.

But the spread of contraception where it was most needed was largely due to her pioneering. The fall in the birth-rate and the corresponding fall in infant mortality and maternal mortality figures were her triumph. Inevitably, those who accused her of shaking the foundations of marriage as an institution by making it possible for wives to be unfaithful without exposure as men had always been, were basically right. It was never quite so solidly established as it had been before.

The change began to show in avant-garde novels, such as

Aldous Huxley's *Antic Hay* and Evelyn Waugh's *Vile Bodies* which described a society in which unfaithfulness is an occupation, as it was in Sheridan's London, as depicted in *The School for Scandal*. In *Antic Hay*, for instance, a husband penitently confesses to his wife that he has been trying to seduce another woman, and finds that she is also having extra-marital liaisons.

'But, cher ami,' protested Rosie, 'you can't seriously expect us to do the Darby and Joan business, can you? . . . You have your life – naturally. And I have mine. We don't get in one another's way.'

'But do you think that's the ideal sort of married life?' asked Shearwater.

'It's obviously the most civilised,' Rosie answered.[11]

The divorce rate had shot up. Before the war, the majority of middle-class and working-class families probably did not know a single divorced couple personally. 'Divorcees' were a rare species, with an aura of interesting wickedness. Between 1911 and 1915 there had been only 3,178 divorces in all. Between 1921 and 1925 there were 13,365 and the rate went on rising until by 1928 there were 4,522 in a single year.[12]

It began with the undoing of hasty war marriages. This was much assisted by one of the awards given to British women for their war services, in the shape of the Matrimonial Causes Act of 1923, which gave a wife the same right to apply for divorce on the grounds of adultery alone as her husband had enjoyed for sixty-six years. From then on, the number of women applying for divorce increased until by the end of the decade there were apparently more of them wishing to free themselves from an unfaithful partner than there were men. But the whole process of divorce was clouded by obligatory deceptions. Since adultery was the only ground, one party had to commit it so that the other could sue. And for a long time the tradition hung on that a gentleman always takes the blame, or possibly the credit, since the seducer – at this period, anyway – cut a better figure than the cuckold.

2. *The Amazons*

The Lesbians, who attracted so much attention during the Twenties, were partly a product of the multilated society; that is, young women pairing together as a second-best because there were not enough men to go round. But it does not explain such love affairs as that of Vita Sackville-West, who eloped with Violet Trefusis after seven years of happy marriage with Harold Nicolson, which survived and, according to her own account was 'actually enriched by' her infidelities.[13] The romantic affairs between women which are part of the literature of the time are a by-product of emancipation, an expression of female exhilaration in feeling themselves successful revolutionaries, admiring and loving their comrades because they were their comrades, a proud affection which had its roots in the fighting suffragette days. A new type of woman, who appealed only to her own sex, came into fashion. Rosamund Lehmann in *Dusty Answer* describes the effect of 'Geraldine Manners' on the undergraduates of a women's college, the broad heavy face and thick neck, those coarse and masculine features, that hothouse skin; what taste Jennifer must have had to find her attractive! Oh no, it was no good saying that . . . she was beautiful, beautiful, you would never be able to forget her face, her form. You would see it and dream of it with painful desire; as if she could satisfy something, some hunger . . . if she would. You could love her in a moment, passionately, for her voice, her eyes, her beautiful white hands, for loving Jennifer – anything.[14]

In spite of this book, which had a great popular success, and in spite of the fact that there were self-advertised Lesbian circles in London and that girls were expelled from boarding-schools or women's colleges for open indiscretions, such as being found in each other's beds, the facts were not publicly admitted until the publication of Radclyffe Hall's *The Well of Loneliness* blew the cover-up wide open. It was first published in 1928 and had a sensational reception. Havelock Ellis and Arnold Bennett defended it on grounds of its quality as fiction, as well as its sociological value. On the other hand the *Sunday Express* (male) critic said, 'I would rather give a healthy boy or a healthy girl a phial of prussic acid than this novel.'

The book tells the story of 'Stephen', a girl whose parents had passionately wanted a son, and who grows up into a tormented spinster because she feels herself male and has male desires. She is hounded out of county society but finds she is needed by her country when the war breaks out. In one of the women's services she meets other Lesbians.

For as though gaining courage from the terror that is war, many a one who was even as Stephen had crept out of her hole and come into the daylight . . . 'Well, here I am, will you take me or leave me?' And England had taken her asking no questions, she was strong and efficient, she could fill a man's place. . . . So side by side with more fortunate women worked Miss Smith, who had been breeding dogs in the country, or Miss Oliphant, who had been breeding nothing since birth but a litter of hefty complexes. . . . One great weakness they all had it must be admitted and this was for uniforms – yet why not? The good workman is worthy of his Sam Browne belt. And then, too, their nerves were not at all weak; their pulses beat placidly through the worst air-raids, for bombs do not trouble the nerves of the invert, but rather that terrible silent bombardment from the batteries of God's good people. . . . Yet now even really nice women with hairpins often found their less orthodox sisters quite useful. It would be, 'Miss Smith, do just start up my motor, I can't get the thing going', or 'Miss Oliphant, do glance through these accounts, I've got such a rotten bad head for figures'.[15]

Stephen falls in love with Mary, one of these feminine women, and they have a happy 'marriage' until persecution from the orthodox makes Stephen decide to sacrifice herself and leave Mary to marry a man. The book caused such an outcry that it had to be withdrawn, and for years afterwards could be bought only surreptitiously. But even its brief public appearance was enough to establish and acknowledge the existence of Lesbianism, and inevitably, to spread it. Though, as E. M. Delafield remarked, it put long-standing arrangements, such as that of two old maids sharing a country cottage 'under the wholly unnecessary strain of being obliged to consider the breath of scandal with regard to a relationship into which such a thing had not hitherto entered'.[16]

Like the original Amazons, who adopted male characteristics themselves because they had to survive without men, the women of the Twenties began to look masculine. The war was hardly over before they discarded curves and flared skirts and fitted themselves into a 'barrel line', with a 'flattener' to hide the bust. The waist disappeared. Up till 1923 skirts were still only just above the ankles; by 1925 they were just below the knee and by 1927 the knees were shown.

A new type of woman had come into existence. The new erotic ideal was androgyne; girls strove to look as much like boys as possible. All curves – that female attribute so much admired – were completely abandoned. And as if to give the crowning touch to their attempted boyishness, all young women cut off their hair. The bob of the early nineteen-twenties was abandoned for the shingle, which made the coiffure follow much more closely the lines of the head. Even older women were compelled to conform, because the cloche hat, which had now become universal, made it almost impossible to have long hair. Early in 1927, even this was not considered enough and the shingle was succeeded by the Eton crop. There was now nothing to distinguish a young woman from a schoolboy except perhaps her rouged lips and pencilled eye-brows.[17]

D. H. Lawrence, predictably, did not care for the new fashions at all. His Lady Chatterley was 'a little old-fashioned and womanly. She was not a little pilchard sort of fish, like a boy, with a boy's flat breast and little buttocks. She was too feminine to be quite smart – not enough like an adolescent boy.'[18]

It is impossible to overrate the effects of this revolutionary change in women's dress. It not only made them look free, but it gave them a physical freedom which even the lightly clad women of post-French Revolution simplicity had not enjoyed. The transformation between girls' clothes in the Twenties and what their mothers had worn was so astonishing that it was a constant reminder, to the wearers themselves, of how women's fortunes had changed. The new clothes made being fashionable a joyful experience, in a way it never had been before and never was again. There were no more corsets, to squeeze the flesh and make any exercise twice the effort it need be. There were no more skirts round one's ankles, to fetter walking and prevent running; no more swathing layers of underclothes; no more elaborate hats which had to be kept pinned at a certain angle on one's hair, with the penalty of looking immediately ridiculous if it went awry.

In the same way, women cut their hair, and everybody said, 'How practical!' nor did anyone bleat much about women's 'crowning glory'. The woman who had experienced the comfort of being able to take off her hat at any moment, without apprehension about the state of her hair, or more disorder than could be put to rights by merely running a comb through it, instinctively realised that here was a passport to freedom in daily life which she was not going to let go.[19]

A girl's brief, light underwear might weigh no more than one pound. The slip replaced the petticoat; she had an elastic belt in place of a corset; she wore beach pyjamas and slacks on holiday.

The Amazons of the nineteen-twenties, who smoked cigarettes in public, drank cocktails or beer, and called each other bi-sexual (or sexless) names, such as Bobbie, Billie, Jackie, Dickie, Ray or Jo, were a product of their time and faded away after it. But they had their roots in British history, in the 'tomboy' who had always been a permitted deviant in society, and who had a name and a definite identity ('a girl who behaves like a spirited or boisterous boy') since the sixteenth century. She was a regular character in children's story-books in the nineteenth and twentieth centuries, always envying her brother his freedom and trying to draw level with him. The moral ending always consisted of her resigning herself to growing up, and becoming womanly. The post-war Amazons improved the story, by refusing to do just that.

When they married, they had no intention of being tied down to house and children as their mothers were. The first number of *Good Housekeeping* in March 1924 announced firmly that 'We are on the threshold of a great feminine awakening. . . . There should be no drudgery in the home . . . the time spent on housework can be enormously reduced in every home without any loss of comfort.'[20] The birth-rate fell to a new low.[21] Only a third of all couples had what used to be the average family size and over. Sixty-seven per cent had less. Of these, 17% were childless, 25% had two children and 25% one. Meanwhile the number of private cars rose, within the decade, from 200,000 to over a million. Engaged couples used to announce that they intended to have 'one child and a car'.

Part of the spate of post-war legislation, directed towards improving the position of women, was concerned with women in their identity as wife, mother or widow. They were given equal facilities for divorce in 1923; equal guardianship of the children in 1925; the first of progressive improvements in widows' pension rights the same year; and the right to legitimise a child by marriage to the father in 1927. The Adoption Act of 1926, which made official the work that had been done by voluntary associations to find homes for 'war babies', made more of a long-term difference to women than was ever anticipated at the time. Once adoption was legal, it became 'first a fashion and then a passion' in Britain, with waiting-lists of eager childless parents. This meant that a girl who had an illegitimate baby could decide for herself whether to hand it over to adoptive parents who could certainly do better for it than she could, rather than have to choose between marrying the father (if she could catch up with him and he agreed) or trying to support the child on her own. It removed a burden from the unmarried mother which she had had to carry alone up till now, and eventually put an end to the old custom of the shot-gun wedding.

But the new Acts of Parliament which affected women as individuals and not in their relationship with someone else made an immediate and noticed change in the lives of career women. Probably the Franchise Acts – the original one in 1918 and the 'Votes for Flappers' one in 1928 – made more difference to them because, as the nurses and the teachers had learned by sour experience, their professional organisations had no power unless members had the vote. And whereas the wage-earning women had surrendered to their men's demand on returning from the war, for 'restoration of pre-war practices', the salary-earning women had struggled to keep their war-time gains where they could.

The two Acts which opened most gates to career women were the Parliament (Qualification of Women) Act of 1918; and the Sex Disqualification (Removal) Act of 1919, which ruled that women were to be allowed to 'assume or carry on any civil profession or vocation'. This meant that the professional bodies which were incorporated under legal charter were obliged to take steps to legalise the admission of women.

It was also supposed to admit them to the higher ranks of the Civil Service. They had reason to expect this, because during the war the number of women civil servants had increased from 65,000 in 1914 to 170,000 in 1919, and they had been employed in all departments and on work interchangeable with men.[22] In fact they had virtually taken over, because recruitment of men had been suspended and the men had both volunteered and been called up for military service in large numbers, so that a continual supply of new staff was needed, and the most available kind was female.

By the end of the war, the segregation of the sexes, which had been one of the Victorian hangovers right up until 1914, had at last been discarded so that women were 'sitting in the same room with men and even at the same table, supervised now by a man and now by a woman according to suitability, and these surprising changes were to be found, not only in the new departments, but also in the old-established offices of Whitehall'.[23]

But as unemployment among ex-servicemen began to bite, and the Civil Service was pressed to make room for them, the women realised that the small print of the Act had a proviso giving the government power to regulate the admission of women. It was laid down that from now on men were to be admitted to the higher ranks by open competitive examination, whereas women were to be chosen by a Board of Selection, and whereas in men's colleges it would be known what students would have to train for, to get in, in women's colleges it would not be known.

The permanent officials, with a sigh of relief, settled down to draw up regulations which would restore the cherished old system by which all higher-grade jobs were rightfully men's jobs, though women were absolutely free to compete with men in the lower-grade ones (a simple and convenient male-chauvinist scheme later adopted by the B.B.C.). In 1921, they snatched one of the plums out of reach of the women by getting an Order in Council 'to reserve to men any branch of or posts in the Civil Service in any of His Majesty's possessions overseas or in any foreign country'. This was a bitter disappointment because these posts had been the way in which a young civilian could get out into the Empire, and the single women who had been doing a man's work in the Civil Service during the war had looked forward to getting the same chance of travel and adventure and seeing the world.

The excuse given was that it was not practicable for women to have diplomatic or consular posts because all the real business in this man's world was 'done over tête-à-tête meals and in clubs and on occasions of that sort'; also that it was doubtful if women could deal with drunken sailors in foreign ports who 'come to the office of the consul with various grievances and if they are not met they are apt to become violent and abusive'.[24] By the time the women were conceded a place in this field of the Service, in 1946, the British Empire was on its last legs anyway, and so the women civil servants never did get the adventurous overseas jobs of which they had dreamed for so long.

But in spite of discriminations of this kind, this was the era of the spinster. At last, after so many years of being grudged the right to exist at all, she came into her own.

For one thing, the war had taken away her reproach among women, the shame of not having been able to attract a man. Everyone knew, now, that a woman between 20 and 35 could easily have lost hers on any one of the battlefields between 1914 and 1918. Anyway, even spinsters who had not really done so could always let it be assumed that was why they were spinsters. And the sex revolution of the Twenties was a most extraordinary and unprecedented benefit to the unmarried woman because it meant that she could take a lover (even if it was only the husband of her married sister or a friend) without feeling that she was taking a step of such magnitude and crossing such a moral Rubicon that her life would never be the same again. The working spinster, with her Eton crop and long cigarette-holder and her brittle manner, began to have a new standing with the married men who worked in the same establishment. And for the first time, the Old Maid began to be a threat to the wife. She was no longer the spare female in the family's life who could always be put upon, but the one who kept a husband drinking cocktails in the bar after work, when he should have been coming home.

Another blessing for the spinster was that the man's world (now becoming rather limp and compliant) had conceded her the right to support herself by her own unaided efforts, for life. There was no need for her to hesitate over whether it was worth taking a long expensive training when her working period between it and marriage might be short. Hers was going to be permanent. This was therefore the time when young women looked round for training places as architects, dentists, veterinary surgeons, dieticians and pharmacists. The Order of Deaconesses, 'the only order for women which bore the stamp of apostolic approval',[25] was revived. Oxford granted full degrees to women in 1920, but restricted the number of entrants. Cambridge granted them a titular degree in 1933. The Sex Disqualification (Removal) Act with the Parliament (Qualification of Women) Act had opened a whole set of new doors, to public service and politics. By 1923 there were some four thousand women serving as magistrates, mayors, councillors and guardians. By the last general election of the decade there were sixty-nine women candidates.

But the spinster's right to an occupation and a livelihood was not to be allowed to extend to women in general, during this anxious time when men's work was becoming steadily scarcer. The Civil Service barred married women; it was impossible to combine being a nurse with being a wife; and woman teachers were required to resign by the wedding-day, though in theory each local authority made up its own mind on this issue. In July 1925 (in the case of *Short v. Poole Corporation*) a married women teacher sued against dismissal. She won the case initially, but the judgment was reversed by the Court of Appeal, which ruled that 'a determination to employ as far as possible women who are devoting their lives and energies entirely to the business of teaching without assuming the privilege of domestic ties cannot be irrelevant to the maintenance of the efficiency of the schools or the cause of education in the district'. The assumption that if women were admitted to a profession they ought, in gratitude for the privilege, to dedicate themselves to it and forego earthly loves was still more dogmatic in the field of nursing. At a time when all other girls were being allowed new freedoms, the nurse's life became harsher and more nun-like. It offered, said Dr Comyns Berkeley in 1920,

Three and sometimes four years of strict discipline under the rule of another woman, accompanied by hard physical and mental work, an atmosphere of sickness and suffering, a perpetual sense of unnecessary restrictions, an exile from the world of art and letters and human progress and the narrowing effect of institution life. And all the time there lurks the spectre of *fear*. For if she thinks for herself and speaks out fearlessly and independently, if she rebels against anything that seems tyrannical or wrong, she will incur the displeasure of the authorities at the present moment, run the risk of losing her certificate and forfeit the help of her training school when she launches out as a fully trained nurse.[26]

Even by the end of the decade, the women in authority, who now made the rules for the profession, had not softened the harshness of their apprentices' lives. The Lancet Commission, making a study of nurses' training conditions, found that

the probationer's life consisted of petty restrictions, petty tyrannies and plenty of heavy domestic work. Attendance at meals was compulsory at 58% of all hospitals. In 84% the nurse was not allowed out after 10 p.m. without a late pass. She often actually had to go to bed by this time. A third of the hospitals did not provide separate bedrooms for the probationers . . . there were hospitals where it was laid down that a nurse should never sit in a ward, even if the job she was doing could be done better in that position. And there were hospitals where the night nurse was forbidden to sit by the fire or wear a shawl.[27]

The dominant spinsters of this post-war world were the teachers. Their number had not changed much – 180,000 odd in the 1911 Census and again in 1931. But their status had risen considerably since the Burnham scale settled their salaries on a national basis. Before it, their union had to argue with each separate local authority, because each fixed the price of a woman teacher according to their views and their county's financial situation. They also had an alarming habit of reducing salaries, in hard times, which meant that there was no fixed standard of living which candidates to the profession could expect and no real security. The new scales, although there was a variation in grades 'as appropriate to each local authority area' meant that the teacher's prospects were clear and definite, and that teachers could live in a certain way and have a recognised social position. The women teachers had salaries which were very good for women, that is to say, not so very far behind men's salaries for the same level of work. A certificated woman class teacher got a minimum of £150, increasing to £324, compared with her male opposite number's £168 to £408. A headmistress got up to £486, a headmaster to £606. Secondary school teachers' pay followed the same line as those laid down for the state-school ones, but was 20% more for trained but not graduate teachers, while graduate men started at £240 minimum, graduate women at £225.

What really fretted the men teachers about these salary-scales was that although the women's were suitably unequal in order to compensate for the fact that men were breadwinning for others, the women only for themselves, the differential did not really bite as they thought it only fair that it should. The woman teacher supporting herself should – according to this belief – be able to live no worse than a man after he had paid out for supporting his dependants. In fact, she lived considerably better.

An elementary school headmistress could have her own house and keep a female relative as housekeeper, and put money in savings as well. Two graduate assistant mistresses, by sharing a home and pooling expenses, could live just as well as a childless married couple where the husband was of their own social class, and considerably better than any male colleague with children to support. These prospering schoolma'am couples were a new phenomenon of the nineteen-twenties. They were a healing way of adjusting to the mutilated society. Two girls who had learned the value of pairing with an intellectual equal at college, with steadily rising salaries, security of tenure and a pension ahead of them, could have a very good life together. They could afford some domestic help; buy books and journals as they liked, go to concerts, perhaps run a small car and take holidays abroad. The British schoolma'am couple became a regular feature of the holiday season in Florence and Venice and Paris, taking an intelligent interest in historical monuments and art galleries and becoming sophisticated tourists. These trips to the Continent riled the married men teachers, whose own holiday was more likely to consist of taking the wife and children to a boarding-house in Margate. In fact it was at this time that teaching as a job for men began to lose ground. Ray Strachey pointed it out:

Since the salary awards of the Burnham Committee... the proportions of men teachers have been steadily diminishing. Some of the men teachers explain it by saying that the salary scales, although attractive to women, are inadequate for themselves (and this in spite of the fact that they are in all cases a fifth higher than the woman's). The women teachers on the other hand assert the fact that they are cheaper is what is causing the increase in their numbers...

but the facts are undisputed; 69% of all teachers of general subjects are women.[28]

This meant that from now on women got a stranglehold on the profession and this resulted in girls' schools having another period of growth and reform, as they had at the beginning of the century.

'In many ways, the present position is very unsatisfactory,' worried *The Times Educational Supplement* in 1922. 'The rich are badly served in respect to the education of their daughters. Some of the costly schools for girls – and the fees in all such schools are very high – are educationally useless.'[29] They were a survival of the old 'finishing schools' which prepared a girl for London Society and the hunt for a bridegroom. But now even wealthy parents were taking the education of daughters more seriously, and during the next few years new public schools for girls were founded, such as Benenden, Wadhurst and Westonbirt, which – although they were aimed at the gentry and the professional classes – offered a broad general education and the preparation of girls for Matriculation, college entrance and scholarships.

At both Oxford and Cambridge, women took the same courses as men, despite a controversy, soon after the war, as to whether there should be separate women's universities instead. Oxford took about 730 women and Cambridge 500 and there were always more applicants than places. Both the girls' public boarding schools and the girls' high schools competed eagerly to get their pupils accepted. The girls' curriculum was now shaped, deliberately, to fit university requirements and therefore became more and more like that of the boys. *The Times Educational Supplement* advised that

> In the first place, parents should co-operate and allow their daughters' education to be directed on the lines of preparation for the university earlier than is often the case. Secondly, the ordinary school subjects, languages, mathematics and English, should be brought up as soon as possible to the standard required by the selected university for matriculation examination. . . . Mothercraft, needlework, cookery and other feminine crafts are excellent for the majority of girls but they are not subjects which are studied at Oxford and Cambridge. . . . Language papers results, specially in Latin, are often very bad. Here again it is a matter of preparation, on definite and limited lines of ordinary school subjects . . .[30]

There was an approving pat on the back for the Mary Datchelor School for

> conducting an encouraging experiment in which the headmistress will not have the girls abandon their short Latin course without a taste of the authentic Virgil, Horace and Catullus. The idea is stimulating. . . . Why not? There are two reasons for knowing Horace and Virgil, the one because of their beauty and the other because all the best minds of civilised Europe for centuries have been familiar with them; if the stream of historic continuity is to be maintained it must be maintained no longer exclusively . . .[31]

The girls' public schools, therefore, now modelled themselves openly on the ideals as well as the studies of the original boys' establishments, and the more expensive and distinguished the school, the more masculine were the virtues it encouraged. Girls were to be courageous, hard-working and hard-playing and Spartan. Tears and tantrums were for 'common' schools where they were still permitted to behave girlishly. It was contemptible to show physical weakness or make a fuss about your health. Girls were expected to attend Communion before breakfast and to kneel unmoving for up to an hour or more. If they fainted, they were removed by the gym-mistress and the matron without comment.

The more talented and scholarly a girl was, the more she was encouraged to follow the traditionally masculine course of study: Latin and Greek above all. The classical sixth was an élite group, just as in a boys' school. English and modern languages were for second-class scholars and Domestic Science and housecraft for the stupid, now that the education of girls in one-sex schools was run by women who retained their self-respect and their identity as a worker, and their value as an individual, although they were not married and had to plan their lives without the prospect of marriage being any part of them.

The hockey-captain and members of the First Lacrosse twelve were the admired 'bloods' just as athletes were in boys' schools. Girls' boarding-schools began to take on the same glamour as the boys had enjoyed since *Tom Brown's Schooldays*, as the base of the élite group among their contemporaries. Girls who had never and would never see the inside of a girls' school dormitory spent their weekly pocket-money on *The School Friend* and *The Schoolgirls' Own* which specialised in long, continued boarding-school sagas, in which the heroines were utterly sexless. Heroines were not even specified as being pretty or attractive. It was their talent for games or scholarship or leadership that mattered. Girls who minded about clothes and coiffures were given ridiculous names such as 'Augusta Anstruther-Brown' and caricatured quite viciously. It was permissible for the ordinary healthy minded, normal girl characters – if not to beat them up – at least to arrange ludicrously humiliating accidents to make them look foolish.

This closed world of élite girls, which was run by the top spinsters of the labour market, had an appreciable effect on attitudes towards marriage. Girls who admitted that they were not interested in a career and simply wanted to get married were made to feel they had chosen to settle for second-class citizenship. In consequence the normal relationship between schoolmistresses and mothers tended to be cautious and distant, and there was strong disapproval from home when a daughter developed a 'pash' for one of the staff. This happened as a regular thing in single-sex boarding-schools. The younger girls would have a pash for the gym-mistress as a matter of routine, partly because she was young, but more because she represented the cult of physical perfection and went around in a short tunic like a page-boy in tights, and with a swinging gait. Later, a scholarly girl would develop a master-pupil type of love affair with her chief tutor for university entrance. Often she would aim at the same college where the beloved one had taken her degree.

3. *The Women M.P.s*

The first decade of women in Parliament was also the one in which all the political parties suffered from a gap in their ranks, where the war dead should have been. The missing men were 'the cream of their generation, the first volunteers, the junior officer; out of Oxford University's total roll of service 2,680 were killed . . . there is no doubt that much of the political weakness of Britain in the inter-war years can be attributed to the paucity of young talent of quality.'[32]

The new blood which Parliament did have in those arid years, in the shape of the first women members, could not really replace these men, because they were still raw recruits, uncertain of their place in the political arena. The men had centuries of tradition to provide them with examples of what a Member of Parliament was like. But neither the British voters nor the first women members knew exactly what kind of an animal a woman M.P. was.

Lady Astor, in spite of being American by birth, stepped into the rôle of the British lady of the manor more convincingly, if possible, than the genuine article. She represented a female figure well known in British life, the jolly, friendly, bossy upper-class woman who keeps the village in order but jokes with them on equal terms. Lady Astor was also easy for the public to accept because she was stepping into her husband's shoes, just as every Lady always deputised for the Lord, when necessary. Mrs Wintringham, the third woman M.P., was also easy for the public to accept because she too was deputising, but for a dead husband this time; and was a slightly less aristocratic lady-in-authority type, a committeewoman and magistrate and (like Lady Astor) a protagonist of Total Abstinence. (Even in the cocktail-drinking Twenties, this was still regarded as an appropriate feminine attitude, right-minded, if tiresome.) The fourth woman M.P. was also stepping into her husband's shoes, because he had lost his seat on a technical error. She had been Mabel Russell, a popular musical-comedy actress who had been 'Fifi' in the original production of *The Merry Widow* and had married Hilton Philipson, the National Liberal member for Berwick-on-Tweed. Gaiety girls had graduated into being ladies of the manor in Edwardian times, so the public and her husband's ex-constituents had no difficulty in accepting her. In the 1923 election, two more joined them, the Duchess of Atholl (described by Mary Agnes Hamilton as 'the O.B.E. type – the sort of woman who did good work during the war') and Lady Terrington, Liberal M.P. for Wycombe, a thirty-five-year-old Diana of a woman who wore expensive furs and pearls and conducted her election campaign on horseback.

But the election of 1923 brought in a new feminine figure, who was to become a part of the political scene and make her mark on the history of the twentieth century, the Labour woman M.P. Three of these won seats, and they were also important because they were the first spinsters to do so. All of them had worked professionally in the women's trade-union movement and could speak with assurance about employment and wages and the cost of living. One was Susan Lawrence, afterwards immortalised by Shaw as 'Lysistrata, Powermistress-General, a grave lady in academic robes', in *The Apple-Cart*. Lysistrata, 'who has evidently been a schoolmistress', can talk all the men in the Cabinet down. When she scolds the Prime Minister 'he sits down distractedly and buries his face in his hands' and his male Foreign Secretary says,

> What do you go provoking Lizzie for like that? You know she has a temper.
>
> *Lysistrata*: There is nothing whatever wrong with my temper. But I am not going to stand any of Joe's nonsense, and the sooner he makes up his mind to that the smoother our proceedings are likely to be.[33]

Susan Lawrence's parents were rich enough to give her an élitist education, ending up with the mathematical tripos at Newnham. Leah Manning (who was elected M.P. for Islington in 1931) described her as 'stiff-collared, mannish-suited and forever smoking cigarettes . . . although not an orator like Margaret Bondfield she could marshal her facts with cold logic and drive home a point with devastating effect. "Don't you shake your head at me", she scolded Austen Chamberlain.'[34] She had been a Conservative and friend of the Duchess of Atholl until, as the first women member of the L.C.C., she discovered the wages of the charwomen it employed, upon which she joined the Labour party, where she worked with Mary Macarthur in the National Federation of Women Workers. In 1921, when she was on the Poplar Borough Council, she went to prison with other Poplar Guardians for failing to collect the poor-rate. 'What a lark! What a lark!' was her comment, and she spent her six weeks there writing a pamphlet on taxation.[35]

THE WOMEN M.P.s

Beatrice Webb described her as

more forceful than attractive. For so able a woman she is strangely emotional about persons and causes . . . she has read enormously and gets up a case exactly like a lawyer, but her remarks are not original and she lacks intellectual perspective. . . . Is she lovable? I have never heard of anyone being in love with her . . . she is an enraged secularist and would be a revolutionary Socialist if she had not a too carefully trained intellect to ignore facts. . . . As a speaker she interests women more than men; her very masculinity and clearness of mind attracts women. Charming, no, able but not charming.[36]

Susan Lawrence upset Beatrice by being 'in a state of emotional excitement – I might almost say exaltation' on the occasion of the General Strike, addressing the workers' meetings in 'a fine spirit of demagogic optimism': 'they – the strikers – have all been heroes, ready to become martyrs . . . the enemy was weakening'. When they heard the strike had collapsed, Beatrice walked off

thinking of the amazing change in Susan Lawrence's mentality . . . addressing her constituents as 'comrades' and abasing herself and her class before the real wealth-producers. . . . What is the good of having professional brain-workers to represent you if they refuse to give you the honest message of intelligence but treat you to a florid expression of the emotion which *they* think the working-class are feeling or ought to be feeling?[37]

But Maggie Bondfield, who was elected for Northampton

at the same time, was really from working-class roots. She was a shop-assistant at 14, came to London with £5 in her pocket at the age of 20, found a job at £15 a year and joined the shop-assistants' Union from reading about it in the newspaper around a purchase of fish-and-chips. She became assistant to Mary Macarthur and took over her place as secretary to the National Federation of Women Workers on Mary's death. She was a small dumpy woman with a round rosy face. She had not the intellectual capacity (or the education) of Susan Lawrence but she combined shrewd political sense with great organising ability, and overcame the antipathy of male trade-unionists to a woman candidate, which was considerably harder than it was for Conservative women M.P.s to overcome the prejudices of their menfolk. After the Flappers' Election of 1929 she became the first woman Cabinet Minister and received congratulations from all over the world.

The third and youngest of the first Labour women to be elected was Dorothy Jewson, for Norwich. Like Susan Lawrence, she was single, and had come from a middle-class professional family able to send her to Cambridge. She had been a suffragette and had worked with Mary Macarthur, like the other two.

By the end of the decade, another prototype for Labour women had emerged – the working-class girl who gets to the top through scholarships. (This in itself indicates a change in the attitude of trade-union fathers towards females since girls needed the backing of their family if they were going to dedicate themselves to study.) Ellen Wilkinson, Member for Middlesbrough, had been born in the mean streets of

Manchester and got scholarships which took her eventually to the university there. She was tiny but a byword for dynamism and was nicknamed 'Red Ellen' on account of her hair and also her leanings towards Communism. Jennie Lee (for North Lanark) was a Scottish miner's daughter who got into Parliament at the age of twenty-four, three months before the Flappers' Election. The *Manchester Guardian* commented, 'It is amusing to reflect that no girl of her own age had a chance of voting for the youngest woman M.P.'[38] She was to have a long, stormy and distinguished career on the left wing of the Labour party, and to become one of the women life peers.

Mary Agnes Hamilton (for Blackburn), a Newnham graduate, was one of the group of pacifist intellectuals which included the Woolfs, Aldous and Julian Huxley, D. H. Lawrence and Lytton Strachey. She was one of the chief biographers of the Labour party, as well as of the Women's Movement. She was one of the first women to become a distinguished broadcaster. During the Thirties, she did her best to fight the growing anti-feminism inside the B.B.C.

Eleanor Rathbone, who was elected for the Combined English Universities in 1929, was the first Independent woman Member of Parliament. She had advocated Family Allowances as the only way to give married women independence and dignity, since the end of the First War, and when she died, at the end of the Second War, with this ambition achieved, it was suggested that they ought to be called 'the Rathbone' as old-age pensions had once been called 'the Lloyd George'.

The era of women who had to manage without men, the

twentieth-century Amazons, ended with Amy Johnson, who achieved world-wide and lasting fame by making long, difficult and dangerous flights about the world, alone. She was by no means the first woman air pilot. When she qualified in June 1929 she was 37th on the list. But her predecessors had been aristocratic young women with money and leisure to pursue a risky, glamorous sport like amateur flying in the best possible circumstances. Amy flew as a career. Like other girls of her generation, she had chafed in the unadventurous, unimportant job of typing in an office. She decided, quite deliberately, to take flying lessons, qualify as a pilot and hit the headlines. She illustrated the difference (which the industrial trade unions found it so difficult to accept) between skill and muscle; and between physical force and physical endurance. Years after her initial triumph, she told a group of women engineers, 'After all, physical strength is purely relative. In engineering there are many jobs beyond a *man's* strength. What do I do when I find a job beyond my strength? At first I used to fetch a real he-man engineer, and if he couldn't do the job, he'd fetch some tool that would. I soon learned to fetch the tool straight away.'[39]

Like other women pioneers since Victorian times, she owed her opportunity to start to her father, who put up money to back her financially. Also like the others she had to put up with the affected amusement of male colleagues.

If she was to fly regularly, she must make it her job. Just how difficult that was to be she learned from the moment she qualified as an amateur and announced her intention of going on to take her

'B' licence which would allow her to fly commercially and carry passengers; and perhaps even her Ground Engineer's certificate.

'But what's the big idea?'

'I thought maybe I could become an instructor.'

'Well, that beats all! It's the first time I've heard of a lady flying instructor. But d'ye really think our members would be willing to take lessons from a lady pilot?'[40]

Before her flight to Australia, she 'learned ju-jitsu, just in case she was forced to come down in some place where men were swine. Her body was spare, lithe and well-muscled like a boy's, and now that the great adventure was so near, her face had the faintly-polished sexless good looks of all true-blue heroines.' She had her public triumph, with larger crowds rejoicing over her than any Roman Emperor ever had.

Her achievement was permanent, because she made her mark at the time when flying was just developing into a civilian occupation which had, without argument and as a matter of course, been allocated to men. She astonished the whole Western world by illustrating that there was no biological reason why this new skill should be more suitable for one sex than the other. She died, still proving the point, early in the Second War; but her great triumph and the peak of her fame belonged to the Twenties, and was part of the Amazon era, of the latch-key girls and the career girls and the women in politics and the public-school girls and of Shaw's Saint Joan, who died for refusing to submit to a woman's rôle; for 'wearing men's clothes, which is indecent, unnatural and abominable' and for 'clipping her hair in the style of a man'; and because she had 'against all the duties which have made her sex specially acceptable in heaven, taken up the sword, even to the shedding of human blood'.[41]

CHAPTER FIVE

DEPRESSION
1930–1939

1. *Unemployed Breadwinners*
Working-class married life was never quite the same again, after the chronic unemployment of the Thirties. In areas where husbands were out of work as a normal state for the depression years, they became a separate class, accepted drones, treated kindly by some wives, nagged and bullied by others. Their authority, which had been based on being the breadwinner, gradually withered away in their own households.

Leah Manning, the Labour M.P. for East Islington, visiting the home of an unemployed constituent at the time of the family's mid-day meal, found them gathered round the table which had on it 'the usual loaf of bread and pot of jam'.

'Careful, Johnny,' said the mother. 'It's got to last all week.' 'Crikey,' the boy answered. 'I'm the only one earning in this family, ain't I? I've got the right to the 'ole pot if I want it.' I looked at the father. He said not a word, but, white to the lips, got up from the table and left the house.[1]

DEPRESSION

Unemployment, which had been the creeping disease of the Twenties, dominated the scene by the time Britain went off the gold standard in 1931, and the number of unemployed began to climb towards three million. That autumn, 'citizens in every walk of life were preparing themselves for such distressful emergencies as had not been experienced in living memory. Many expected that the pound would go the way of the mark and the rouble, that the comfortable would lose their savings and the uncomfortable would starve.'[2] During the depression which followed, the number of unemployed was never below a million. It averaged 14.2% of insured workers. The Unemployment Insurance Fund, which was supposed to be self-supporting through the weekly subscriptions of those in work, was drained dry by the calls for benefit and in debt to the Treasury. The government therefore set up the Unemployment Assistance Board to support those whose benefit had run out. It was under this regime that the hated Means Test was imposed, a regulation which was still a byword in Lancashire and Durham and Clydeside, forty years later, and which so eroded the dignity of husbands and fathers that they never fully recovered their old status afterwards.

The Means Test meant that in order to draw the Dole a man had to prove that he had no savings or assets of any kind left. But the real indignity was that the earnings, savings and assets of all members of his family were called upon to support the unemployed head of it.

Thrift was penalised and improvidence rewarded. Family solidarity was undermined . . . sons and daughters forced to support parents in a way which frayed the tempers of both generations . . . the children would move into lodgings in order not to be 'dragged down' by having to support their parents. The Means Test was an encouragement to the tattle-tale and the informer and to petty tyranny on the part of the Labour Exchange clerks and managers.[3]

The breadwinner's humiliation and despair would start with the sudden curt announcement on the weekly visit to the Labour Exchange, 'They've knocked you off dole.'[4] Walter Greenwood's documentary novel, *Love on the Dole* describes a typical scene in Salford.

'Y' what?' he asked, staring incredulously at the unemployment exchange clerk on the other side of the counter.

'A'y deaf? There nowt for 'y. Sign on a Tuesday for future if y' want y' health insurance stamp. Who's next?'

Dreamlike, he turned and paused, holding the dog-eared yellow unemployment card in his hand. This was catastrophic; the clerk was joking, surely a mistake must have been made.

'You've a couple of sons living with you who are working, haven't you? . . . In view of this fact the Public Assistance Committee have ruled your household's aggregate income sufficient for your needs, therefore your claim for transitional benefit is disallowed.'

'The swine . . . th' eldest lad's getting wed . . . 'as 'e to keep me and th' old woman?' . . . but the policeman collared him and propelled him outside roughly, ignoring his loud protestation.

In the end he has to accept the degradation of being given money his daughter has earned through becoming the mistress of the local bookie. 'Living on a woman, his daughter, whom he had once dismissed for living on a man! . . . Oh, why the devil couldn't they give him work? The canker of impotence gnawed at his vitals. He felt weak, as powerless as a blind kitten in a bucket of water . . . Sal was independent now. He had not the slightest authority to interfere with her. Nay, financially, he and his wife were her dependents.'

Physically, it was a harder life for the wife of a long-term unemployed man than it was for him. She was the one who washed and cleaned without soap, who wheedled fat out of the butcher to melt down for fried bread for the children's breakfast, who patched and re-patched clothes so that they had something to wear for school. The unemployed, as magistrates used to observe disapprovingly when they got into trouble for stealing or debt, continued to have large families in spite of their lack of money. It was, perhaps the only way in which the unemployed husband could assert his masculinity. The wife of a ship's riveter, who had worked a total of one year during the twelve and a half they had been married, lamented that she had five children. 'But it means expense to avoid them. I know all about the avoidance part, but I haven't the means to carry it out. I know a baby costs more when it does arrive, but we just haven't the pence to spend to prevent it.'[5] The worse gaps in the Health Insurance system were those affecting mothers and children. Wives were not provided for at all, except at the actual time of childbearing and then it was only £2 4s. 'A doctor's fee is two guineas so ever since the first I've had a woman – a certified midwife – because it's cheaper. I had chloroform for the first baby but I haven't been able to have it since. And I always have long, lingering times. . . .' Maternal mortality was 19% higher in the county boroughs with heavy unemployment than in those with little. In 1935–37, the National Birthday Trust Fund conducted an experiment in a depressed area with two groups of pregnant women. One, comprising 10,384 women, was given special food during pregnancy, at a cost of 13s 4d per week per woman. The other (18,854 women) was not. Maternal mortality in the first group was 1.63 per thousand; in the second 6.05.[6]

But spiritually, the wives were undefeated. It was their battle. They could keep the children fed and cared for and the household running by their own ceaseless effort and grim endurance. So long as the mother did not give up, the home was secure. Her status increased as that of the unemployed father diminished. As Colin Cross described him, 'He acquired a characteristic slouch, the result of hanging around street corners with his hands in his pockets. As the months passed, his hands grew whiter, softer than those of his wife.'[7]

In a culture in which the man's standing and his weapon of authority had been the living wage he brought home, he was now completely disarmed.

The man brings the dole in, and he's finished – the woman's got all the rest. Many a week he's given it to me, and I've just said, 'Put it in the fire.' It's just like an insult to a mother to bring in 33s to keep her home and five children. I've often said to my husband, 'Don't you feel ashamed at bringing this home to keep all these on?' And he'd say, 'What can I do?'[8]

The only thing he could do was women's work. There was always plenty of that about. Women could get a job twice as easily as men, because they could do domestic work, scrubbing, cleaning, washing and baby-minding. When the wife took on paid work of this kind, it meant that the unemployed husband had to stay at home and do all that she used to do. By 1936 even older men, who had to conquer a lifelong taboo against it, would succumb to the need. As Ray Strachey reported:

> Although the tradition that it is shameful for men to do 'women's work' is a very strong one, the actual necessities of the last few years have been breaking it down. During the peak period of unemployment when in so many families the only people who could find work were the adult women, it became necessary for the fathers, when they were not totally heedless, to attend to the daily care of the children. Crèches and infant-welfare centres became accustomed from 1929 onwards to the arrival of fathers in charge of toddlers and as the cases increased the sense of oddness and peculiarity wore down. At the same time, 'men's work' being so scarce and domestic service so steadily in demand, parlour-men, house-men and men cooks began to increase in number. A crack in the tradition really seems to have opened and it is not wildly impossible now to expect a world in which men and women will share between them, in accordance not with tradition but with their actual strength, capacity and leisure, the common family tasks.[9]

Among the younger unemployed men, 'marrying on the Dole' became a common custom. ('They're all doin' it. Tarts go out to work nowadays while the ould man stops at home.'[10]) Thirty-five per cent of the unemployed men between 18 and 25 in Liverpool did so, and 31% of those in Glasgow. It was better than no family life at all, and the State did not discourage such marriages because two could live better than one, on the scale of unemployment allowances. Often the wife would continue at work, supporting the husband. The newer industries, such as tinned food production, light engineering and rayon clothing, employed more women than the older declining industries had done.

In households where the breadwinner was female, she gradually became accepted as the decision-maker.

When I was first married, we had the one room. I had the four children in it, and then I had the chance of three rooms and though it was twice the rent I took the responsibility. . . . I couldn't expect to bring four children up decently in one room. But it meant not only twice the rent but I had to furnish them. So I bought sixteen pounds worth of furniture and I paid it off week by week out of the dole money. It took nearly two years. My husband gave up his cigarettes and we did without something that mattered each week to pay for it.[11]

Husbands lost status when they became impotent breadwinners in the white-collar classes as well. J. B. Priestley's 'Mr Smeeth' who lived with 'the one great fear, the fear that he might lose his job, who, after a bit of fried liver or toasted cheese had refused to be digested' would dream that he was out of work for evermore and 'walking down vague dark streets with nothing on but his vest and pants'. When the terror finally does catch up with him and he has to go home and break the news to his wife, her stature grows as his diminishes.

'I can work,' cried Mrs Smeeth fiercely. 'You needn't think there'll be me to keep in idleness. I'll go out charring first.'

'But I don't want you to go out charring,' Mr Smeeth told her, almost shouting. 'I didn't marry you and I haven't worked all this time never missing a minute if I could help it, and we didn't save and plan to get this home together, so that you could go out charring. My God, it's not good enough.'[12]

And Mr Smeeth's employer, ex-public-school man, Mr Dersingham, is most of all afraid of facing his wife with the fact that he has failed to keep his business going, and gets the crushing contempt he anticipated when he does.

'Oh Howard, you have been stupid. Yes you have. I'll never believe in you again as a business man.' But after the first shock Mrs Dersingham realises that now her husband is down and out the family's future depends on her courage and resourcefulness.

She was not depressed. At this moment she might just have had good news instead of bad. Unlike her husband, who appeared to be only half the man he usually was, a listless lump, she felt twice her customary self.... The situation, leaving him crushed, challenged her and there was something exhilarating in accepting the challenge. Plans by the score, some of them born of old idle daydreams, were stirring in her mind and now, while he listened, sometimes shaking his head, sometimes looking at her hopefully, they came tumbling out: 'Of course, we'll have to give this place up as soon as we can – we ought to get a decent premium too, look what we've spent on the decoration – and then I'm sure Mother would take the children for a few months. . . .'

In areas where women had long been established as skilled manual workers, for example in the Lancashire textile mills, women who were laid off because of unemployment suffered the same shock and loss of self-respect and feeling of being exiled from the community as did the miners and shipyard workers when it happened to them. Like the men, these women felt their job was their identity. Without it, they were anonymous, belonging nowhere.

The *Manchester Guardian* reporting on the unemployment among women in Lancashire explained that:

Most spinsters and self-dependent widows used to remain at the mill till sixty at least, not only because of the employment but because of the company and habit. I have known many whose objection to the old-age pension was that it meant an end to mill days. In Blackburn alone, there are about 1400 wholly unemployed single women between 55 and 65 – many of these self-dependent widows, out of work for six years, who, because of a long and intensive training in cotton only, and because of the physical disabilities of ageing, can never establish themselves in a new industry and will never be re-absorbed into the old. . . . The tremendous amount of inherited and acquired skill and habit, sustained and continued interest in work, are disappearing among these women and girls.[13]

DEPRESSION

The Lancashire family budget was unusual in that it was based on the idea of a dual income, produced by husband and wife, fairly equally, and later added to by boys and girls, also fairly equally. Males and females in cotton weaving, for instance, were paid on the same piece-rate list where they were engaged in the same work (with the exception of some weaving operations on automatic looms where men could manage more looms at a time).[14] Therefore, in Lancashire, women in 'the mill' had never thought of their natural place as a lowly one, compared with women in industry in other parts of the country. They had been proudly independent for generations. Even the old woman, married or single, could retain her independence. Being deprived of it, as she was by the unemployment of this time, was the most bitter misfortune that could have happened to her.

According to the 1931 Census there was, at any given moment, 37% of the whole female population between the ages of 14 and 65 working for money. The slump never hit them quite as badly as it did the men partly because, as Beatrice Webb had pointed out long ago,

Unemployment involves, to a woman, usually less suffering and less danger of demoralisation than to a man. She has nearly always domestic work, with which to occupy herself usefully. She can be much more easily provided for by enabling her to improve her qualifications in domestic economy than an unemployed man can be found any other occupation other than the demoralising and costly relief works.[15]

Apart from this, women could find jobs where men could not, for the old reason that they were cheaper. Ever since 1919, there had been a silent agreement between employers and trade-unionists that equal pay was not to be pursued with any enthusiasm, but that the old hit-and-miss definitions of 'women's jobs' and 'men's jobs' – often varying from area to area as well as by industry – would do very well for a bit longer, anyway until the work situation picked up.

The other reason why women workers were more acceptable was that they were apt to give up a job, very conveniently, just about the time when they should have been given a rise in pay and a promotion. During the nineteen-thirties, the high peak of percentages of women at work came at the age-group 18–20. From then onwards, the girls began to leave every job for the alternative occupation of marriage. At 18, four out of every five girls were working. By 21, it was 65%; and by 25, until 34 years of age, it was only 36%. There was thus a very welcome disappearance of female workers before the moment when promotion for long service might be expected.

A girl's chances of getting married were now considerably improved. By the mid-Thirties, the gaps in the mutilated society of fifteen years before were getting filled up. The generation of boys who had been still at school when the war ended were now marrying age. Their ranks had been further swollen by some 565,000 disillusioned men who had emigrated to the far-flung Empire when Lloyd George's land fit for heroes to live in failed to materialise.[16] Now they had trickled back, having found the situation out there just as bad as at home. (Like the pre-1914 emigrants they got back in time for the expected war with Germany.) Besides these, there was a small but steady flow of political refugees from the various European countries now engaged in establishing dictatorships. Adding all these factors together, the proportion of men to women had increased, and restored the normal chances for a girl to find a bridegroom. In the age-group 15–49, the proportion of women to men fell from 110% in 1931 to 106% in 1939.

But that still left some two and a quarter million women over 30, still seeking a livelihood. Many of these were the mate-less victims of the great battles of the war, who had got to support themselves till they died. For these, the position during the chronic unemployment period was grim. Most employers of females, in both manual and white-collar jobs, were looking for someone to do routine work only; and much preferred young girls, mainly because they were cheaper, but also because they were pleasanter to have about than ageing spinsters or widows with a built-in grievance against life. Women growing old in underpaid routine work therefore did not dare to change their job, for fear of not being re-employed, or to ask for higher wages, for fear of being dispensed with altogether.

Comfortably-off married couples, advertising fruitlessly for living-in domestic servants, were once again utterly perplexed by the number of girls who did not want to come and share their pleasant home.

'It is not the actual work which is unpopular', Ray Strachey explained.[17] 'Hotels and institutions (where the physical volume of work is often much harder than in private service) are comparatively easy to staff, even though their hours are sometimes cruelly long. But they do not carry that element of loneliness or of enforced association with only one or two others, which attaches to private service.' Private domestic service, in spite of more comfortable and liberal conditions, was in fact duller than it ever had been before. Now that the great houses had been broken up, the chance of learning a recognised job, with good prospects, under a skilled expert, in a hierarchical community, was no longer available. (It was only the young, liberal mistresses of the nineteen-thirties who thought that the girl must naturally prefer to be treated as an 'equal' and share lunch democratically with her, chatting about politics and art, to the ritualised snobbery of the old Servant's Hall. The actual servants involved had always found that it added greatly to the interest of the job.)

But by now 'domestic service' meant starting in straight away as cook-general or house-parlourmaid, or more likely as the amorphous, badly paid 'Mother's Help' who had no training, no professional standing of any kind and no social standing either. The job had gained in leisure-time and in material living-conditions, but now it had no status. It was no longer a craft, with an apprenticeship and rising pay.

Two efforts were made to revive it and attract more recruits. One was to resurrect the special training for domestic work which had been tried out when the munition-girls had been laid off after the war. This time, the bait was offered to the sacked white-collar woman-on-her-own.

The Times described the scheme:

DEPRESSION

Another London centre has been started to deal with the difficult problem of the older unemployed woman, the feminine equivalent of the 'black-coated worker', who, after many years of employment in office or shop is overtaken by the trade depression and, once unemployed, has little chance of resuming her ordinary occupation. Since January 1933 there has been a class for these women held in the kitchen of the YWCA ... it has been found that they can be trained in cooking and places found for them with ease, because many employers, in cases where it is intended to place upon them more than ordinary responsibility, prefer the older women to the girls.[18]

This was the second effort to make use of the domestic-servant shortage to deal with the perennial problem of the ageing untrained spinster (who, incidentally has no opposite number in the male sex: there has never been a problem of the unemployable untrained bachelor).

The other attempt to revive domestic service aimed at restoring its status as a skilled craft. This was in the development of the Nursery Nurse training colleges. The oldest of these (the Norland) dated back to 1892; and the others had been founded between the beginning of the century and 1930. But now the curriculum became much more elaborate and scientific, to match the middle-class mother's new knowledge of modern baby-care methods, which had already helped to push the infant-mortality figure down still a little further. The colleges offered a two-year training course to girls whose parents could afford the fees. When they qualified, they could take their choice of places in which they would live 'as family' and never be asked to help with the housework. Young mothers who would make any sacrifice to get their baby looked after, waited on the college-trained nannie when necessary.

She got up to £100 a year and all found; that is, she got as much, for pocket-money, as a 'Lady Clerk in a City Office' was offered,[19] on which to support herself, and a third as much again as a man on the Dole got for himself, his wife and five children to live on entirely.

2. *Pin-money Wives*

Under the shadow of unemployment and the fear of unemployment, resentment against women in regular work once again became as widespread and hostile as it had been just after the war. 'Take a school-teacher, a young lady', said a shipyard worker, who had worn out his only pair of boots, tramping the streets of Glasgow in search of work. 'She has suffered a wage cut. She feels very bitter about it. She feels she has really been struck by the depression; she has had twelve shillings a week cut off her wages. But that's not suffering. What she got cut off doesn't matter so much. It's what she has left that counts. She had five pounds twelve shillings a week. Her share of the suffering is that she now gets five pounds a week.'[20] Unemployed men in depressed areas felt antifeminist about teachers because they were the only well-paid women who impinged on their lives. Young teachers giving P.T. lessons in the schoolyard had to do it in the teeth of barracking from the local fathers, who were killing time by leaning on the school-fence and making loud remarks to each other about girls who got paid five quid a week for showing their bloomers. Local authorities who, in less difficult days had made concessions about keeping valuable women teachers on even though they got married, now withdrew them. Wives who needed the money – perhaps because a husband was out of work – were driven to pretending to be still single, perhaps wearing their wedding-ring on a chain round the neck under the clothes, for reassurance.

The Twenties' liberalism towards professional women began to go out of fashion. The small but steady increase in the number of female recruits to medicine, dentistry, law and accountancy was arrested. Girls who had been edging into newer professions with a shorter training – such as pharmacy and radiography – found fewer openings. And broadcasting, which had looked very promising for women in 1927, now began to play down sex-equality in employment.

The British Broadcasting Corporation had been, from the beginning, unusual in its treatment of women employees, far more so than the Civil Service itself. *The Women's Leader*, in 1931, praised its enlightened attitude: 'As regards women on the staff, the B.B.C. has set an example which is not always to be found in public bodies. Women are not compelled to resign on marriage and equal pay for equal work is on the whole respected, while married women are not debarred from applying for jobs.'[21]

Ethel Snowden, the famous left-wing feminist, was one of the first five governors of the B.B.C. and the earliest example of the 'token woman'. The Postmaster-General had chosen her because 'he had to find a representative of Labour and a woman' and 'had done well to find them in one person'.[22] The four male members of the Board found her a trial. 'There were few weeks without complaints from Mrs Snowden,' grumbled John Reith. 'Minutes were unsatisfactory; the Board should meet much more frequently . . . newspapers were continually discussing matters of the gravest importance of which she knew nothing . . . the B.B.C. was far too prone to give in to the press; someone had only to be nasty in print and the B.B.C. would concede anything. . . . ' Her colleagues discussed asking the P.M.G. if she could be removed, but eventually resigned themselves to the fact that the 'statutory woman', always armed against a surrounding male majority, is liable to be either defensive or truculent and they would just have to learn to live with it.

The two departments which were to be Britain's most outstanding achievement in radio, and used as models for other countries to copy all over the world, were both the brainchildren of young women, who were recruited in the days when the B.B.C. was a consciously modern, experimental organisation, bent on proving it was not like the stuffy old Civil Service with its outmoded attitude towards the female sex. Mary Somerville, one of the starry-eyed girl graduates of the Amazon period, had dreamed of using the harvest of her own privileged education by taking part in 'the diffusion of knowledge' by 'a fraternity of itinerant preachers'.[23] When she listened to Sir Walford Davies broadcasting, as she sat in a country schoolmistress's parlour, along with the schoolmistress and three enthralled pupils, she knew how she could do it. ('Things happened in all of us, in the children, in their music-loving teacher and in me.') The system of schools broadcasting which she devised 'became the envy of educationists in every other country' and made a 'fourth dimension' of imagination and new ideas in the ten thousand odd classrooms which came to depend on them for brightening up the curriculum.

The other pioneer woman of the period was Hilda Matheson, who had been put in charge of the 'Talks Section' in 1927. During the following four years, she created the 'Broadcast Talk'; which was neither a lecture, nor a sermon, nor a lesson nor a written essay read aloud, but an art-form on its own, created on the basis of the qualifications of the medium, just as the silent films had been. It was to be listened to, not read; and heard in private, not in public. The editor of *The Listener* grumbled that she objected when he edited the text of talks and changed 'won't' into 'will not', thus 'spoiling their beauty as talks'.[24] She resigned at the end of 1931 because she had so many battles with her fellow-members of the Programme Board. The *Daily Telegraph* reported that she had pressed her views 'from a feminine standpoint in the face of overwhelming masculine opposition'.[25] A subsequent report on the recruitment of women to the Corporation was reassuring that there was a 'good proportion of women to men' on the staff.[26] But by the middle of the Thirties the *Manchester Guardian* was beginning to point out that the B.B.C. was becoming 'an exceedingly masculine institution' and asking:

Is there a career at Broadcasting House for women? In the early days of the B.B.C. there were almost as many women chiefs of departments as men, but gradually this has changed until it looks as though every one of the higher-paid jobs at Broadcasting House will soon be in the hands of men. With the departure of Miss I. D. Benzie, who intends to leave when she marries shortly, only one important post will be occupied by a woman – that of Schools Director, held by Miss Mary Somerville. Women governors, Mrs Mary Hamilton and Lady Bridgeman are said to be concerned about the alleged evidence of anti-feminism in the B.B.C., particularly the tendency not to employ married women.[27]

It was unlucky that broadcasting, which had started as an entirely new career, without any hampering traditions of men's jobs and women's jobs, should have had to develop its organisation at the exact time when women were being edged out of the labour market wherever possible because of unemployment. The campaign against 'pin-money wives' gave the Corporation a good excuse for ceasing to make much effort to break new ground by giving women equal responsibilities with men. During the Thirties, it developed into a male stronghold and stayed that way longer than any other public institution except the Church of England. It had the correct token women on the Board of Governors and on Advisory Councils. But once it had got rid of these upper-rank ones on the staff, who had been appointed in its early progressive days, it did not replace them. This enabled the men to dig up the traditional excuse (used by the Civil Service when refusing to appoint women to consular posts) that so much of the real business was done over drinks in clubs that a woman would be hampered in trying to keep abreast. As one man in a senior position at the B.B.C. explained it to an enquiring researcher from P.E.P.: 'It's the women just below the Alpha Plus level that are discriminated against. . . . Take a regular management meeting – every Monday morning say. It's a closely knit little circle of men meeting – it knows its own mores, language – and then suddenly a species with entirely different reactions is introduced into it. . . . They don't like it.'[28] Another man in a senior position added: 'I think we were a male society. We had an unspoken sense of male camaraderie – a kind of lingua franca. . . . There was a high-powered woman there, but she didn't have it. She didn't speak our language. She would talk very loudly at meetings as long as she could. . . . We didn't like it.' Gradually, as the women Controllers and Assistant Controllers retired and were replaced by men, it began to seem perfectly natural that there should never be a woman on the Board of Management.

The government which took over in 1931 had been put there by an electorate which now had 15,600,000 women compared with 13,500,000 men. The Conservatives had ten new women members in the House. The Labour party returned only fifty members, none of them women. No woman was given a post in the government. It was a lean period for feminists; and one of the government's first ideas for economising was to make their own attack on pin-money wives.

This was to cut unemployment benefit to married women. They could do this simply by imposing the Anomalies Regulations which had been passed under Labour, who could not therefore complain if they were put into force now. The basis of these regulations was that married women could manage without the unemployment benefits for which they had been insured and towards which they had subscribed before they were married. But now (the ever-popular argument ran) they had husbands to support them and did not need money of their own. This meant that if benefits were allowed to them, they would simply be pin-money.

The new rule was that unless a married women had *since marriage* paid a certain number of contributions – that is, had actually been in work for a number of weeks, she would be disallowed her benefit. No matter how many contributions she had paid before marriage, unless she could prove that she was 'normally employed, would seek work and could reasonably hope to obtain such work' in the district where she lived, she could get nothing. It was unlikely that she could qualify for these conditions, since in the Thirties, except in areas where women workers had a special standing, such as the textile districts of the north-west, it was unusual for an ordinary married woman to have an insurable job. Fewer than one woman in eight did so, in 1933, as compared with more than one in three in the nineteen-sixties.

The results of putting the Anomalies Regulations into action were immediate and drastic.[29] By the middle of November 1931, 5,000 married women had been struck off benefit in Glasgow alone, 2,800 in Bootle and 2,000 in Birmingham. By the end of the year, 134,000 married women had been disallowed. This was a modest triumph for the government, who were desperately trying to cut down on their spending. They had already cut not only the Dole, but salaries of Ministers, judges, Members of Parliament and teachers and the pay of the police and armed services. But it was a sharp put-down for women, because it re-established the old formula that women were either wives or workers, and if they were wives they were already in possession of a sufficient income for their needs. The women's real loss of ground, during the Depression, was the return to the choice of marriage or a career. The re-establishment of this tradition (still very dear to many male hearts) affected everything; from girls' education to women's place in trade unions. Now it was possible – twenty years after Dilution had been successfully practised by women workers in the engineering shops of Glasgow – for a speaker at the Conference of the Amalgamated Engineering Union to get up and denounce women as 'a danger to the State' without anyone in the audience having to ask what he meant.

3. *Marriage – the Perpetual Honeymoon*
The proper interest of women, in this attempt to return to the good old ways of the pre-war world, was not work, but all aspects of marriage. A female's identity was daughter, sweetheart, wife and mother, not engineer or broadcast talks producer. The state of the economy made it essential that women should go back home and stay there; and there was a great propaganda drive to coax them into doing so. The theme was built up by newly established 'woman's pages' in national dailies.[30] These were read more by the well-to-do group of the population (earning over £500 a year) than the working-class group. The *News Chronicle* woman's page was

earnestly disapproving about middle-class daughters who would rather live in independent squalor than at home with kind and tolerant parents. A quarter of a century after *Ann Veronica*, it seemed, in the late Thirties, that nothing had changed after all.

Sally lives very uncomfortably in a bed-sitting room near Victoria, rather than in a comfortable home with her family in Knightsbridge. Her married brother [a re-incarnation of Ann Veronica's married brother] asks her, 'Why on earth do you starve in this garret instead of living at home?' Her answer is that the family gets on her nerves. . . . Sally's mother asks nothing more than that her daughter accepts the convenience of home without taking on any of the responsibilities . . . she need have no pin-pricks of conscience that she keeps meals about, waiting for her to eat them, and always happens to have a date on her mother's bridge evenings and is never up on Sunday morning to take a walk with her father. . . . Is she worrying that her 'twenties' are on the wane and marriage is not yet in sight?[31]

The *News Chronicle* also ran a feature about a 'pin-money wife' who found that after all she was worse off financially than if she had stayed at home and done the housework herself.

'An 8-years married woman reader was offered a £3 a week job and jumped at it, but after 3 months experience says, 'I can't afford to work. The money was tempting. I could see a long holiday at the seaside for all of us, new furnishing for the home and a nicely growing account in the savings bank. But after three months, I have less in hand than before.'[32] By the time she had paid a char, her own lunches, business dress, and lost money on doing the laundry at home and on not shopping thriftily each day, she was out of pocket. The moral was the anti-social foolishness of the pin-money wife, who took a job when breadwinners needed any that were going, neglected her family and lost money. 'But it taught us a lesson. We now know my value in the house in hard cash. This week I hand in my notice. I can't afford to go out to work. My place is in the home.'[32]

But the most important propaganda machine was 'a string of new magazines which appeared in the Twenties and Thirties, appealing directly to women, which instantly succeeded and within a few years had a combined sale of probably two million copies a month'.[33]

Between them, these journals spanned the social system from the Council house to the stately home, with the shilling magazines (*Homes and Gardens* and *Ideal Home*) suggesting expensive settings for gracious upper-class married love; to the new sixpenny ones for middle-class women: *My Home, Modern Woman, Woman and Home, Wife and Home, Mother*; all with much the same formula; all much alike except to the regular subscriber to whom her own was cosily familiar, with each of its pundits her own personal guide, philosopher and friend. They all rammed home the same messages; that a man's enduring love was the only important thing in the whole of a woman's life; and that if you did not find the whole absorbing world of shopping, cooking, knitting and bringing up children sufficient to occupy your time and talents, it could only be because there was something the matter with you. The Amazon of the Twenties who, only a few short years ago, had been praised for her sexless achievements and her refusal to be tied down to fussing about her appearance and her house, had now become a monster, as Molly Carmichael advised the readers of *Woman and Beauty*.

The Peter Pan Girl

You've often seen her. Attractive when she's young, she gets very embarrassing as she reaches the Forties, for she will persist in being girlish and skittish. Very often she's been hockey captain at school and sees no reason to develop her sphere of efficiency. She continues to wear the suits she wore as a girl, making no attempt to dress with dignity and grace . . . her skin uncared for, weather-beaten, and her hair-style untidy. . . . Grow up Peter Pan girl! Put a little polish on your character and your finger-nails! Develop a style of your own in dressing, taking Kay Francis as your model.[34]

Fashions went back to hampering women's movements, with longer skirts by day, long flowing sleeves, wide shoulders and slender hips with the material drawn tightly over them.[35] Curls and elaborate coiffures came back; so did hats, perched over one eye. There were butterfly sleeves and romantic chiffon dresses with full-length skirts for the evening, and by the end of the decade there was the final tether for women sandals with enormous cork soles, on which they teetered like Chinese women with bound feet.

It became a moral duty to keep yourself attractive to your husband, so that he could get his money's worth out of employing a permanent mistress and also for the sake of your family's future, because only if you remained sufficiently alluring could you be sure of keeping him and his support of the home. The Women's League of Health and Beauty which was Britain's answer to the mass physical-fitness cults on the Continent differed from them in its earnest appeal to wives and mothers to keep fit in a graceful womanly way. All through the Thirties hundreds of thousands of them gave public displays of callisthenics, bare-armed, bare-legged, at Olympia, in the Wembley Stadium, beside the lake in Hyde Park or in their village hall.

The question of what sort of a thoroughly feminine image husbands really liked was discussed at wearisome length. 'Most husbands like the bright accent of lipstick but they aren't crazy about looking at lipstick stains on handkerchiefs and towels.' The assumption was that marriage, in these days, was an ecstatic honeymoon which lasted for life if the wife worked hard enough to assure this. E. M. Delafield mocked the popular illusion in her *Diary of a Provincial Lady*. She made a whole generation of middle-class middle-aged matrons sit up and begin to notice what their everyday life was really like, with her sketches of the emptiness and boredom which has afflicted the comfortably-off provincial lady since Madame Bovary.

Dec. 10 Robert this morning complains of insufficient breakfast . . . cannot feel that porridge, scrambled eggs, toast, marmalade, scones, brown bread and coffee give adequate grounds for this, but admit porridge is slightly burnt. How impossible ever to encounter burnt porridge without vivid recollections of Jane Eyre at Lowood School! say I parenthetically. This literary allusion not a success,

MARRIAGE – THE PERPETUAL HONEYMOON

Robert suggests ringing for Cook and have the greatest difficulty in persuading him that this course utterly disastrous.

E. M. Delafield was part of the literary group which included Viscountess Rhondda; and which supported the now old-fashioned feminist view that women should be adult, sensible and realistic about their emotional relationships and be more concerned with the state of the world around them than with their own little world indoors. Miss Delafield put her middle-aged 'provincial lady' into a highly successful play, *To See Ourselves*, in which she tries to live up to the women's-magazine concept of married life as a perpetual romantic honeymoon.

Caroline: Do you still think me at all pretty?

Freddie: (rising) What on earth's the matter with you to-night, old girl? I'm sure you're not feeling well.

Caroline: But *do* you?

Freddie: I've never thought about it.

Caroline: (desperately) Think about it now!

Freddie: This is all great nonsense. You look just as nice as any other woman – of your age, I mean. Though I must say I wish you'd keep you hair tidier.

Caroline: Freddie, I know you'll think me idiotic – but say you love me!

Freddie: (Kind but awkward and slightly annoyed) Shouldn't have married you if I didn't, should I? (He pats her face hurriedly) There, is that what you want?

Caroline: Women want such unlikely things – romance and adventure and excitement – but what's the use?

In the end, Caroline, like Ibsen's Nora, realises that she is living in a false, sugary Doll's House, without enough to do or enough to think about. But, unlike Nora, she knows she has not quite got the conviction or the courage to break free of it. She decides she must 'accept the limitations of her surroundings' because 'it isn't the limitations of one's surroundings that matter. It's one's own limitations.'

All this emphasis on marriage as a delicious, perpetual love-affair was rudely interrupted, in the mid-Thirties, by a great scare about the falling birth-rate.

In 1934, Dr Enid Charles told the Royal Economic Society that 'whatever changes in mortality rates ensue, nothing can arrest a continuous decline of the total population unless something happens to increase fertility above the present level'. She followed up this warning by a tract, called *The Twilight of Parenthood or The Menace of Under-Population* in which she drew attention to the fact that the replacement figure for 1933 had been 0.845, that is, less than par, showing that the population was not even replacing itself; which meant that by the year 2000 at the present rate of decline there would be no more than 28,522 Britishers in the world. The annual number of births had been falling steadily throughout the Twenties. The spread of birth control clinics had made it possible, and women's insistence on personal freedom had made it fashionable. As a Royal Commission on Population reported, later,

The influence of social example should be noted. Once the movement for smaller families had gathered some way, social example and fashion helped to spread it. The wealthier and more leisured families were the first to be influenced by the cultural movements that favoured family limitation and ... they set the fashion in family limitation itself and also in many things that tended to make it appear desirable or necessary for other social groups.[36]

Because there was a higher standard of living available, it mattered more to have to struggle to support children, and therefore the gulf between parents and non-parents was more noticeable. 'More leisure, along with higher standards of living, more ways of spending, increased facilities for recreation and pleasure outside the home, the private motor-car, cheap transport, development of holidays away from home all tended to emphasise the advantages enjoyed by those with few ties or none over parents and members of large families.'[37]

'A nation is decadent which considers a motor-car a greater possession than a child', said Sir Leonard Hill, castigating the one-child-and-a-car marriage of the Twenties, at the Annual Conference of Sanitary Inspectors in 1936. 'The physiological need of every woman is unsatisfied if she does not bear children. The proper number of children in each family to maintain the nation is 3, not 1. Wide limitation of family size is a national disaster.' And the Chancellor of the Exchequer, deprecating his own lavishness in raising the income-tax-relief allowance from £40 to £50 for second and subsequent children explained that it was to encourage couples to have more children, confessing that, 'I looked upon the continual diminution of the birth-rate in this country with considerable apprehension. The time may not be far distant when the countries of the British Empire will be crying out for more citizens of the right breed and when we in this country shall not be able to supply the demand.'

Whether he meant it or not, it sounded remarkably like the reasons that the two most menacing dictators, Hitler and Mussolini, were giving for encouraging their women to have larger families, as future gun-fodder for the Fatherland. The young British parents of this era could remember the war and its aftermath vividly and were not prepared to have children at all under the threat of a repetition.

'The recent statement that a child below 4 or 5 cannot wear one of the gas-masks being got ready for the rest of the population', wrote one young husband to the *News Chronicle*,[38] had decided his wife and himself not to bring one into a world so dangerous and unwelcoming. In fact the young couples of the Thirties had the fewest babies in British history.

4. *Divorce*

They were also the most divorced generation so far. But this was one facet of the new romantic concept of married life as an endless honeymoon. The difficulty of achieving it was partly responsible for the rise in the divorce rate. As the King's physician, Lord Dawson, said in the House of Lords, when pleading for a more enlightened divorce law:

We must not think that increase in divorce means a corresponding increase in marriage failures. In former days, married people were better able to live with failure because the wife was dutiful. She fitted in. She had no more equality in sex than she had in the law. The war accentuated the coming of freedom and equality to women . . . and women now expect sex-satisfied life just as they demand equality of companionship. . . . It follows therefore that women do contribute more to marriage failures than they did in days gone by when woman was a more submissive partner. On the other hand it is my belief that marriages which are successful today reach a higher level of happiness than at any previous period.[39]

The young couples of the Thirties certainly thought so. They believed that their households, in which young husbands did not disdain to help in the kitchen or push the baby out in its pram, were more friendly and enlightened than those of their parents and even than those of their elder brothers and sisters of the Twenties. The film stars on whom millions of young men and girls modelled themselves had made divorce a highly romanticised and glamourised proceeding. They looked upon it (as they explained to a million fans) as part of the search for the perfect marriage, which was always just around the corner, to be achieved eventually by the one who would go doggedly on, trying out one marital partner after another.

'Doug Fairbanks (junior) and I believed we were just right for each other, once', said Joan Crawford, summing up one such effort. 'We were both so happy. Life was such fun. And we were like children together, doing our house. Everything that he wanted! Everything that I wanted! We might have known that it was too magical to last . . . but some people just haven't known such happiness at all. At best, they've just been comfortably contented.'[40] To the young romantics of the Thirties, this was a contemptible, spiritless kind of married life. The mood was that it should be perfect, even if it couldn't last. 'Let's say goodbye and leave it alone', as Noël Coward was fond of suggesting in a score of different, haunting lyrics. Therefore divorce, on stage and screen (though not on radio) and in the Society magazines, was represented as not so much a failure as a not quite successful experiment to build the perfect relationship.

It was this popular fantasy about divorce which made the new king, Edward VIII believe that he would be able to make a divorced woman his queen.

He had apparently no inkling of the difficulties which he would encounter. His personal friends were out of touch with respectable opinion. Mrs Simpson knew only the American code in which marriage was essential and divorce a harmless formality. . . . Like others of his generation (Edward) exaggerated the decline in traditional standards of behaviour. England was a laxer country than she had been 30 years before. But appearances were still kept up in public. Divorce still carried a moral stigma and still drove men from political life.[41]

Nevertheless, in spite of the moral stand taken by all except a noisy minority ('the King's party') that Britain could not have a divorced woman as queen, nor a man married to a divorcee as king, the nation was in fact ready and waiting for the Divorce Law for ordinary people to be liberalised, and accepted its drastic reform the following year.

DIVORCE

Ever since the progressive Gorell Commission of 1909 there had been continual efforts to reform the Divorce Law by extending the grounds on which divorce might be allowed, on the lines of the Gorell recommendations. Each effort, so far, had come up against the stubborn Puritan morality that divorce was a punishment for adultery and that the future of Christian marriage depended on this remaining unaltered. In the end this citadel of righteousness was stormed by a distinguished barrister, Alan Herbert, who was also as 'A.P.H.' a well-known author, dramatist, composer and wit; and who was the Independent Member of Parliament for Oxford University.

He defeated the moralists by exposing the absurdity of their case in a satirical novel, *Holy Deadlock*. In it Mr Boom, a solicitor who specialises in divorce, explains to the upright civil servant who has come to an agreement with his wife that their marriage was a mistake, what he will have to do in order to enable her to divorce him without unnecessary scandal.

The law regards physical infidelity as the vital element in the marriage bond. Thus, without an act of adultery on one side or the other it is impossible to obtain a divorce. And a single act of infidelity is sufficient cause for the dissolution of a long and happy marriage, although that act may be begun and ended in five minutes – a sudden, unpremeditated act, the fruit of a passing craziness, jealousy, temper or desire. So dearly does the law regard the purity of the marriage bed. . . . One would think, then, that where *both* parties have violated the fundamental clause of the contract, there was twice the reason for dissolving the partnership. Not a bit of it. We say that in that case there is no good ground for divorce at all.

The story describes how the hero and heroine, because they both want the divorce, and because they are simple, honest people who keep on blurting out the truth, fail to get their decree, every time they attempt it, and in the end, after months of embarrassment and the outlay of a great deal of money, they are, as the solicitor explains, 'as much married as you were before. But Chastity, Decency and Truth have been upheld and the institution of Christian marriage has been saved again.'

The Matrimonial Causes Act of 1937 – the 'Herbert Act' as it was justifiably called, after the man who coaxed, persuaded and talked a whole nation into a more rational attitude – introduced new grounds for divorce besides adultery. This was A.P.H.'s triumph, although the extensions were not startling. It broke the ice and paved the way towards allowing divorce for marriage breakdown. The 1937 Act, however, in itself, merely added three new grounds on which divorce could be granted. One was wilful desertion for three years and upwards; the second was cruelty, and the third was incurable insanity after five years' confinement. The stage direction for Clemence Dane's play of 1921 about this last situation ('The audience is asked to imagine that it is 1933 and the recommendations of the Gorell Commission have become the law of the land') thus came true, though four years later than she hopefully predicted.

5. *Peace Ballot*
The decade which had started with slump and unemployment ended in war.

George Lansbury had observed sorrowfully that, up till now, the women's entrance into public life had been a disappointment, after all the splendid promises of sweeping reform, made in suffragette days. In fact the progressive young women of the Thirties were cool about the suffragettes who had been bourgeois and jingoistic while they themselves were left-wing and pacifist. They were at least a comfort to George Lansbury, and had the same ideology as his dearest suffragette friend Sylvia Pankhurst. At the time of the Peace Ballot, he acknowledged that 'On one vitally important matter, women's influence has been enormous. This is on Peace.'[42]

The Peace Ballot was the most important of all the Peace movements which had been burgeoning since Stanley Baldwin had remarked in the House of Commons that 'the bomber will always get through', also that if war came it would be the fault of the young men for allowing the old ones to make a mess of things. The following year, the young men of the Oxford Union voted that 'this House will not fight for King and Country', and the same year the pacifist parson Dick Sheppard inaugurated his Peace Pledge Union in which a hundred thousand men signed a pledge on a postcard. 'I renounce war and never again will I support or sanction another and I will do all in my power to persuade others to do the same.'

But the Peace Ballot, the women's main effort, was less idealistic and more practical than the straight pacifist movements. It rejected the ordinary old-fashioned war, between two well-matched sets of nations which would go on until one of them won, and based its case on collective security as represented by the League of Nations. The people who joined in the ballot were asked to vote on how far they would be prepared to go in supporting the League to stop an aggressor.

The project involved the distribution of forms to every possible household and collecting them again with the answers and the signatures. It was mainly the left-wing women's organisations which 'wore out their shoe-leather', as one observer said, in tramping round patiently doing the work.[43] The results were announced on June 28, 1935: 11,500,000 voted in favour of Britain's continued membership of the League; nearly 10,500,000 in favour of all-round disarmament and the abolition of the private manufacture of arms.[44] And over 10,000,000 voted for the use of economic sanctions against an aggressor.

Eleven and a half million votes could not be ignored, and the National Government which had been backing away from collective security was obliged to make some gesture towards supporting it. They subscribed to the League's plan of 'economic sanctions' against Mussolini who was conducting an old-fashioned imperialist adventure against Abyssinia, until it came to the dangerous moment of stopping oil supplies, which they were afraid would lead to war. The last of the high hopes of the League, which was founded in 1918 in order to insure that the Great War should be the War to End War, was destroyed by the Hoare-Laval plan to sell out to Mussolini, and in this atmosphere of giving way Hitler re-occupied the Rhineland.

During the years of appeasement, the peace movements lost their conviction as though they had now been convinced that war was a natural disaster, no more to be prevented by human effort than an earthquake or the eruption of a volcano.

There was, as Malcolm Muggeridge said, 'a strange apathy ... occasionally broken when some event, exceptionally violent, impelled attention. Then for a little while voices were raised, demanding an explanation, prophesying woe, pleading that it was still not too late if only at this eleventh hour. . . . Soon this clamour died away and the old apathy returned, the waiting, no-one knew for what.'[45]

Between 1935 and 1938 the annual number of marriages went up slightly (from 373,000 to 397,000) and so did the annual number of births (689,000 to 703,000)[46]; either because couples thought they might as well take the chance while they were still in command of their own destiny, or because there were more jobs in every field, and more money, as Britain began to re-arm. After Munich, and the air-raid trenches dug in Hyde Park, there was no more doubt. Arrangements began for moving mothers and children out of the areas in which it was expected there would be casualties of 600,000 dead and 1,200,000 injured.[47] The experts anticipated that the Germans would drop 100,000 tons of bombs on London in the first fortnight and that each ton of bombs would cause fifty casualties.

CHAPTER SIX

WOMEN IN UNIFORM
1939–1945

1. *Evacuation*

On September 1, 1939, there were coffins, shrouds and 1,000,000 burial forms ready and waiting in Britain's supposedly doomed cities. At dawn, a mass exodus started: some 827,000 unaccompanied children, 524,000 mothers and children, 7,000 handicapped persons and 115,000 teachers and helpers. By the third sunset it was completed without a single accident or casualty.

Back in the cities, notices were posted on the school gates to tell those left behind that their children were safely installed in the countryside, and all the papers, together with the B.B.C., painted a rosy picture of happy little boys and girls believing they were on a holiday treat. 'Children were taken to the doors of their new homes, introduced and given a meal and a wash. Some of them were soon eating high teas beyond their dreams and many went up into bedrooms larger and airier than they had thought possible', wrote *The Times* reporter, taking it for granted that children brought up in the cosy fug of a slum had been privately wishing for this kind of accommodation all their lives. 'An empty cot, a stray slipper, a doll lying face downward on the floor', lamented the leader-writer, describing 'A Childless City. It's dull in our town since the children left.'[1]

In the country, the host families really did want the scheme to work. Women who had seen their husbands off to the War to End War in 1914 were now seeing their sons off to fight the same enemy. All the Peace Movements and the policy of Appeasement had failed. They needed to feel that there was some difference in the situation, twenty-five years later, that some kind of human progress had been made; otherwise there was no hope at all. Offering a home to other people's strange children, in order to save them from the enemy, was something new to do. It created morale. So, the mass evacuation, in the last hours before war was declared, was a focus for sad and anxious patriotism and national unity, which was quite unlike the war-fever of last time; and the country people made up beds, and waited, uncomplainingly, in the parish hall for the evacuees to arrive, determined to do their best by them.

Their disgust when the guests did arrive filled the correspondence columns for several days. 'There were scenes of horror in the village streets.' 'The heads of some of the children could be seen crawling with vermin.' 'Some of the women arrived in a verminous condition which has contaminated bedding and wallpapers in houses where they are billeted. The owners are asking if compensation will be forthcoming.'[2] It was also a shock to the country hosts to learn that when a single lavatory is shared among half a dozen families in a city tenement, continual improvisation is necessary. 'You dirty thing', said one Glasgow mother to her six-year-old child. 'Messing up the lady's carpet like that. Go and do it in the corner.'[3] The *Lancet* noted that, 'Somewhat unexpectedly, enuresis has proved to be one of the major menaces to the comfortable disposition of evacuated urban children. Every morning every window is filled with bedding, hung out to air in the sunshine. The scene is cheerful but the householders are depressed.'

So were the slum mothers, who felt as if they were cast away in some terrifying wilderness, which sank into silence and darkness at black-out time every evening. Meanwhile no bombs were falling in their home cities and they began to wonder how their husbands were filling the gap where wife and children used to be. 'It is very disturbing to learn that certain women having been evacuated expensively are returning to their homes in the danger area', commented *The Times*, and Lord Ravensdale rebuked them for being so ungrateful. 'Surely, after the immense labour and expense laid out in settling them most comfortably in farms and cottages, the parents of these children should not be permitted to walk out at a moment's notice and return to the big cities because they feel so lonely.'[4]

The fact was that the non-appearance of the Luftwaffe had upset the whole scenario. Attitudes taken up to face a danger so immediate and so terrifying that class distinctions were wiped out became ridiculous when no enemy attack of any kind materialised. The evacuated mothers, who on

EVACUATION

September 1 had been pathetic fugitives, fleeing from their doomed cities with their babies in their arms, had now dwindled into untidy sluts, taking a country holiday at someone else's expense and hating it. By the beginning of 1940, nearly two-fifths of the unaccompanied children and nine-tenths of mothers with children under five had gone back, unmoved by government posters which showed a mother sitting in a country meadow, her children playing safely and happily at her feet, while the ghost of Hitler whispers to her, pointing to the distant city, 'Take them back! Take them back! Take them back!'

All the same, this first evacuation, which seemed so unrewarding at the time, had far-reaching results. It sowed the first seeds of welfare legislation, which was to set ordinary mothers free from many of the burdens which had always been looked upon as their biological fate. You could only escape them by being rich, until the setting up of the welfare state. And it was the traumatic shock of seeing how the other half lived, in September 1939, which prepared the ground for the respectable self-supporting classes to accept the principle of subsidising the submerged tenth. It was not only the lice and the nits which shook their hosts. In any case, some cities sent fewer of these than others. Among the Merseyside children, for instance, the proportion of infested children was between 22% and 50%[5]; whereas from London it was only 8% to 35%. But it was also distressing to find how insufficiently clad many of them were. They were invariably sent in their best clothes; but if they came from areas which had had a long period of unemployment and depression, they were not likely to have either mackintoshes or boots, let alone spare underwear or nightwear. One report about Manchester and Liverpool children said that the little girls had no knickers and never had worn any.[6] In order to pacify foster-parents, the Ministry of Health was obliged to distribute about £15,000, for clothing grants among local education authorities in the reception areas. It did so on the condition that the transaction should be kept a strict secret, in case of opening floodgates to similar requests.

But most of the schemes launched because of the shock of the first evacuation only began to show when the second took place, which was when the Luftwaffe at last made its long advertised appearance over Britain, in the summer of 1940. Britain's casualty-roll from air-raids was larger than any other member of the United Nations; about half of them registered in London. A year after the war began there was a heavy raid on the East End starting at 5 o'clock in the evening and going on until 4.30 in the morning, and another the next night. At that, there was a great new exodus, a spontaneous one this time, queues of women and children with their possessions done up in pillow-cases fleeing vaguely west, or taking trains from the main-line stations to wherever they could reach. During the next fifteen months, some 1,250,000 were helped by the government to leave bombed cities, and soon the number of evacuees billeted in reception areas was only about a hundred thousand short of the total of the first exodus.

From this time on,

the original role of evacuation as a means of transferring children to safety diminished in significance. Instead, it operated as a receiver of social casualties; it took into care, for instance, the children of mothers who were ill or expecting another baby and whose husbands were in the Services, the children of mothers who were forced by shortage of money to work, or who preferred to work, children from homes where strife had broken out, children who were out of control and at cross-purposes with society, children of parents who had no satisfactory home and could not get one. The evacuation scheme, designed as an integral part of civil defence, increasingly assumed the form of a social welfare agency; an agency which placed children in temporary boarding-homes or residential nurseries and hostels . . . [7]

In fact, here was the embryo of the 'children's charter' (the Children Act of 1948).

Before the war, plans had been made for sending expectant mothers out of cities, and allocating their hospital beds to air-raid victims. In London, the hospitals had arranged to transfer three-quarters of the midwives to casualty work and two-thirds of the maternity beds. No one had arranged for the same number of beds and nurses for confinements in the reception areas. The Ministry of Health had asked the Treasury to sanction expenditure for the purpose, and the Treasury had replied vaguely to the effect that some makeshift maternity homes could easily be run up, in the country, if it turned out they were needed.[8] In fact that was exactly what did happen and for the first two months farm-houses and castles, disused public institutions and private homes were hurriedly equipped with bathrooms, lavatories, sinks, sluices and cooking facilities, for the purpose. (The shortest time taken from first inspection to readiness was five days.)[9]

But if the babies were not to be born during an air-raid, mothers had obviously got to leave the cities early in their final month; and accommodation had to be provided; and while they had a place to stay, it might as well be used to keep them for a month after the birth, the way that middle-class mothers always rested until the 'monthly nurse' departed. The Ministry therefore set up pre-natal homes as well as emergency maternity hospitals, and coaxed or coerced the pregnant women away from the city as early as they could get them to go.

Some of this emergency accommodation was in one or other of the stately homes of England, lent for the purpose for the duration, which the mothers found excessively bare and draughty, but which were a godsend to journalists whose job it was to write propaganda paragraphs suitable for American readers who were touched to learn that the babies of Cockney slum mothers were being rocked in the ancient cradle of the young heir. But the truth was in fact better than this harmless conceit. It was the fall in maternal mortality and in such usual complaints as post-maternal sickness and disabilities, among the hitherto underprivileged mothers who had a rest, with adequate food and medical inspection before the birth, who were looked after and waited on by professionals during the confinement, and who had the convalescent period after. Maternal mortality dropped from 497 per 100,000 to 232 per 100,000, while the infant mortality figure, after a bad start between 1939 and 1941, then declined by 28%, the biggest decline since records were kept, except for the post-war period from 1918 to 1923.[10]

2. Conscription

In the autumn months after the outbreak of war in 1939, there was no war-work for women, any more than there had been in the autumn of 1914. 'No words can bring out the sense of frustration, of sheer impotent anger of some woman who has spent the day looking for a job everywhere and has only been confronted with newspaper placards, "Big Increase in War Effort!" "Call-Up Accelerated" and "Increase of Women's Unemployment"', lamented Elaine Burton in the *Evening Standard*.[11] Out of over 6,000 registered with the Women's Employment Federation, more than half were wholly unemployed or employed below their capacity.

'Ring up five more influential friends between 9 and 12 to ask if they know any national work I can undertake', reported the 'Provincial Lady'.[12] 'One proves to be on duty as an L.C.C. ambulance attendant, at which I am very angry and wonder how on earth she managed to get that job – and two more reply that I am the tenth person at least to ask this and they don't know of anything more for me, and the remaining two assure me that I must just *wait* and in time I shall be told what to do.' *The Times* told the same story: 'Thousands of women have offered themselves since the war began for some form of emergency service . . . in an unending stream they visit the various depots and try to enrol.'[13] A patronising government pamphlet advised them to stick to the housewife rôle for which providence created them, but to do it patriotically.

What must I do? I remember that this is a war job, too! – and I try to do it even better than usual. I shop with special care. I waste nothing.

I save paper, tins, bones. I try to keep myself and my house trim and cheerful. I take special pains with the cooking because I know this keeps the man's spirits up. I send the children to bed early and I *don't* stay up listening for sirens. I remind myself that in this way though I may not be winning medals, I am certainly helping to win the war![14]

In October 1939, the number of women totally unemployed went up by 198,998, because 'non-essential occupations'[15] (assigned to women by long-standing custom) had been curtailed, while war-work was not yet sufficiently advanced to make up for it.

Everything changed suddenly, in the early summer of 1940, just as it had in the summer of 1915. Once again, the enemy was on the doorstep. Once again, it was put to the women that the only hope of Britain's survival was for them to go out to work. They were to forget everything that had been said about women's rôle being the care of husband and children, and woman's place in the home, and the expression 'pin-money' became archaic. This time, the order to switch rôles was even more peremptory, because they were to be conscripted as soldiers as well. Even their own feminist preacher, Dr Maude Royden, had long ago laid down that 'women are by deep instinct debarred from soldiership'. And while it was not going to be compulsory for them to kill, it was represented to them that it would be convenient if some of them could overcome their biological repugnance to taking life instead of giving it.

On May 20, the German armies reached the Channel

coast, and were so close to Britain that housewives drew the black-out, in the mornings, hoping not to see parachutists floating down like dead leaves, as they had in Holland. On May 22 changes in the position of women were made which would have taken months of discussion and protest in the ordinary way. In less than three hours, the House of Commons passed an extension of the Emergency Powers (Defence) Bill through all its stages. It gave the Minister of Labour and National Service power to direct each individual in the United Kingdom to perform such services as might be required of him or her. On the same afternoon the Minister, Ernest Bevin, reached agreement with the Amalgamated Engineering Union, the National Union of General and Municipal Workers, and the Transport and General Workers' Union, about the temporary relaxation of peace-time customs, in order to allow Dilution (the breaking-up of skilled work among a team, as practised in the 1914 War) and also for the employment of women in processes usually closed to them by trade-union customs which made them 'men's work'.[16] The agreement securing to women on 'men's work' the men's rate of pay, when fully trained, was also signed, on the same day.

Ernest Bevin, whom Churchill had appointed to the War Cabinet in this crisis, was the second statesman of the century to help women make a 'great leap forward'. Like Lloyd George he was no feminist. But, as he said in the House, when defending his policies for women's employment, 'I yield to none, not even the most extreme feminists, in the work I have done for the women of this country in my trade-union efforts.'[17]

Churchill had brought him in because he was probably the only man who could take the unions along with him, in organising labour on a total-war basis. It was in achieving this that he gave women a place in industry which they had been denied since the Industrial Revolution, except between 1915 and 1918.

Once his war machine got under way, no skilled person was to do what could be done by an unskilled person; and no man was to do what could be done by a woman; and women could undertake anything within their physical strength.

At the time he took over, the Germans had overrun five countries, knocked France out of the war, and twice driven Britain into the sea. Britain had a population of 47,676,000. The population of 'Greater Germany' exceeded 75,000,000 and the German government also had at its command the vast labour resources which it could compel the occupied countries to provide. Also, Germany had been preparing for war since the Nazis came to power, and her production had been on a war footing for some time, while in Britain the turnover from peace-time economy to war-time was not yet achieved. Production in the factories was still on a limited scale and the entire equipment of the British Expeditionary Force had been lost at Dunkirk. Britain's services had to be manned – including Civil Defence; labour had to be provided for food production and war administration; and the war industries had to have workers on an unprecedented scale.

The only untapped source of labour was married women. Unmarried women now supported themselves as a matter of course, and nine girls out of ten worked from school-leaving until marriage (apart from the recent period of temporary unemployment). Bevin's plan was first to move women who were free of hampering ties into men's places, and then move the childless married women into theirs; and so on. Eventually he had to scrape the bottom of the barrel, conscripting grannies and using such hours of the day as mothers had to spare from their children. Two legends about good wives were now discredited and never recovered their old status. One was that looking after family and home was the most important work a woman could do; and sacred. The other was that a woman running a home as it should be run was fully occupied. During Bevin's direction of woman-power, it was acknowledged at last that housewifery is more subject to Parkinson's Law than any other human activity.

In April 1941, the Registration of Women began at the employment exchanges, under the Registration for Employment Order. It started with those born in 1920. From then on, women registered with their age-groups at regular intervals, until by October 1942 all those from 45 downwards had registered.

The National Service (No. 2) Act became law in December 1941. Its main purpose was the provision of an adequate supply of recruits to the Women's Auxiliary Forces. Those called up were able to choose between service in the Forces and whole-time work in essential industries. Younger women were 'conscripted' while eighteen-year-olds and older and married women were subject only to direction by the Minister of Labour. This distinction, however, made little difference as the order had to be obeyed.

This drastic mobilisation was achieved without the patriotic fervour which had celebrated women's involvement in the First War, but with remarkably little friction. Bevin was a skilled negotiator, who took trade-union taboos more seriously than sexual ones. He knew when to press the men, and when to be flexible. When sheet-metal shops in the Midlands (an old craft, threatened by automatic tools and the power-press anyway) flatly refused to accept the introduction of women, he let them get away with it. But Dilution, on the other hand, was absolutely essential, though still dynamite with some of the craft unions. (As one Ministry of Labour official said despairingly, 'Whenever dilution is mentioned we seem to come up against a ghostly army of unemployed boilermen.'[18]

However, in January 1943, the A.E.U., which had always maintained that engineering was by nature a man's job, at last recanted and admitted women to the Union 'on a footing of equality with their men comrades'.[19] By August 1944 it had 143,000 women members out of a total membership of 920,000. The two general unions (N.U.G.M.W. and T.G.W.) had increased their female membership to 250,000 and 269,354 respectively. In London Transport there was 100% organisation of women. In all, the number of women trade-unionists nearly doubled between 1938 and 1944.

Women workers were now divided into 'mobile' and 'immobile'. The main source from which it was still possible to bring some fresh labour into the war effort was the large number of women who could not be transferred to where they were most needed, because of domestic responsibilities as wives and mothers. By finding them employment within reach of their homes, it was possible to release other women who could be moved. Up until 1943, women who were running a home and looking after children or sick or elderly people had been left to find their own part-time work. In April 1943, however, Bevin issued an order requiring them to undertake work to which they were directed. In July, he announced that as part of his plans to release women for work in aircraft factories, the government intended to proceed with the registration of women up to 51.

The 'conscription of grannies' unexpectedly aroused a storm of emotional protest. The press was hostile and refused to believe it was necessary, 200 Conservative M.P.s signed a motion objecting to the scheme. Bevin replied that no one had uttered a squeak of protest when he registered nurses and midwives up to 60 years old, or ex-cotton operatives up to 55, when he needed women back in the cotton trade; and that he did not really believe the protests came from the women at all.

A war-time social survey found that over 97% of women agreed emphatically that women should do war-work. But although they accepted the necessity and liked the money, they were not as starry-eyed about it as the munition-girls had been in the First War. 'Working in a factory is not fun', said one eighteen-year-old.[20] 'To be shut in for hours, without even a window to see daylight, it's grim. The noise is terrific and at night when you shut your eyes to sleep all the noises start again in your head. . . . Night-shift is the worst, the ghastly sensation of never feeling really awake and meals all different times and the work so monotonous ... boredom is our worst enemy.'

The outsider, the resented shirker, was the married woman who had managed to dodge both being conscripted and being directed. A rising young left-wing M.P., Dr Edith Summerskill, asked in the House of Commons, 'Is the wedding-ring to act as a magic charm, to release the wealthy, independent childless married women living in hotels or delightful country reception areas?' The reference was to wives of serving officers who moved to be near to wherever their husbands were stationed ('well-to-do camp followers', said Dr Summerskill) and who therefore managed to avoid registration. In fact this was a concession to masculine sentiment which had originated with Churchill himself, who had been told that men serving in the Forces were upset at the idea of their wives being sent away from the marital home. From then on, servicemen's wives were not classed as 'mobile' (although in fact many of the young-marrieds did not have a marital home of any kind) and could not be sent away, to where labour was needed, as other women without pressing domestic responsibilities were.

More importantly, the House debated the question of who was to mind the baby, while the mother was on work of national importance? Churchill pointed out that 'married women, or women doing necessary household work, which meant some 11,000,000 persons, were now the largest reserve for industry and home defence. Many varieties of arrangements were possible to enable women to divide up domestic tasks and be free to work close to their home, in factory or field. You could have crèches and public nurseries. . . .' More nursery accommodation for workers' children was supplied during the war than at any time before or since. In December of 1941, *The Times* reported that 'vast strides' were being made all over the country to provide children with a hot mid-day meal at school, thus saving their mothers the trouble; and a few days later a correspondent improved on the idea by suggesting that married women on war-work should be relieved of the care of their children altogether. 'I am surprised that no-one advocates residential nurseries in safe areas. . . . this would bring the obvious advantages of evacuation within reach of the under-fives, while enabling their mothers to work full-time in factories.'[21]

By the end of 1943 there were 1,450 nurseries under local authorities, with places for 65,000 children; and more than double that number of under-fives had been given places in elementary or nursery schools; while by 1945 one child in three was being fed at school, in place of one child in 30 at the beginning of the war.[22]

When the conscription of women was first announced, along with other new measures, on December 2, 1941, the comment in Parliament and in the press was chiefly to ask why it had not come before, rather than why it had come at all. It was not that the girls wanted it for themselves, but that their elders approved of it for them in principle. Mass-Observation, the new social organisation which had started in the late Thirties and used voluntary 'observers' amongst people all over the country sounded some of the young women whom it affected. A typical answer came from a typist who spoke for her generation, 'I can lay my hand on my heart and truthfully say that I have not yet met a woman in her twenties who is not in *an awful state* about conscription.'[23]

The girls who liked the idea had volunteered for the women's services long ago. By December 31, 1939, there had been already 43,000 eager recruits. The volunteers, however, tended to come from the better-off sections of society. They were girls who had enjoyed boarding-school or college and who – like some of the ex-public school young men – foresaw that service life would offer some of the same satisfactions. Also, it was the middle- and upper-class girls who opted for travel and adventure if they could get it through a war-time opportunity, while the working-class ones made marriage their priority. Mass-Observation found that 'Wanderlust is very widespread in the women's services. The uppermost feeling seems to be a negative one, "I'll never be able to settle down again."'

Just as the girls' public schools had taken their pattern from those of the boys, so the women's services copied those of the men, with officers from the upper and middle classes, non-commissioned from the lower-middle and upper-working class. Mary Lee Settle, an American girl who had come over in order to volunteer for the W.A.A.F., described the 'Admin' officer whose duty it was to lecture the new recruits on hygiene. 'Throughout the whole lecture she never moved her head, straight on her thin neck above her absolutely centred tie, her officer's cap straight on her pulled-back Eton crop ... she clipped out information about diseases, told about crabs, warned about toilet-seats', and ended by announcing, 'One thing I must warn you about. I absolutely forbid my girls being seen talking to American niggers.'[24]

But there was also Flight-Officer Trimingham, 'an ex-tennis player, a good sport and an absolutely unquestioning snob', who was just and affable with defaulters. 'Well, ACW Settle, we've been a bit of a fool haven't we? . . . let's just have one day confined to camp since it's a first offence . . . let's be more careful in future, shall we?'

In spite of her disillusionment, Aircraftwoman Mary Lee Settle found that:

When we had formed companies and begun to learn drill, our pride resurged . . . a corps pride. Marching with the others, the loss of self and the gain of communal pleasure came without realisation. . . . The girls around me had begun to fill out and glow. Their skin was losing its thickness. They looked seventeen. In what seemed to me a life without joy, which was imposed on them without their choice, they were beginning to thrive . . . air, exercise, regular meals, the very act, for some of them, of sleeping above ground for the first time in years were making the blood run better through their bodies . . . the morning air in the new after-breakfast dawn was tinged white from our breath . . . over the flat face of the square, through it in the distance the yell of a sergeant seemed to float over the stamp of feet as we dressed ranks, wheeled, counted, slapped shoes, hollow-sounding on the concrete, snapped turns, 'By the right, qui-ick march'. I thought of Kipling, of all the roles, the acquiesence to orders yelled in the same Cockney voice, all the way from Danny Deever to ACW Settle.

There was the same brutality in this world where women were the final authority as in men's military services since the Roman occupation of Britain; but in women's communities it was feline. Sergeant Smerd, for instance, was 'a tiny sadistic bundle of wire', whose way of punishing a girl was to ride a bicycle, herself, through the station, with the culprit running behind like a dog, 'while the men turned away, as they often did, disgusted at the blatancy of so much W.A.A.F. punishment.' One girl in the camp, who was being treated both for nits in her hair and for being a bed-wetter, driven by the humiliation to despairing self-hatred, tried to hang herself 'by the cord of her WAAF pyjamas to one of the toilet struts'. But there was one way out, for the girl who found that this final equality with the other sex, of being liable for military service was too hard to be borne, and that was to 'work your ticket' to get pregnant in order to be discharged under Paragraph Eleven in the King's Regulations. 'Cap off with a grab, I see them as one girl, slowly grinning, "I'm aht". The sergeant's scrawny hand reaching for the tan papers, all lecturing stopped in face of that easy triumph of natural insolence, saying "Paragraph Eleven?"'

The girls in uniform who had the most romantic aura of all female conscripts were those on Anti-Aircraft gun sites. The reason was that they were the only women who shared the men's licence to kill. The fact that they were 'by nature' barred from this had been the ultimate argument against their being allowed to vote, in pre-suffrage days. In all other service jobs, they were merely keeping the war-machine running; but in the anti-aircraft batteries they were actually helping to fire the guns which, it was hoped, would kill as many German airmen as possible.

'No woman, although compelled to join the A.T.S., will be compelled to go into battle', Churchill explained.[25] 'It is a matter of quality and of temperament, of feeling capable to do this form of duty which every woman must judge for herself, and not one in which compulsion should be used. Women may be compelled to join the A.T.S. but only volunteers from within the A.T.S. will be allowed to serve with the guns.'

The first mixed battery started training in the spring of 1941. It was thought that the shock to old soldiers, of sharing a gun with women, might be too severe, and so only new recruits formed the male part of the team. The officer whose mixed battery was the first to make a kill, said proudly that 'If I were offered the choice of commanding a mixed battery or a male battery I can say without hesitation that I would take the mixed . . . the girls in my opinion are definitely better than the men on the instruments they are manning.'[26] By 1943, the first women Technical Control officers were beginning to replace male operational officers on gun-sites in the Home Command. These women were responsible for co-ordinating the attack on enemy aircraft and the Gun Position officers had the order to fire on their information.

3. *Planning Utopia*
Just as the First War resulted in women getting Suffrage and the Sex Disqualification (Removal) Act, the second one promised them equal education and equal pay. These awards

for war-work were in both cases planned and announced before the war ended, at a time when there was at least light at the end of the tunnel, and it was possible to think of reconstruction plans for the post-war world without feeling it was tempting Providence to discuss them.

The Education Act of 1944 opened the path to élite university education to any child who could profit by it, no matter what sex or class the child might be. No Local Education Authority was to be allowed to charge fees in its schools, though all would have the power to buy places in public schools or in 'direct grant' grammar schools. These arrangements about money affected girls' chances directly, because parents had always hesitated about making sacrifices for a daughter, who was going to give up her career on marriage, whereas the investment in a son's future was for life. A girl who got into a grammar school, through an examination to test her ability at the age of eleven, was on the direct road to university. If she qualified for a university place, the Local Education Authority would allow her a grant sufficient to see her through to graduation, according to the means of her parents. Although the system laid down by this Act was later discredited (because of social injustice inherent in the 'eleven plus' test), it did give so many more girls the stimulus and the chance of getting to college that within one generation the words 'university student' and 'undergraduate' became bi-sexual, whereas in the Twenties and Thirties one had still referred to 'women undergraduates', though never to 'men undergraduates'.

A slight cloud marred the otherwise cheerful and hopeful

parliamentary discussion of this new education bill, which was perhaps the most important milestone of all on women's road to equal opportunity. The House of Commons voted to amend it to include giving equal pay to women teachers, which seemed to them a logical extension of a bill for equal education. It did not strike the Prime Minister in this way at all. He denounced the impertinence and made the Commons revoke their decision.

However, in response to war-time pressures and the strength of the feeling that now was the time to consider post-war reconstruction, a Royal Commission was appointed in the autumn of 1944 to examine 'the existing relationship between the remuneration of men and women in the public services, in industry and in other fields of employment and to consider the social, economic and financial implications of the claim of equal pay for equal work'.[27] Since the agreements made with unions providing that women replacing men in the factories could receive equal pay with men when fully trained and if able to work without extra help or supervision, it was no use anyone pretending that the case for equal pay did not exist, nor hoping that if one took no notice the whole issue would disappear after the war. The bus conductresses in London had got it; so had the textile industries and some sections of the engineering industry. In fact the opposition did not come from the craft unions which realised, as the A.E.U. had long ago, that equal pay was a security for craftsmen, since there was no logical reason why any employer should prefer a woman if she was just as expensive, and several reasons (such as muscular strength) why one should prefer the man.

Compared with the engineers, the National Association of Schoolmasters was fretful and nervous about the issue. To them, it did not represent a safeguard against being undercut, but a threat to their status and living standard. They did not argue about the fact that women did much the same work as men in teaching. They simply said that if married men only got as much as spinsters, teaching would be a profession of well-off women and badly-off men and no ambitious worthwhile man would take it up. 'The interests of education in general and of the boys in particular called for a ratio of 39% men to 61% women teachers and the concession of equal pay to women would reduce the male percentage below the 29% at which it stood in 1938.'[28] The Permanent Secretary to the Ministry of Education said that it was not so much the question of different standards of living between married men teachers and women; but there would be a 'psychological disinclination' to enter what would tend to be regarded as a woman's profession.

The majority of the Commission came to the conclusion that women were less in demand and got lower wages because they were not so strong physically; because they were oftener absent from work; because they were less resourceful in dealing with unexpected situations; and because they looked upon full-time paid work as only temporary, a way of filling in the time till marriage, after which they seldom returned.

A dissenting minority of the Commission (Dame Anne Loughlin, Dr Janet Vaughan and Miss L. F. Nettlefold) argued that the superior physical strength of men was getting progressively less important since newer industries needed 'manual deftness or machine operations' rather than brute force; and because 'the war has greatly accelerated the use of mechanical devices and gadgets to reduce physical effort in numerous operations in nearly all industries'. They agreed that women had a higher absenteeism rate, due to family responsibilities and also to their 'psychological attitude' to employment; but did not believe it justified a whole policy about wages. Was an individual woman who was never absent to get less than an individual man with a poor attendance record because on the average men have a better rate of attendance than women? They queried the assumption that women were less instantly adaptable, and suspected that it was based on war-time experience when large numbers of women with short training doing a variety of new jobs were compared with men with long experience of different jobs. Anyway, they added, the traditional sphere of women's work, like housekeeping and children, is full of 'surprise situations' such as the morning after a blitz.

They found that the same generalisations were being applied to the superior 'career value' of men, who were expected to stay longer in the job and so got better wages. They accepted that most women were less eager and ambitious than most men; and that therefore the average earnings of women were less than the average earnings of men. 'We should certainly expect, under a regime of equal pay and equal opportunity, that more men than women would be found in the most highly skilled, responsible and highly paid posts. But this neither accounts for nor justifies sex-differentiation of rates of pay at any particular level of skill.'

In the opinion of the dissenting minority, an important reason for women's wages being lower was that their bargaining power was puny compared with that of the men, who had getting on for a century's experience of collective bargaining since Tolpuddle. But there were also 'conventions and pressures' restricting the employment of women, much more irrational and whimsical than any barriers put up by women against men; for instance that there was so little objection to women being aircraft ferry pilots that this particular skill now had the aura of being a 'woman's job', whereas to suggest that a woman might be a London taxi-driver was a shocking idea, an unnatural concept. Among these taboos, the most important were 'those which have their origin less in the sentiment that "this is something which women can't do," than in the sentiment that "this is something which only men should be allowed to do."' The three dissenting women entirely appreciated that this resistance against allowing women into new occupations was not just stubborn male prejudice; but an understandable fear of unemployment, with the misery of the Thirties still raw. But, they reminded the men gently, the threat of being unemployed again was 'enhanced by the very fact that women's wages are lower than those of men'.

Although the 1944 Commission failed to reach any conclusion on the introduction of Equal Pay (since in the first place they could not decide how it was to be defined), they did provide a study of the causes of and the reasons for unequal pay, which proved extremely illuminating in the approaching discussions of the issue, which were to go on, as the women's suffrage ones had, for some thirty years after it had been established that Equal Pay, like Women's Suffrage, was a piece of social justice which must clearly be enacted sooner or later, but preferably later.

This was the time for planning post-war Utopias. Soldiers, kicking their heels in drab and tedious camps, waiting for the Second Front to start, were kept docile by educational discussions about post-war social reform. Tired women in factories, their fingers busy on a monotonous process, their thoughts running on whether to lay out the family's 'points' on a tin of Spam, hummed refrains from one of the many songs about a better post-war world which had now become as much a part of working-class culture as the Moody and Sankey hymns about 'pearly gates' had been, in an earlier generation.

(There'll be love and laughter
And peace ever after,
To-morrow, when the world is free.)

The determination that the long-drawn hardship should result in some kind of a new world was shared by the middle and the working class. The upper class was unenthusiastic, foreseeing correctly that the best they could hope for was to go back to a society in which some of their privileges still held.

But as early as 1941, the T.U.C. had sent a deputation to lobby the Minister of Health about improving health insurance, which did not cover wives and families and which in any case dealt out only meagre benefits. The Minister thereupon appointed William Beveridge to make a comprehensive survey of all existing social insurance schemes.

The story of the Beveridge Report, which was to be the catalyst for a whole period of social reform, had started some forty years earlier when the Webbs invited 'the boy Beveridge' to breakfast to consult him about their own scheme for Utopia – which was to break up the old Poor Law and use the pieces to create a network of remedies and preventives against the ordinary misfortunes of everyday life; that is, cradle-to-grave insurance. This was the substance of Beveridge's CMD 6404, which was published on December 1, 1942.[29]

His version differed from the original Fabian scheme, which had assumed that the social security bill would be paid by society. His was a contributory scheme, based on flat-rate contributions. Two assumptions in it were important to mothers. One was that Family Allowances would be paid directly to them (a scheme for which Eleanor Rathbone had been agitating since the early Twenties), which meant that they would have a (small) weekly sum for children which was not dependent on the father's financial state nor his mood. The other was that there should be universal insurance for free medical treatment under a National Health Service.

The public, dreaming of their post-war millennium, queued outside the Stationery Office shops to buy the Report and read it hungrily. A fortnight later, the Gallup Poll ascertained that 19 people out of every 20 had heard of it, and 9 out of every 10 believed its proposals should be adopted.

The Cabinet was embarrassed by its success. Already, the private insurance firms were mounting a campaign against it;

it was extremely unlikely that the Coalition would ever agree to vote for it and Churchill thought it would distract the nation, too early, from the business in hand of actually winning the war. The government hastily tried to smother it, which made an extremely bad impression on the electorate. In fact it was perhaps Churchill's failure to realise that both the weary but dogged civilians, and the servicemen fighting without any military-romantic illusions, all meant to see some solid results for their efforts, which lost him the 1945 election.

4. *Whose Children?*

By the middle of 1943, among women between 18 and 40 years old, 9 in 10 single women and 4 in 5 married ones were either in the services or in industry, and living conditions in Britain were much what you might expect of a home in which the housewife never has time to do more than the bare minimum and is always trying to catch up on her sleep. The number of babies who were suffocated in their cots or in their parents' bed was greater than the entire total deaths from war operations of all women in the armed forces.[30] War-time Social Surveys found that absenteeism from school was very marked every Monday and Friday; the days on which shopping had to be done and bills paid. On those days, the 'unpaid domestic servant of the poor, the eldest child in the family' took over, staying at home while the mother went to work, in order to deal with the coalman, the insurance man, the rent collector and the sick baby sister. 'Children are seen in queues at 8.30 a.m. and by the time they return home it is too late for them to go to school.' A welfare officer in an industrial town producing urgent war supplies reported that 'the mothers on night-shift keep children up to school-age in bed with them all day while they try to get some sleep and at night the child is put to bed again with the father'.

It was no longer automatically virtuous to be conscientious about caring for your own child. It might even be a form of self-indulgence. A Sheffield housewife with one son over 14 asked at the labour exchange whether she might work a short week, so as to leave her time to look after him. 'Now it was a young lady of the superior self-confident type to whom I addressed my petition. She spoke with a Girton accent and she proceeded to lecture me. The country was at war, she said, it was my duty to accept the job that was offered me and my boy was old enough to look after himself.'[31]

No Medals by Esther McCracken, which was a long-running and popular play, put the case for the ultimate Cinderella, the full-time housewife, whose sister in the women's forces despises her.

. . . Oh, the conceit of you women just because you're dressed in khaki! . . . I at least look after the health and comfort of two Wrens, one naval officer and one airman . . . rising every morning at 6.30, and rarely getting to bed before midnight. Do you clear out grates and re-lay fires before 7 a.m.? Do you stand in queues most of the morning, so that your people may have a balanced diet? Do the washing and mending and darning for all these people every week? Nor do you firewatch. If there's a raid, you're exempt, and it's I and others like me who go bobbing into the street to see your flat doesn't catch fire, while you hog it in bed – and yet they give you a better tin hat than they give me!

WHOSE CHILDREN?

With husbands and sweethearts sent overseas, and so many allied troops stationed in Britain, women's sex-life, like their homes, became increasingly disorganised. In Birmingham, the number of irregularly conceived babies born to married women trebled. In Yorkshire a back-street abortionist was prosecuted for helping too many soldiers' wives out of an awkward situation. British soldiers, who felt creased and shabby beside the newly arrived Americans, could not quite laugh off Lord Haw-Haw's suggestion that these were sleeping with their wives in their absence. (According to a figure quoted by Mrs Frances P. Bolton, in the U.S. House of Representatives, American soldiers fathered 70,000 illegitimate children in Great Britain.)[32] Syphilis and gonorrhoea went up by 113% among male civilians and servicemen, by 63% among women, according to a Birmingham survey. The illegitimate birth-rate soared to 93 per thousand live births, in 1945.[33] This did not necessarily mean, however, that young women were less chaste than they had been before the war. Three mothers out of ten had conceived their first child out of wedlock in 1938–39, but 70% of them had married the father in time for the birth. In 1944–45 there were fewer irregularly conceived babies of the kind, but far fewer shot-gun weddings, because the fathers were overseas. A great many of them did marry the girls later, when they got home.

A curious feature of the illegitimate war babies was the number born to older mothers; almost twice the average to spinsters between 30 and 35, and 20% more than average to those between 35 and 45.[34] They were, perhaps, the last of the women left without a mate by the 'mutilated society' of the

Twenties; the result of the First War. Now, in the second, they took the chance of society being disrupted and the rules relaxed, and lonely men needing companionship in order to have a war-time affair before it was too late.

It was not socially acceptable to sleep with an American if your husband was actually fighting; nor to have so much as a harmless flirtation, at any time, with Italian prisoners of war (who tended to be around loose, helping on the land). But there was never the vicious bitterness about such contacts in Britain, as there was in occupied countries, against women who became the mistress of a man of the occupying army.

All the same, it was no time to have an illegitimate baby, since it was a problem to find enough women to look after the legitimate ones. Service women were discharged as soon as 'Paragraph Eleven' was invoked; and war workers lost their official billet. There was no place where a mother could keep her baby and work, unless it was in domestic service – and there she was an easy target for exploitation.

On July 15, 1944, Lady Allen of Hurtwood wrote to *The Times* about the little children who had been dumped in institutions because there was no one to care for them or to care what happened to them, in war-time society: the '100,000 wards of the community', who were living under Dickensian conditions, but 'this time they have no Dickens to plead their cause; those who have suffered must themselves be their own advocates'. In a pamphlet 'prepared for a single purpose – to stir into action the government, members of Parliament, Local Authorities, the general public' and called *Whose Children?* she quoted examples of the way children were being treated:

Meals in compulsory silence . . . children forcibly fed by holding noses . . . food kept over from meal to meal until finally eaten . . . a 3-year-old child put to bed in a dark room as punishment for a temper tantrum . . . indiscriminate cruelties such as the wrenching of ears, the twisting of arms, the pulling of forelocks . . . and I have seen a boy of 7 years stand all day in the main lobby on a cold winter day, partly clothed, as a punishment for accidental incontinence . . . during those long hours the lad was not allowed to talk at all or to lean on the lockers for support . . .

In consequence of the public agitation raised by these revelations, a Committee was appointed to make an intensive study of the care of children in institutions, which underlined everything that *Whose Children?* had said. The recommendations of this Committee eventually became the Curtis Act (or Children's Charter) which created a whole new order for the child deprived of normal home life and let loose a whole new culture of social work on post-war Britain, on the basis that every child has a right to individual care and the pursuit of happiness.

Meanwhile, the authorities were so much alarmed by the public reaction that when they discovered they had some 5,000 evacuee children still left on their hands after the rest had gone home, they dared not put them in public institutions, but went on making interim arrangements for them 'without any stigma of the poor law', at great inconvenience to all departments involved, until they were able to hand the last 1,500, thankfully, over to the newly constituted Children's Department.[35]

CHAPTER SEVEN

WIVES AND MOTHERS AGAIN
1945–1960

1. *Woman's Place in the Home*

The difference between the peace of 1945 and the peace of 1918 was that this time so many more of the men came home. During the First War, there had been between 9 and 10 million in the forces, and 947,000 of them were killed. In the Second War there were only between 5 and 6 million fighting and 256,000 were killed. This time, the death-toll among civilians was high; 60,000 killed in air-raids. In the 1914 War it was the families safely at home who dreaded the sight of the telegraph boy. During the worst months of the Blitz, the telegram was as likely to be received by the serviceman, telling him that his wife and family had been wiped out.

Therefore, although more men than women were killed, post-war Britain was not a mutilated society, as it had been in the Twenties. As early as 1951, the numbers of the sexes had equalised, in age-groups up to 30. There was a great marrying year in 1947, with 401,210 weddings. The pre-war annual average had been 325,813, but it had gone up to 370,997 during the war years.[1] Therefore, when demobilisation took place, a phenomenal number of young husbands and wives settled down to live with each other for the first time.

At first, it was all they wanted. Living in camps and hostels and eating in canteens had created a passion of affection for the ordinary things of home life, for plushy armchairs by the fire and beds with sheets, and clean curtains fluttering in windows from which the black-out had been joyfully ripped down. Shortly after the end of the war, there was an 'Available Later' exhibition of furniture. Every day, from morning till night, an endless stream of shabby men, women and children shuffled by the glass cases, like hungry children outside a baker's shop-window, just to stare at what they could not buy.

The young wife who had spent her girlhood as a conscript or a directed worker asked nothing better than the kind of routine which her mother had found so frustrating and imprisoning. She was quite willing to stay at home, while the breadwinner turned out in the cold morning dusk, and have an extra cup of tea before she started the housework. It was one of the things she had dreamed of, when she had rushed to clock-in herself, or to turn up on parade or clip tickets on the first bus. She was quite glad to throw aside her all-purpose siren suit or her factory overall suit, and to play with the idea of buying a humble version of Dior's 'New Look' which had been first shown in Paris in 1947.

A tight slender bodice, narrowing into a tiny wasp waist, below which the skirt bursts into fullness like a flower. Every line is rounded.

There are no angles in this silhouette. Shoulders are gently curved. Bosoms are rounded out with padding, hips are very full, stiffened with padding or swelling with pleats, stitched from waist to hips and then released . . . every house in Paris shows day skirts twelve inches from the ground, with even longer skirts for the afternoon. . . .

This fashion became a moral and political issue, a focus on the question of what women's rôle was to be in the post-war society. The wearer of a New Look outfit was illustrating that as far as she was concerned freedom of movement, economy and practical working usefulness came second to looking sexually and romantically attractive. To the old-guard feminist, and particularly to the left-wing one, this was counter-revolutionary on both political and sexist fronts.

'Utterly ridiculous, stupidly exaggerated waste of material and manpower, foisted on the average women to the detriment of other, more normal clothing!' exploded Mrs Mabel Ridealgh, Labour M.P. and ex-Regional controller for the Board of Trade's war-time 'Make-do-and-mend' campaign. She warned that she would get its manufacture controlled and would not tolerate fashion experts decreeing 'longer this and padded that, and proceeding to push women around to wear them. . . .' ('She thinks padding and artificial aids are extremely bad, because they make for sexiness' reported the girl who interviewed her.[2]) 'Our modern world has become used to the freedom of short, sensible clothing . . . the New Look is too reminiscent of a caged bird's attitude. . . . I hope our fashion dictators will realise the new *outlook* of women and will give the death-blow to any attempt to curtail women's freedom'[3] and Labour M.P. Bessie Braddock added that the longer skirt was just 'the ridiculous whim of idle people'.

But the generation of girls who had never thought of going out to work as a mark of the emancipated woman, since they could be sent to prison for failing to do so, were unmoved by these old-fashioned feminist sentiments. To them, Labour M.P.s who lectured them about wearing 'sensible' clothing, suitable for productive work, were the same breed as the women officers who had routed them out of doorways where they were having a good-night kiss, and sent them back to camp; and as the forewoman who had shouted at them for spending too long in the Ladies while Russia was waiting for aeroplane-parts. Now they did not have to listen to lectures about hard work and freedom any more, but could think about being feminine and glamorous. 'Seductive' became the favourite fashion-writer's expression. There was a boom in frills and silly hats and the national dailies rejoiced that women were 'no longer Amazons, but nymphs'. Girls spent three times as much on cosmetics as they had in the Thirties. In amusement arcades you put pennies in a Love Test machine to find out whether you were 'Red-hot', 'Passionate', 'Flirty' or 'Ardent'. A survey among young-married couples found that two in every three favoured a double bed rather than twin ones, because it 'encouraged sexual spontaneity'.

The rôle that really mattered, however, during the postwar period turned out to be neither nymph nor Amazon, but housewife. Once the war was over, the public had a chance to become obsessed by their own living conditions; by the lack of homes; the misery of icy winters combined with a fuel shortage; by the continuance of meat-rationing and sugar and butter and 'points' rationing, and by the beginning of bread-rationing and of the new and nauseating food-stuffs such as whale-meat; by the only available consumer goods being army surplus such as used blankets, some with stains on them which looked disagreeably like washed-out blood. In this atmosphere of dismal poverty for all, male politicians could hardly open their mouths without being slapped down by irritated housewives, who resented such statements as 'the gentleman in Whitehall really does know better' – than they did about buying the right things for health and nutrition. For this reason, women candidates for Parliament found, for the first time in their short history, that being female could be a definite advantage. They took up the stand that only one sex could really comprehend the 'mystery' (in its original sense of a trade secret) of housewifery, just as the A.E.U. had always claimed that only one sex could really comprehend engines. They peppered their speeches with the technical jargon of housewifery – 'sides-to-middling' sheets, and 'wasted grimy crust on unwrapped bread'. In the 1951 election there was a record number of women candidates, 42 Labour, 45 Liberal, 29 Conservative and 11 others. It was called the 'Housewives' Election'; and Bernard Shaw, writing a letter in support of the Labour woman candidate for Croydon East, said that 'Women who all have to manage homes and rear children are practical and know where the shoe pinches.'

The landslide Labour victory of 1945 had already installed a record number of women members. Many of these had been the undeniable heiresses of both the women's movement and the Labour movement, come to power at last. Teachers were very well represented, as indeed they might be, since they had been the most influential group of women in the nation since before the First War, and were still the largest women's profession, except for nursing. (In 1951 there were 207,100 teachers, compared with 237,000 nurses. Women teachers comprised 60% of their profession, nurses 89% of theirs. But nursing, in spite of having the largest number of professional women, has never sent one to Parliament.) Dr Summerskill, as Minister of Food, was doubly armed, as housewife and as qualified doctor. She needed to be, as the most-attacked Minister of all during the first five years after the war.

The identikit woman M.P. of the Parliament which changed the face of Britain with its welfare legislation, was middle-aged, middle-class, qualified in and having practised a profession, and had entered political life through public service or local government or trade-union work. One of them, Barbara Ayrton-Gould, was one of the few active suffragettes ever to reach Parliament. She had ridden at the head of a procession as Joan of Arc, in the legendary days of the women's rebellion.

The three youngest members of the first post-war Parliament represented a different kind of left-wing feminist. Alice Bacon and Margaret Herbison were miner's daughters, scholarship girls and school teachers. Barbara Castle (at thirty-four the youngest woman member) was grammar school, Oxford University and a successful journalist. These were part of the generation who had grown up into women's suffrage as a right. They could not remember an election in which they had not had a vote. They were not emotionally involved in sex warfare as such, and if they made jokes about being females in a man's world, it was as a kind of friendly courtesy to their older colleagues, whose jokes they were. All of them were more interested in women as workers than in woman as the oppressed victim, or in whether they were nymphs or Amazons. But no woman Member of any kind, at this period, dared to forget to describe herself as a 'housewife', on every possible occasion, and each made a point of springing to her feet to voice the 'housewife's point of view' on any question.

Women, at this time, were drifting back into the kitchen, willingly or unwillingly. There was never the crude elbowing-out of women from war-time jobs which there had been between 1918 and 1920. One reason was that Bevin had vowed that his achievement with the labour force was not going to end that way. 'The government is not going to let an ex-service-man or anyone else stand in a queue outside the labour exchange this time.'[4] If a man found that there was 'nothing doing' within three weeks of signing on, he was to be found a job in an entirely different calling and if necessary trained for it. So the men's return went smoothly. But this was also partly due to the fact that some 2 million – mostly married – women workers melted tactfully away when they began to feel unwelcome. At the T.U.C. conference in 1946 it was noted that the number of workers in munitions production and in the armed forces had fallen, in a year, by some 2 million, but that the numbers in industry had risen, in the same period, by only 400,000, with some 840,000 men still halfway between the Forces and Civvy Street. The reason was given that 'a number of married women and elderly persons have left industry'[5], the assumption being that they had only been waiting to do so until the end of conscription and direction set them free. But in fact only a few weeks before the end of the war, a survey made in 228 factories by the A.E.U. had shown that two-thirds of the women meant to stay on if they could. The over-fifties were the most keen, and the ones between 20 and 25, whose thoughts were concentrated upon starting a real married life at last, were the least interested, but even among them over half wanted to stay.

Nevertheless, when the men were demobilised, there arose as a general reaction the old feeling that the jobs ought to be left for them, and that the women should make way. Firms who had organised shifts to suit women now stopped doing so and many war-time nurseries were closed down. By 1947, the number of married women in gainful employment had shrunk to 18%.

Once again, as in 1920, the feminists themselves began to question whether women had to be workers in order to be first-class citizens. War-time measures to meet the needs of women workers had amounted to a social revolution. But, as Ray Strachey had said after the First War, should one give the business of earning a living a sacred aura which 'that somewhat dreary necessity' does not really rate? Eleanor Rathbone had first campaigned for Family Allowances in order to give dignity and independence to the non-working wife and mother. Now, since 1946, all mothers with more than one child drew them.

The home-and-motherhood school of thought now acquired some unexpected allies. Since the earliest days of the Women's Movement, it had been the highly educated young women who fought for their right to a career. Wives' attitudes to going out to work have always been in reverse ratio to the economic necessity to do so. At the top of the pro-work scale were the wives whose husbands were able and eager to keep them in comfort without their stirring a finger to earn money; and at the bottom were those who had to go out, in addition to housework and child-minding, in order to prevent the family from starving.

But now there was a change of opinion. The Royal Commission on Population, originally appointed to examine a falling birth-rate, reported, in 1949, that it had discovered a curious change in family building habits, that it was now the top section of the Registrar-General's occupational groups which tended to favour large families, whereas ever since the introduction of birth-control the reverse had been true. Judith Hubback, who during the Fifties conducted a private survey, *Wives Who Went to College*, carried this discovery a stage further. She established that graduate wives had more children than non-graduates and that further, 'the average fertility of those . . . who obtained first-class degrees is distinctly higher than that of women with other classes of degrees . . . it does look as if higher education had not led them to restrict their families as other women of approximately the same social class and income. On the contrary, higher education seems to be associated with higher fertility.' This undeniably élite group of women – university women were only 1 % of the population at this time – also made it clear that they did not despise housewifery as a second-class occupation. 'I feel very strongly that running a house and caring for a husband and family is vastly more than "unmixed domesticity" and is a career and profession in itself.' 'I personally am *delighted* to give up work. I love gardening and dressmaking, and I compose cookery recipes with the exultation of an ode.'

The back-to-the-kitchen movement had already been endorsed by educationalist John Newsom, whose recommendations to that effect in his book, *The Education of Girls*, had a preface by the Rt. Hon. R. A. Butler (of the Butler Act, which offered free secondary and higher education to students of either sex who could use it). Newsom grumbled that, 'In many girls' Grammar Schools the more intellectually able pupils take a second foreign language while the less able are allowed to take domestic science, forgetful of Samuel Johnson's dictum that "a man is better pleased when he has a good dinner upon the table than when his wife talks Greek"'; thus taking the girls back to Square 1, where pleasing a man was woman's priority.

It was the graduate wives, making a career of motherhood and setting the fashion for large families, who were mainly responsible for spreading the teachings of Dr John Bowlby among the general public in Britain. He had been asked by the Social Commission of the United Nations to make a study of the needs of children who were homeless and without family care in their own country and who had to be looked after in foster-homes or institutions. Dr Bowlby's monograph for the World Health Organisation on this subject, *Maternal Deprivation and Mental Health*, became a classic and started a whole new school of child-rearing methods. His book described the damage done to babies and infants by early and prolonged separation from mothers or mother-substitutes. It was abridged and sold as a paper-back, *Child Care and the Growth of Love*, and its theory was explained and recommended by sociological journals and women's magazines. Conscientious young mothers who drank it all in became afraid to leave the baby at all in case it developed 'maternal deprivation'. Dr Bowlby explained that 'the absolute need of infants and toddlers for the continuous care of their mothers will be borne in on all who read this book, and some will exclaim, "Can I then never leave my child?"'

The answer was that 'Leaving any child under three years of age is a major operation only to be undertaken for good and sufficient reasons . . . and when undertaken, planned with great care.' The mother was to bear in mind, like a hair-shirt taken with her on holiday, that in consequence of her self-indulgence 'she must be prepared for her child to be upset by her return. Though he *may* fulfil her hopes by greeting her warmly, she must not be surprised if he is cool and stand-offish for a few hours or a day or two. . . . The holiday whilst granny looks after the baby, which so many mothers (or fathers) of young children pine for, is best kept to a week or ten days.'

Grannies were, as a matter of fact, completely bewildered by the new mystique because in their day the up-to-date progressive mothers had reared their babies according to the doctrine of Truby King, which meant that they were fed strictly by the clock and never picked up if they howled between times, because they had to learn not to demand their mothers' attention unnecessarily by not being able to get it just for the asking. The Bowlby system, of the mother being continually on tap, seemed to the grandmother generation of the period to be regressing to their own grandmothers' method, which had been to carry the baby around with them and let it suck whenever it fancied. (Incidentally, 'demand feeding', as a trendy new system, did come back again, as the babies' share of the permissive society of the Sixties.)

Meanwhile, the graduate mothers of the post-war era, who stayed dutifully by the baby's side for fear of doing psychological damage, were probably the first highly-educated women in history expected to make themselves the bodyslaves of their own child, since any mothers before them who had been in the financial group able to allow girls to become learned had taken care to pay someone else to mind the baby.

This movement towards a return to *Küche und Kinder*, if not *Kirche*, disturbed many of the leading feminists of the period. Margaret Mead wrote:

There is at present a growing insistence that child and biological mother must never be separated; . . . this is a new and subtle form of anti-feminism in which men – under the guise of exalting the importance of maternity – are tying women more tightly to their children than has been thought necessary since the invention of bottle-feeding and baby-carriages. . . . It may well be, of course, that limiting a child's contacts to its biological mother may be the most efficient way to produce a character suited to lifelong monogamous marriage, but if so, we should be clear that this is what we are doing.[6]

And in 1956, the Swedish feminist and sociologist Alva Myrdal combined with her opposite number in Britain, Vera Klein, to warn the younger generation that this was an ancient device for keeping women from making a choice between, or of combining, the two possible rôles of home-maker and worker.

A cult of Homemaking and Motherhood is fostered by the press and propaganda. The sentimental glorification which these activities receive may flatter housewives but sometimes the glorification has a suspicious air of persuasion . . . the sentimental cult of domestic virtues is the cheapest method at society's disposal of keeping women quiet without seriously considering their grievances or improving their position . . . it has been successfully used to this day and had helped to perpetuate some dilemmas of home-making women by telling them on the one hand that they are devoted to the most sacred duty, while on the other hand keeping them on a level of unpaid drudgery.[7]

Practical benefits were also awarded to the family, besides Allowances. Food was still rationed by coupons rather than price. In the early fifties the only place where you saw a traditional-sized joint of roast beef was on the table of an outsize household with a fistful of ration books, and the only way you could skip up the waiting-list for a council house was by increasing your family at top speed.

In 1947, the Bulge was born, 881,025 babies in a single year, who were to be a planner's nightmare for the next thirty, as they crowded primary schools, secondary schools and the juvenile labour-market and then started coupling and having children of their own. In the 'Twilight of Parenthood' period of the Thirties, the annual figure had been 580,413. Even after the post-war birth-rate had slowed down, in the mid-Fifties, the generation which had married during the war or just before it still went on having more children than their parents ever had done.[8]

2. *Broken Homes*

All sorts of supportive organisations were set up, to safeguard the family. They were needed because, in spite of all the propaganda and all the babies, the family as an institution was in worse shape than it had ever been before.

To begin with, families had been physically disrupted on an unprecedented scale. Between the summer of 1939 and the end of 1945, 38 million civilians had had 60 million changes of address. This had at least contributed to the number of marriages which had broken up. In 1947, the number of Maintenance Orders made by magistrates' courts rose to 20,000 as compared with 11,177 in 1938, and it is reasonable to suppose that this was only the tip of the iceberg, since tidying up the wreckage of your marital battle by getting a court order to regularise the position was an unusually organised and methodical next step. Affiliation orders were up by 2,000 over the pre-war figure, while the number of illegitimate babies still being born, after it had passed the 1945 peak of 93 per thousand live births, was settling into an annual average of between 48 and 51, instead of its pre-war 43. The Curtis Committee, patiently visiting all the places where unwanted children were dumped, had discovered some disturbing traces of old-fashioned baby-farming. Divorces multiplied to ten times their pre-war number. There was an unknown number of 'unofficial families' in which one party was really married to another person, perhaps hoping to get a divorce. When a child was born they often settled down together, allowing the neighbours to suppose they were a married couple.

But the most obvious sign of the decline of the family was the number of children without a functioning one. There were 65,000 such children in public care, as a regular part of the national life, at any time during the post-war years. Few of them (so far as could be ascertained) were literally orphans; though over a third had both parents missing and over three-quarters had one or both parents either missing or dead. Some of them had been taken into care because the court had ruled that their parents were not fit persons to look after them. Others were there because nobody claimed them. And the rest (who were significant of the change in government and public attitudes, since the experience of Evacuation during the war) were there because their parents had asked the Children's Department to take them in.

The Children's Department was the offspring of the Children Act of 1948, which was the offspring of the Curtis

Committee's Report on the Care of Children deprived of their natural home. The difference between the 'Curtis Act' and previous legislation about homeless children was that it was concerned with the welfare of the child, whereas previous Poor Laws had worried first about who was to pay for his support. As late as 1930, the Poor Law Act had laid upon the local authority the duty 'to set to work or put out as apprentices all children whose parents are not, in the opinion of the Council, able to keep and maintain their children'. But the 1948 Act was most concerned about intervening only 'when it is necessary in the interests of his welfare' and ordered the local authority 'to further his best interests and to afford the opportunity for the proper development of his character and abilities'.

The 'Children's Department' plan put all homeless children under one umbrella – the Home Office – and required each local authority to set up a network of care for them in its area. The foundations of such a network had already been laid, after the second large-scale evacuation, when the scheme became a social welfare agency, without the Civil Defence authorities having exactly intended it. Now (also unintentionally) the existence of the Children's Department gave the working-class mother a freedom which she had never had before, at any time in history, to break up her marriage and desert her children, without being penalised, and without feeling unduly remorseful, because she knew that someone else was looking after them, at least as conscientiously as she had been doing.

The Children Act laid upon the Children's Department

the duty 'to receive the child into care' when he had neither parent nor guardian, or had been lost or abandoned; also when the Authority judged it necessary for the child's welfare and also when his parents or guardian 'are, for the time being or permanently, prevented' by incapacity or infirmity, or by 'any other circumstances' from looking after him properly. In other words, if a mother could establish that she was unable to manage it, the Children's Department had got to take over.

This changed everything, for the working-class mother in difficulties. If she was ill, or about to have another baby, or had just been turned out of her house, she could send her children to be looked after and kept as cheerful as possible in a Short-stay Home. This new amenity (however much disgruntled ratepayers might grumble that it was destroying family life by freeing the mother from responsibility) was intended, above all, to shore up the family. The idea was that if parents were helped over a daunting domestic crisis, they would make an effort to go on keeping the family together, instead of giving up the hopeless struggle altogether.

The Children Act of 1948 felt like the beginning of a brave new world in which the government was concerned with the terror and the despair of each deserted child. Working in one of the new Children's Departments gave the staff a sense of excitement, of being part of a new crusade that mattered more than anything else. A whole new army of social welfare workers – the majority of them women – had been trained and let loose in the former jungle of poor-law care for unwanted children. No effort was too great, no detail too trivial in the care of the vulnerable human material of the job. Welfare officers who had spent all day trudging from one boarded-out child to another would turn out again in the evening, uncomplainingly, to re-visit a single charge whose foster-parents had not been available during the day. The memory of Dennis O'Neill, who had died of ill-treatment because no one had cared and whose death had touched off Lady Allen of Hurtwood's campaign, still haunted all the new Children's Department workers.

They were in the exhilarating situation of seeing reforms take place under their hands; of moving children out of a soulless barracks put up by some late-nineteenth-century philanthropist into a country house where Edward VII used to stay, and where they would have the freedom of the overgrown gardens; or into a 'Small Family Home', a council house or suburban villa in which a 'substitute family' was collected and installed, under the care of 'substitute parents'.

It cost the nation some £21.5 million a year, that is, almost £7 a week per child, and any local authority who got back an average of 6s weekly in parental contributions considered itself lucky. About half the children were boarded out with private families (many of whom also took a dedicated, idealistic view of trying to 'make up' for the child's deprivation); a third were in local-authority homes or residential nurseries; a small fraction (about 4,000) in homes run by voluntary organisations but now also under the wing of the Children's Department, and the rest were in hostels or homes or boarding-schools for handicapped children.

The critics who prophesied that this scheme would weaken the bonds of marriage were almost certainly right. Women who would have stayed with an intolerable husband, for the children's sake, could now leave him. So could wives who merely thought they would like a change. When these set up house with another woman's husband and seemed likely to stay put, the welfare officer might suggest that they should make a home for the children of the original marriage (or indeed of both discontinued marriages) because the cardinal principle of child care at this time was that any kind of a stable family unit, however irregular in form, was better than the most perfect institution. Welfare officers were inclined to regard 'stable co-habitation'[9] (a union which seemed set to last in spite of having no marriage lines or else the wrong ones) as a good second-best to a conventional union, and often happier and more secure, for the children, than a real marriage which had broken up and which the couple had been persuaded to resume against their inclination.

But the very efforts which the Child Care workers made, in those early years, to humanise the system, worked against the preservation of an already shaky family unit. When a mother put her children 'temporarily' in a short-stay home, the welfare officer always urged her to visit them so that they should not feel deserted. When the mother found them sleeping in a spacious dormitory, with Walt Disney curtains in the windows, eating meals at a table with a vase of flowers on it, playing in a garden with a swing and a sand-pit in it, she was as certain she was doing the best for them, by leaving them there, as a middle-class mother visiting her children at their fee-paying boarding-school. In any case, she might well have been a child evacuee, in the days when it was the duty of a good mother to leave her children where they were and resist any maternal instincts to the contrary. So she would put the children off, when they begged to go back with her, by making vague promises that as soon as she and their new father had found a place of their own, with enough room, they would come and fetch the children to it. Usually, she half-believed that one day she would do so. And the children, weaving fantasies of their own, and boasting about them to their companions in exile, would also grow up half-believing that they really did have doting parents, with a big house, waiting anxiously for the time when the family could be reunited.

3. *Failed Marriages*
Broken homes were not limited to the working class; but middle-class ones were usually dealt with by enlisting the help of relatives and boarding-schools rather than that of the Children's Department. In the same way, the custom was for the proletariat to get a 'Separation' from a magistrate, the gentry a divorce from a judge, although the practical basis for this, which was that a divorce was so expensive, no longer held since the Legal Aid and Advice Act of 1949 had increased financial aid to litigants. The rate of the new petitions thereupon jumped for a few years, with couples who had been waiting to part from each other at cut price. But even after they had been accounted for, the annual number of divorces stayed at six or seven times its pre-war figure – for instance, 27,417 divorces in 1954 compared with 4,735 in 1937.[10]

The Royal Commission on Marriage and Divorce, which was appointed in 1951 to consider whether there should be changes in the law, was a disappointment to those who had hoped for easier divorce. On the contrary, its members were so much alarmed by the way that marriage and the family seemed to be going to pieces, that they would have liked to tighten up the law, rather than relax it. 'There are some of us who think that . . . it may become necessary to consider whether the community as a whole would not be happier and more stable if it abolished divorce altogether and accepted the inevitable individual hardships this would entail.'[11]

The Commission considered all the excuses for breaking up marriages which in the past would have held together; such as the lack of a marital home because of the housing shortage; the teaching of psychologists that the individual had a right to pursue personal satisfaction regardless of the consequences to others; the undue emphasis on the overriding importance of a satisfactory sex relationship; and the social and economic emancipation of women, who were 'no longer content to endure the treatment which in past time their inferior position obliged them to suffer. They expect that marriage shall be an equal partnership, and rightly so.'

The commissioners had no doubt that the 'happy and healthy' marriage which they were there to promote was by definition monogamous and for life. They were also quite sure that the laws which kept it this way should be retained except for cases of real hardship. But when it came to interviewing witnesses they found themselves up against the question asked by Shaw's *Don Juan in Hell* some fifty years earlier. 'Those who talk about the blessings of marriage and the constancy of its vows are the very people who declare that if the chain were broken and the prisoners left loose to choose, the whole fabric would fly asunder. You cannot have the argument both ways. If the prisoner is happy, why lock him in?'

Some of the witnesses argued that the time had come to recognise a new principle, namely that the basis of a divorce should be that the marriage had irretrievably broken down; that is, divorce by consent. But the Commission almost unanimously agreed that the doctrine of the matrimonial offence must be retained; that is, the principle that divorce was the remedy for an unoffending partner who had a large and justified grievance against the other. Some even felt that the Herbert Act of 1937, which had released couples from the obligation for one to commit adultery or pretend he had, if they wanted to be free, had been of doubtful benefit to society. Anyway, they felt that 'to give people the right to divorce themselves', or to allow them to believe that there could be such a thing as 'a wholly blameless way of terminating a marriage', would lead to social disaster. What they wanted was a less permissive attitude towards the marriage bond; and more organisations set up to keep marriages going, to shore up the shaky structure and to do maintenance and repair work on individual marriages which were threatening to collapse.

This was already done for couples who brought their quarrel to the magistrates' court, and had it referred to the probation officer who was often able to report to the magistrates that their separation and maintenance order would not be required after all, as the parties had decided to go back to each other. Many individuals in marital difficulties were in the habit of taking a short cut and going straight to the probation officer without any preliminaries. In 1954 the probation service dealt with nearly 40,000 matrimonial cases in which both husband and wife were seen, and another 36,000 in which only one party was seen.

But the white-collar classes, who were mainly responsible for the divorce rate, told their troubles to their own class, to clergymen and doctors and of course to their solicitors who were paid to listen and who, on the whole, did try to keep it in mind that they ought to work for a reconciliation, even if it meant losing divorce case fees. Since 1938 there had been committees, usually set up by these informal consultants, to deal with marital problems of this kind, and after the war a training board for 'counsellors' was started. This new voluntary organisation, along with the Family Welfare Association and the Catholic Marriage Advisory Council, were given government grants and an official standing as subsidised voluntary organisations for preserving the institution of marriage. The Royal Commission warmly recommended that they should be given more help and more standing.

From now on, Marriage Guidance became an accepted part of everyday life and wives would recommend each other to go to a certain practitioner as they did for a dentist or an osteopath. 'People are getting more willing to talk about problems which, before, they kept behind their front doors', as one counsellor explained.[12] More of the clients were white-collar workers than their proportion in the population – 70% of them had secondary education; and about 10% were professional people. The 'cardinal rule of counselling' (as in most social work of this time) was 'not to tell people what they ought to do but to help them understand their situation and reach their own decisions'. However, 'Principle Five' had to be subscribed to by all counsellors. It was that 'the right basis for personal and social life is that sexual intercourse should only take place within marriage'. Twice as many women as men sought the Council's help, and very often they were afraid of the husband finding it out. 'He would beat me up if he knew.'

J. H. Wallis, who became one of the best-known practitioners of this new calling, said that the standard opening to a first interview would be: 'Well, I don't know if you'll be able to help me very much . . . well, my next-door neighbour she knew someone who came to see one of your counsellors and her husband used to beat her up, but I don't have anything like that happening . . . we just don't seem . . . we can't talk together any more, I think I must be doing something wrong but I've asked him and sometimes he doesn't talk to me for days. . . .'[13]

As this new service to the public became accepted, public interest in its discoveries mounted. It became the fashion for Counsellors to write – not only books about their work, but regular magazine features, and for them to take part in radio discussions and give lectures. What their audiences wanted to hear were case histories (with the names changed, of course) because then they could find that their own secret doubts and humiliations were shared. The spread of Marriage Guidance did at least as much to inform one half about how the other half lived as Mass-Observation had done.

What came to light in this great flinging open of front doors was not so much the individual tales of fixed wretchedness – like those of the couples who lived together for years without speaking to each other – but the extraordinary and naïve expectations pinned on the married condition.

Most people take it for granted that marriage and happiness are so closely linked that if a marriage is not happy there must be something wrong. Most people feel that if a marriage is basically unhappy and nothing seems to get it right, then it should be ended. People often say, 'Don't you *ever* advise divorce?' Husbands had been taught, chiefly by articles and advertising copy addressed to women, that a proper wife should be competent in managing the home and children . . . she should be a stimulating sexual partner, willing to please her husband at all times and yet never intruding her own desires.[14]

The high expectations of sexual performance which had been encouraged among women ever since Havelock Ellis became fashionable set a very difficult standard for mid-twentieth-century husbands. Since the great women's liberation of the Twenties, books had been piling up, describing the sexual enjoyment to which they had a right. (In the old days of sheltered girls, brides had no clear expectations but accepted what they were given, which made life a great deal easier for husbands than it became later.) The

Marriage Guidance Counsellors of the Fifties uncovered a great mass of worry and uneasiness among husbands.

Many clients try to overcome their difficulties by recourse to books on sexual techniques . . . this is much commoner among men than women. . . . I had quite a long sequence of husbands, doing technical work of a highly skilled kind, with sexual problems they had been trying to cure through the theory and practise of sexual techniques. Eventually I came to realise how differently these husbands, and indeed most husbands, think about sex from their wives who do not want to think about sex at all. Sometimes literally . . . the husband had the book at the bedside. The much-vaunted progress from prudery to candour, has helped some people but added to the latent difficulty of others . . . a young man who was soon to be married asked me to arrange a sperm-count . . . what would it have solved? . . . it is difficult for a woman to understand a man's sensitivity to any slur on his virility. . . . Thus a husband will cross-examine a near-frigid wife as to whether she achieved an orgasm of the kind the book describes. . . . 'Next time it will be better' comforts him as little as 'Never mind, we'll open a tin of something' soothes her wounded self-esteem at a spoiled supper.[15]

4. *Affluent Working Wives*
The latter years of the Fifties were boom years. A million more jobs became available and since there was already full employment married women were once again in urgent demand. Even those careers once sacrosanct to dedicated spinsters – teaching and nursing – were involved. The

Ministry of Education put out plaintive appeals to trained wives to 'Come back to teaching', and the Ministry of Health, short of 48,000 nurses for the National Health Service, urged hospitals not only to accept married ones part-time but to arrange shifts for them which would not inconvenience their husbands and children.

The largest flow back to work was in industry, the second largest in domestic work, such as cleaning and canteen service. The 18% of married women working in 1947 rose to 33% by 1957, and by 1961 more than half of all women in paid employment were married.

These working wives of the affluent society were a new phenomenon. They were not going out to work on feminist principles, nor from necessity. Rowntree and Layers, in a survey of *Poverty and the Welfare State*, discovered an 'apparent paradox' that it was the better-off working-class wives who went out to work. When asked why they did it, most of them admitted that it was in order to buy things they wanted (as opposed to needed) and also for the pleasure of meeting other people instead of being cooped up in their homes all day. Their husbands were in full work, and with the Welfare State to look after doctors' bills, dentists' bills and education and with subsidised housing, they could have lived comfortably enough on the single wage. But there was a new complaint among housewives, christened by the papers 'New Town Blues', and much discussed by sociologists, which consisted of the kind of malaise suffered by bourgeois provincial wives in Chekhov plays. The government offered a subsidy for wives' clubs which combined entertainment with education, but the complaint only vanished when the women went back to work on the tide of the great spending spree of the late fifties, when the country's hire-purchase debt alone ran up from its pre-war £100m to £942m in 1959.

Now there was a stimulation in the air, an atmosphere of challenge and excitement such as the Victorians had enjoyed, during their years of expansion and prosperity, when 'bettering yourself' was a pleasant and worthy objective. 'Why should we not aim to double our standard of living in the next twenty-five years?' asked R. A. Butler when he was Chancellor of the Exchequer[16]; and ordinary families, acquiring more and more middle-class goods, and putting them in their new or improved houses, felt themselves part of this cheerful project.

It was the wife's earnings, over and above those of her husband, which made the new life-style possible. In the double-income household it became a custom for the husband to go on paying the basic bills as usual, while the wife paid for new things for the home. This mean that the family budget was not so tied to the wife's job that it would create a disaster if she gave up working for a time, though hire-purchase was a complication; and goods chosen on some cheerful Saturday afternoon shopping expedition, at the end of a week which included the husband's overtime and the wife's earnings, could become a millstone when the husband was down to basic pay and the wife not working because she was pregnant.

The incredulous pleasure of being able to have luxury goods – matching suites and sprung mattresses and labour-saving electrical appliances – set the double-income home apart from its predecessors, in which the working-class family was geared to what it considered necessities. Pearl Jephcott described the typical Bermondsey family's shopping spree on Saturday afternoons to buy something new for the house. 'Once back home, parents, children and neighbours shared in the excitement of seeing how this week's buy set off the rest of the house.'[17] But besides this, the double-income family could have holidays, perhaps buy a car, pay for the children to have ballet lessons and go on the 'school journey' – all the expanding opportunities of the prospering society in which they were living.

In neighbourhoods where it became the custom for wives to work, few husbands felt it threatened their status; and these were usually the older ones, whose wives had a 'little job' rather than a serious one. In Bermondsey, Peek Frean's, who employed most of the married women, ran a special evening shift for them which depended entirely on the husband being willing to stay in and mind the children every week-day.

Meanwhile the social and moral theory of the immediate post-war years, that home-making was a sacred duty and woman's most worth-while career, had faded and died. The working wives of Bermondsey, for instance, 'took the line and with no appearance of self-justification that the neglectful mother is not the one who works, but the one who is too lazy or indifferent to take advantage of to-day's opportunities to raise her family's standards'.[18] A Mass-Observation survey established that the stay-at-home housewife spent between 60 and 71 hours a week on the housework and always had. When she acquired labour-saving devices which cut down the time on certain jobs, she spent the time saved on some other kind of housework, which she had not thought necessary before. As Myrdal and Klein suggested: 'Though lamenting it, most housewives are fundamentally proud to say that 'a woman's work is never done' and there is a suspicion that housewives often unconsciously expand it in order to allay their feelings of frustration by producing evidence that they are fully occupied and indispensable.'[19] Or, as the Bermondsey working wives, who got through their housework on a fixed routine before going in to their shift put it, describing a non-employed neighbour: 'She's a right muddler, just sits around, gossips on the corner, doesn't really get any more time off than us.'[20]

Disapproval of working mothers, however, developed into the most-talked-of moral issue of the day. The Minister of State for Scotland suggested that, 'Perhaps the greatest of our contemporary social problems is that of the mothers in industry. No-one could doubt that the absence of parental control is the cause of much of the lawlessness and instability of character of the young.'[21] A magistrate coined the term 'latch-key child' when he was 'deeply distressed by numbers of young delinquents who came before him mostly because post-school and holiday hours meant all the temptations of street life, with the home motherless, cold and often locked up. . . . The home has ceased to be the best place to go to, the centre of leisured activities, a safe and happy background.'[22] The conviction that working mothers automatically had neglected children got to the point where the first question asked about any child in trouble, from a tendency to chest complaints to failing exams, was, 'Both parents working I suppose?'; with the implication that everything would be cured by the mother giving up her job. The most vocal protagonists of this view were (male) Medical Officers of Health and (male) juvenile court magistrates, and clergymen. The National Council of Women found no proof of this cause-and-effect sequence, and Simon Yudkin with Anthea Holme, who made a study of *Working Mothers and Their Children*, pointed out mildly that 'the criticism that mothers of young children who go out to work are neglecting them and causing them serious harm is based only on prejudice and not on evidence'. They also pointed out that Dr John Bowlby's theories of maternal deprivation had 'been distorted to apply to situations which they did not cover and which Bowlby himself specifically excluded. . . . His arguments and conclusions were derived almost exclusively from studies of children who were completely separated from their families, often in institutions.'[23] In any case, he himself had modified his original strict advice to mothers to stay on the job, and by 1958 was willing to allow that 'it is an excellent plan to accustom babies and small children to be cared for now and then by someone else – father, for instance, or grannie or some other relation or neighbour'.[24] None of this, however, prevented government departments who wanted to dodge having to provide day-nurseries and nursery-schools from bringing up what they claimed was Bowlby's veto on mothers of small children going out to work at all, as a reason why such amenities would be socially and psychologically a bad thing.

CHAPTER EIGHT

EMANCIPATION
1960–1970

1. *The Teenagers*
The girls who had been born during the Second World War grew up into a position of sex equality for which they had not had to fight. During the Sixties, demands made by their mothers and their grandmothers were officially conceded, beginning with equal opportunities in education, and ending with the promise of equal pay. Freedoms which 'Ann Veronica' had dreamed about, hopelessly, came true for them. She had longed for a chance to live her own life, as her brother did, to be able to do without the support and protection of a husband, and to be able to defy her father's authority. The 'teenage daughter' of the Sixties could do it all.

The 'Teenagers' who dominated British social life for the best part of a decade were in some ways the successors of the 'Bright Young Things' of the Twenties. Like them, they had their own music and dancing, defied their elders, led an irregular sex life and wore their own outlandish clothes to identify with their own group. (The rebel girls of the Twenties had shortened their skirts to knee-length; their successors went one better with the miniskirt.)

They also shared with the earlier rebels a Narcissus devotion to their own image. They, too, believed that they were the first generation to make the most of being young. 'There's one mistake about teenagers that's bigger than all the rest put together', said Cathy McGowan, in one of the many television programmes devoted to explaining the breed to the adult world. 'It's the belief that they all want to be adults, as soon as they can. Nothing could be more wrong than that. The only thing they dread is getting old. The absolute limit is 25. After that you've probably got married, got a car, a house and a steady job. You know exactly where you're going for the rest of your life. Who on earth would look forward to that?'[1]

Forty years earlier, Somerset Maugham's young rebels of the Twenties, who did not wish to live after they were 29, were explaining to their elders that,

You can't be so unintelligent as not to realise that nowadays the only thing that counts is youth. And it's because we've discovered that, that our generation is so much ahead of every other. . . . In Daddy's time, when they were young they just wanted to be older. And we don't. We're young and we want to enjoy our youth. For the first time in the world's history we've realised the immense value of it.[2]

The Teenagers were created by prosperity. The idea of their being a separate section of society is said to have been invented by an American manufacturer, who was considering how he could coax the high wages of working youth out of their pockets and into his own. He produced 'teenage clothes' which were neither for children nor adults, but unconventional, picturesque fashions with a hint of children dressing up to caricature their elders. The fashion was copied and became a uniform, which made teenagers into a closed group, which therefore developed its own culture and taboos. By 1957, in Britain, Mark Abrams reported that they were spending £830m a year on their own special toys; clothes, records, musical instruments, transistors and 'teenage magazines' which described them to themselves.[3]

Whereas before the war, the average youth had earned only 26s a week, in a menial job (which he was only offered because he could be paid less than his father) and a working girl had earned 18s 6d a week, the teenagers of the Sixties were offered skilled jobs, the boys in engineering and building and the girls in shops, hospitals and offices, for wages which averaged £8 a week for a boy, and £6 for a girl.

Mark Abrams defined teenagers as 'young people who have reached the age of fifteen but are not yet twenty-five and are unmarried'.[4] In 1960 it was calculated that there were some 5,000,000 of them, of which some 2,000,000 boys and 2,000,000 girls were at work in business or industry, and the other 1,000,000 in school or college or – if they were unlucky enough to be males caught in the last lap of National Service – in the Forces.

The teenage girl of the period was unique in one respect. She was the first ordinary, average girl who did not have to worry at all about getting a husband. Her society was slightly overstocked with nubile males of her own age.

The balance of the sexes in the population which both before and after the 1914 War had been overweighted with marriageable women now had too few of them. At birth, there were 105 boys to every 100 girls, and boys went on being the majority until both reached 39, when the sexes exactly balanced. By the time they reached 75, almost half of the weaker sex had died off before their wives, and the overall majority of females in the population (2 million) was visible in everyday life.[5] Everyone took it as a matter of course that there were more elderly widows about than widowers.

In the same way, the teenage girl could expect to find plenty of boys available, with self-conscious groups of them, partnerless, at the edge of the dancing-floor (just where there had been a group of self-conscious, partnerless girls in the Twenties). This mild shortage of girls was reflected in the tribal customs of the five million teenagers. It was the boys who began to dress in eye-catching clothes, with peacock colours and trousers drawn tightly over neat, slim loins, the boys who warbled songs about being left alone. They were willing and eager to tie themselves down much younger than any of their predecessors, and married younger and younger girls. In the Thirties, only one bride in ten had been under twenty years old; in the Sixties it was one in four.[6] (She was also four times as likely to be divorced.) During 1960 there were 25,827 brides who were only 18, and 18,367 who were younger still.

The teenage culture was a working-class one. Other fashions of youth had always come down from the boys and girls of the leisured classes. 'Crazes' had started in Society, or Oxford and Cambridge, and had been humbly imitated, some years later, in working-class suburbs and factory towns. Now they started there and were copied by university students and debutantes.

It was the female teenager who reaped the emancipation which had been achieved, step by step, through the twentieth century. She was the darling of the advertising industry and the favourite target of middle-aged moralists. Dr Leslie Weatherhead, the most popular Nonconformist preacher of the day, attacked her in a campaign headlined 'A Nation in Danger'. He pointed out that one in twenty of all births was illegitimate, one in six brides pregnant on her wedding-day (one in four when brides were under twenty-one), and that venereal disease was on the increase. The papers followed up with reports of relevant incidents which had come to their notice,[7] such as 'The Night a Mother Chased Her Daughter', '"I am to blame", sobs father', 'Fourteen to wed Eighteen', and 'Badge of Shame', which referred to the home-made miniature yellow golliwogs said to be worn on the gym-tunics of sixth-form girls as a boast, rather than a confession, of non-virginity. Girls'-school headmistresses told an enthralled public that so far as they knew there was not a single virgin in their fifth or sixth forms, and raids on school satchels were said to produce an impressive haul of contraceptives.

The fact was that the original 'Teenagers' were a living, walking justification of the rose-hip syrup and blackcurrant juice, the free cod-liver oil, the green (privileged) ration-books and the subsidised milk and school meals of war-time and immediately after. They were the tallest, strongest, healthiest generation on record. They were also the earliest-maturing. Girls reached puberty at thirteen and their full height between sixteen and seventeen. They looked and felt like women long before they came to the end of their official childhood.

At home, the earning teenage daughter simply did not subscribe to the old taboos about the protection of a virgin. She went out when she liked and ignored the rituals about being in at a fixed hour – ten o'clock, or eleven, or even the stroke of midnight – which had always been believed to be a magic charm against seduction. Now, like her brother, she came in when she had had enough of the party. The parents' Waterloo was the all-night teenage party. Its object was frankly erotic (though laced with music and dancing) and its fixed condition that there should be no adult anywhere on the premises. Most worrying of all, they were open-house parties. Teenagers would wander around the streets until they found a house with their kind of music blaring from it and most of the lights out so that couples could dance with 'mouths glued'. The police grumbled that it was impossible to prevent thefts and that the whole system invited trouble. But it seemed as if the whole adult nation was bemused by the teenagers. Everyone else's parents (said teenage daughters) lent their house for parties and it was humiliating to admit to such unemancipating relatives as one's own. It was socially discreditable to disapprove of the teenagers, and correct to tell one's neighbours, patronisingly, that personally one understood and admired them, with the implication that one was approved by the golden lads and girls themselves.

The working-class father's authority had dwindled still further now that more incomes were being added to the household budget. His wife was likely to be gainfully occupied and had her own money to use as she wished; and his daughter's pay-packet might be nearly as heavy as his own. In the old days, when he was the undisputed authority, there used to be a point in family scenes at which he was called in. ('That settles it, my girl. Now I'm going to tell your dad.')[8] It was not a bit of use summoning him now because his ultimate deterrent, 'I'll turn you out of the house', had been taken away from him and could be used against him. 'I'll run away from home' was no longer the pathetic threat of a dependent child. A teenage daughter could run away, get a job and move in with a friend who rented a room, probably a male one at that. Losing her in this fashion was not only distressing, but discreditable. The neighbours would agree among themselves that you had never been able to get on with her (as they got on with their own daughters) and the welfare officer and the magistrate – if it came to that point – would hesitate to order her to go back to living with her parents, since they knew it was unlikely that they could enforce it.

The classical family crisis – the unmarried daughter getting pregnant – happened oftener than ever. The proportion of illegitimate babies in the birth-rate had gone up from 4.7% in 1955 to 7.7% in 1965 and by the end of the Sixties to 8.4 %, and the mother's age continued to fall (although the under-twenties were still more subject to shotgun wedding pressures than other girls were).[9] The Pill, which was to transform the sex-life of females, had been tested in the Fifties and was generally available, in Britain in the mid-Sixties. It was a great advance in birth-control methods, because it eliminated the human fallibility risk almost entirely. Women who took it as automatically as they brushed their teeth were safe from any risk of pregnancy; and did not have to consider, when going out to a party, whether or not to make contraceptive preparations in case of an erotic adventure. (This need for a cold-blooded decision was the main reason why it was the habitually chaste girls who got 'caught' while the promiscuous ones did not.)

But the teenage daughters of the Sixties hardly profited at all from the existence of the Pill because it was not then available on the National Health Service for ordinary contraceptive purposes, and very rarely indeed to unmarried girls, who would be lucky if they found a sufficiently progressive doctor, or birth-control clinic, to prescribe it privately, on a paying basis. Therefore they were subject to much the same hazards as their mothers had been, and had more illegitimate babies – a third as many again – as their mothers did when they were young. But in fact the proportion of babies *conceived* outside marriage remained much the same, though more of them were born illegitimate.[10] The difference was the decline in cover-up weddings.

To the daughter of the permissive society, the situation which had been the ultimate shame and tragedy to all her great-grandmothers was little more than an inconvenience. It made all the folk-songs about being deserted and ruined sound absurdly sentimental. Having a baby, if properly handled, was not going to reduce her value in the marriage market, because one feature of the teenage culture was that brides did not need to be virgins, any more than bridegrooms did. It was a question of the physical tiresomeness of pregnancy and childbirth, of having to go into purdah, away from the fun and freedom of everyday life, and of making all the necessary and boring arrangements and deciding whether it was worth trying to keep the facts from the neighbours by going to a Mother-and-Baby home when the bulge began to show. Finding such a refuge was no problem, because religious denominations and lay voluntary societies and local authorities all ran them, and by now there was no fear of their supposing that giving a girl house-room gave them a right to lecture her, because it was accepted that this was not only laughably old-fashioned, but in a curious way bad form as well. So the girl would move in, bored and irritable rather than tragic, and very probably the child's father would call on her there, as unmarried fathers were encouraged to keep in touch. But even the most progressive matrons of Mother-and-Baby homes used to be perplexed at the way that a girl would turn down his offer of marriage, although she had liked him well enough to be his mistress. 'I don't love him any more, not after all this fuss', was usually the off-hand explanation.

Although the teenagers took so many nibbles at the condition of marriage, before they launched on it, they were still expecting it to provide a sensation of quite unprecedented strength and ecstasy, just as it did for lovers in stories who had to hunger and long passionately for the time when they were allowed to consummate their love.

All this cool detachment about having the illegitimate baby was only possible because of the popularity of adoption.

The Adoption Societies' waiting lists of childless but child-loving couples were always comfortably long, and nine out of ten girls who refused a cover-up wedding did so on the basis of having the child adopted at the earliest possible moment. It was only this that enabled the unmarried mother's parents to take her situation so calmly and to think of their grandchild in the same category as an appendix, which would be taken away by some competent official after the operation and never seen again. What did happen was that only one in four of illegitimate babies of this period ended up with an adoption order.[11]

The reason was that two philosophies were involved in the proceedings. One was that of the permissive society, that sex was for enjoyment and should not be hedged about with long-faced restrictions. The other was that of the social-welfare society which believed that family relationships mattered more, and should be supported whenever possible. Therefore the girl could get her baby adopted without trouble, and be cheered up and sent out into the world, again free from the burden of motherhood. But first she must be given the chance to establish a bond with her baby, so that if it grew strongly enough they could stay together and have some kind of a family life.

The girl was therefore asked to stay with the baby for six weeks and to breast-feed it if possible. If, at the end of the time, she still stuck to her original adoption plan, the baby would be handed over to the would-be adopters, whose identity the natural mother must never know.

The process of allowing the mother to become attached to

the baby and then taking it away from her, and refusing to let her know where it had gone, had in fact originally been invented by the husband of Chaucer's 'Patient Griselda'[12] when he was trying to find out how far you can torment a young woman before she reaches breaking-point. Its effect on the unmarried mother of the Sixties was that she would decide she could not part with the baby permanently, though she had no prospect of providing it with a home. A generation earlier she might have persuaded her own parents to pass it off as a later arrival of their own, but now they were very clear that it was the local authority's responsibility. So a courageous girl, encouraged by her social worker, would set out to keep the baby herself. But the economics of the permissive society were still geared to the male-breadwinner system. The female-sized income – as the unmarried mother quickly found out – would not even run to a roof over the baby's head. Landladies feared and hated such tenants, not only because of the nappies and the baby's crying but because there was no male protector to pay up the back rent in the end. Sex equality had not yet reached the unmarried father, and affiliation orders were as ludicrously ineffective as they had been in the days when it was ruin and disgrace to have a child out of wedlock. And while the boy was probably generous enough at the beginning and gave her more than the magistrates would have ordered, when he moved out of the district or got a new girl-friend, the money stopped. The end was, almost invariably, that sooner or later the baby joined the 84,000 children now in public care.

2. *Abortion*

In 1967 a new Abortion Act came into force, which allowed an abortion when two doctors agreed that having the baby would involve a greater risk to the mother's mental and physical health or to that of the children she already had, than the risk involved in ending the pregnancy, or that the child, if brought to birth, would have a serious handicap.

The operation had to take place either in a National Health Service hospital or in a licensed clinic. A great many private ones were set up, for fee-paying patients, and during the next five years some 49,000 women a year came to London for an abortion, from countries with more restrictive laws, mainly France and West Germany. It was this which touched off a campaign to get the Act repealed, which developed into a hell-fire crusade against sexual permissiveness. This, in its turn, provoked an equally angry counter-campaign against those who wanted to regulate other people's lives to suit their own moral views. They accused the anti-abortionist crusaders of wanting to punish loose women by forcing them to bear a child against their will. (According to the records of the original Abortion Law Reform Society most abortions were asked for by 'exhausted mothers'; that is, married women who feel physically and mentally incapable of launching on the long effort of bearing and bringing up another child.)

The opponents of sexual permissiveness preached that its logical consequence was the heaps of 'screaming' foetuses regularly (as they alleged) being thrown into hospital and nursing-home furnaces by innocent virgin nurses forced against their will to do it. The protagonists of the new,

American-inspired 'Women's Lib' movement, not to be outdone, proclaimed that 'the abortion issue is the cornerstone in the liberation of women. The debate on whether a woman may have control over her own body is a debate on the place and role of women in society'.[13] They began to represent abortion not only as a right but as a positive pleasure, protesting that women ought to be allowed to drop into hospital regularly and have one by the latest method if they did not want to have to take the Pill.

The abortion dispute, by becoming the kind of angry feminist and anti-feminist battle which had hardly been experienced since suffragette days, obscured the most important issue of all, which was about its use as a safety-net to prevent the birth of a congenitally handicapped child. The development of the antibiotics – particularly since the war – meant that doctors could now keep alive children who would otherwise have died of a congenital handicap, soon after birth or in early childhood. The consequence was that by the mid-Sixties, according to the Invalid Children's Aid Association, there was one handicapped child for every street in Britain. The social-welfare theory was still that every child needed above all to be brought up in its own family circle, and so pressure was put on the mother of the child to devote herself to its care. Usually the irrational guilt she felt, towards the child, made her agree that she ought to do so. This meant that children with spina bifida or hydrocephalus or fibrocystic disease, or autistic children, had to be cared for at home, probably in the kitchen of a small house. A child handicapped to this extent cannot help dominating the life of the household entirely, wearing the mother out and spoiling the childhood of its siblings. Since such children can be kept alive now they obviously must be kept alive. But since it is possible to diagnose certain conditions pre-natally abortion could prevent their being brought to birth. A National Opinion Poll about whether abortion would be justified in these circumstances showed that over three quarters of all voters considered that it would.

3. *The Churches and the Permissive Society*

1967 was a watershed. There were 70,000 illegitimate babies born that year.[14] After that, the number began to fall, partly because of the Abortion Act, but also partly because the Pill was steadily becoming accepted. It was safe, it was very little trouble and it was continual. The security which it provided changed women's outlook. It meant that embarking on a sexual relationship was not going to hurt anyone else. Without any risk of having an unwanted baby, there was no need to worry about one's family getting involved. Soon, there was no need to worry about the neighbours finding out. In 1960, the average young couple at university who were lovers had kept it secret except perhaps from one or two close friends. By 1970 they did not even bother to keep it from their parents.

The rapid change of moral outlook was a problem to the Churches. It was difficult for them to keep what was left of their younger members anyway. But chastity was so much at the centre of Protestant teaching that they could hardly ignore what was happening. Some made a public effort to dispel their Puritan image. The President of the Methodist Conference said that 'Promiscuity points to the awful loneliness, even in the crowd, that afflicts modern life', and reminded his colleagues that this was 'the first generation of the emancipation of women'. The Bishop of Woolwich, giving evidence at the prosecution of the publishers of *Lady Chatterley's Lover*, said that 'What Lawrence is trying to do is to portray the sex relationship as something essentially sacred . . . as in a real sense an act of holy communion.'

The Quakers were also troubled by the fact that when their younger members wanted guidance on sexual problems, the Church's traditional view was no longer any answer to them. A 'concerned' group published a pamphlet, *Towards a Quaker View of Sex*, which finally destroyed the popular image of them as a picturesque group of old-fashioned Puritans. They accepted the fact that it was now common for 'young men and women with high standards of general conduct and integrity to have one or two love affairs, involving intercourse, before they find the person they will ultimately marry'; that it was even more common to have intercourse before the marriage ceremony took place, and that 'this is true, probably, of the majority of young people in all classes, including those who have a deep sense of responsibility'. They also acknowledged the high incidence of extra-marital intercourse and that 'there must be many instances which do not lead to divorce or obvious harm and which are kept secret'. Their conclusion, after this calm and thoughtful look at the facts, was that 'love cannot be confined to a rigid pattern', adding that they had a right to give their views on the subject of sex because 'the Society of Friends has maintained throughout the three hundred years of its history the complete personal and material equality of the sexes'.

The Church of England also made an effort to adjust its thinking to the entirely changed situation. It had lost ground, among its own members, over its opposition to Alan Herbert's proposals for the 1937 Matrimonial Causes Act and its stand against any liberalising by the 1955 Commission and against Mrs Eirene White's proposal for divorce after seven years' separation. Now a study group, appointed by the Archbishop of Canterbury, produced some far more flexible suggestions. The Church (it said) must be free to treat the marriages of its own members in accordance with its doctrine and rules. But, since it was the Church who had originally made the rules on which the secular law was based, its view on this still mattered; and it was (in essence) that it was now time to give up the Matrimonial Offence as the ground for divorce, and to accept that marriages could break down so irrevocably that all the law need do was to pronounce them dead. This was quite an important change of heart, to a great many people who only went to Church perhaps twice a year, but still liked to be christened, married and buried by the Church of England. This report, called *Putting Asunder*, was also notable for its compassionate reminders that in most divorces someone got very badly hurt, and it was usually the ageing wife who had believed herself safe for life, until she was abandoned for a younger and more sexually attractive woman.

4. Equal Education

In 1962, the first children born to free secondary education and the chance of higher education for all reached university age. They had grown up to take the effects of the 1944 Education Act – streaming and eleven-plus selection and the rush for university places – as the normal, ordained steps up the school ladder.

Applications for a university place snowballed from 1956 onwards. Like most teenage fashions this one spread right across the age-group, irrespective of social distinctions. It was also irrespective of sex, because the chance of getting a university education no longer depended on parents being willing to continue paying education bills which would reach their peak at university, for a daughter as for a son. The outstandingly clever girl, in a good high school or a well-known girls' public school had always had her chance of winning a scholarship to college. But the one who was merely competent, academically, had had to settle for teachers' training college, and the girl from the middle of the form mark-list had no need to trouble herself with the idea of competing for higher education, but might as well settle for typing or nursing straight away. Meanwhile – until the 1944 Act – the semi-literate athlete from a well-known boys' public school could get pushed and helped and given a leg up into Oxford or Cambridge provided his parents could afford it.

But under the new system of competing for university places and being grant-aided if you got one, the girls who could profit by higher education had their chance to get it, which made the quarter-century when the schools were dominated by the 'eleven-plus' exam the most fruitful period yet for female education in Great Britain. According to John Newsom, in 1948, 99% of girls had finished their education by the time they were eighteen. In 1962, according to the Robbins Report, 8% went on to some form of higher education, of whom 2.5% went to university, 4% to teacher training and the rest to some kind of academic study (as opposed to training as secretaries, nurses, medical auxiliaries and so on).

Within ten years, the number of seventeen-year-olds still in school increased by 66% and sixth forms were full to bursting-point. The competition changed the atmosphere of girls' schools, giving them a sense of being pioneers trying to break into a man's world they had not experienced since the Twenties. There were 45,000 applicants – of both sexes – for 25,000 university places.

'The sixth-form spends its second year in a state of continual excitement', said the headmistress of the Mary Datchelor School (the very school which had been praised by *The Times Educational Supplement* in 1923 for giving the girls 'a taste of the authentic Virgil, Horace and Catullus'). 'We urge a philosophical outlook, but the strain of waiting for the offer of a place is terrific, with the suspense mounting as the months pass by.'[15] The uncertainty of the system by which the victors were actually chosen gave it the flavour of a gamble. 'The school's model pupil, the Head Girl, may be turned down everywhere, while the nonentity with scraped A-levels gets an Oxbridge place.' A new image on which they should model themselves was put before the girls – the 'university type'. She was not on any account to be a 'blue-stocking'.

('Dons have got a definite thing against them.') She was to be academically competent (more so than her opposite number from a boys' school); sociable, outgoing and with wide interests. She was to be capable of taking up the 'dual role' for which schoolgirls were now openly trained; marriage and a career.

Girls at a high-pressure school with a modern dedicated Headmistress were told to choose their G.C.E. subjects with an eye to their career and to think of it as lasting for life, with a few years' leave from it to have children. It was explained to them that since there were only just enough of them to go round as wives they must all prepare to marry, but that married women already comprised a third of the country's labour force and 200,000 more would be needed for the new 'Technological Revolution'. In schools with a feminist tradition, the black sheep of the form was the one without ambition ('If I want to annoy a staff, I say I just mean to get married and do nothing').

But in spite of all the enthusiasm and the effort, twenty-five years after girls had been given equal opportunity in education, the position of women in the main professions was still much the same as it had been. They were 90% of nurses, but 15% of practising doctors; 75% of all primary-school teachers, but only 40% of head teachers; almost half of all university students, but less than 2% of university professors.[16]

However, in their traditional fields of work, women's conditions had improved because girl entrants to them now had a scarcity value. Nursing, for instance, had been transformed since girls starting dropping out of it to get married earlier; and also since auxiliary medical services began to offer girls hospital jobs which required a shorter training and a less arduous work routine. (In 1961, 73% of all radiographers were women.)[17] Therefore, as early as 1948, a great drive began to make nursing attractive to school-leavers. Instead of being 'probationers', they were given 'full student status'.[18] Hostels were set up, with single rooms and every comfort. Tennis courts were provided, and free time to play on them. Pay was greatly improved; hours shortened and divided into more convenient shifts; and Sisters were encouraged to treat young beginners gently (and be seen to be doing it) and not to be tough with them for the benefit of their characters. By the Seventies, the hospital nurse had quite a new image, no longer a dedicated virgin, but a girl who 'enjoys the warmth of patients' gratitude'[19] and who is worth advertising for in a sexy magazine.

Teaching had a new image; still a job for life, but one with breaks in it and changes of situation. The typical young woman teacher was married and took time off (to the absorbed interest of the sixth form) to have a baby. If her husband moved to a new place, she took another post in the new locality. The dedicated spinster of yesterday, who had stayed for life and provided continuity, was much missed in the schools, where the Head was often hard put to it to find a First Mistress with sufficient experience. But the supply of entrants to the teaching profession kept up to strength, mainly because it had long ago offered the best incentive of all, to a girl hesitating as to which career she should chose;

that is, it had accepted the principle of Equal Pay in 1955 and had got it fully implemented by 1961.

5. *Equal Pay*

The Equal Pay Act of 1970, to be fully in action by December 29, 1975, laid down that women must be paid the same as men if they are employed on 'like work'. This means either identical or 'broadly similar' to the extent of rating the same terms and conditions of employment. They should also be paid the same in jobs which, though different from those of men, have been given an equal value under a job evaluation exercise.

Secondly, it said that women should get equal terms and conditions of employment; thirdly, that their equal pay is not to be affected by, for instance, the protective legislation of the Factory Acts or such factors as maternity leave and women's earlier retirement. In negotiating for equal pay, women can also claim it by comparing their pay and conditions with those in an 'associated' situation, such as another branch of the same firm. Collective agreements between trade unions and employers must be brought into line by Equal Pay Day. If an employer believes there is an undeniable difference between what a man can do for him, as opposed to a woman, it is up to him to prove it.

This forty-second and final effort to get equal pay on to the statute book was the work of the first woman Cabinet minister to make a mark on history in a field which could not be classified as a 'woman's-role' one – Barbara Castle, who, as Minister of Transport, had managed to arrest the apparently foredoomed rise of traffic accidents, year after year. This success where men Ministers had failed gave her an extra edge in getting the country to accept equal pay.

She was Secretary of State for Employment at the time of the strike of 183 female machinists at Ford's Dagenham factory. These women may find themselves canonised, in feminist history, along with the Match-Girls of 1888, and may well be bewildered, since their strike was not about Equal Pay at all in the first place. It was about whether the process of sewing covers for car-seats was worth 8s 5½d an hour, or, like the next women's grade up, 8s 10½d an hour. The newspapers presented this as a fight for equal pay (though if that had been true the women would have been asking for 9s 9½d an hour). But the press concluded that since it was a strike of women engaged on a female-rôle job (sewing) and since they were discussing it over cups of tea with a female – and therefore probably feminist – Secretary of State, and since they had reached an amicable agreement with each other, then it must obviously be a plan for equal pay, and this became a self-fulfilling prophecy because it emerged that there was a differential between men and women doing the same job. The women thereupon got an immediate increase of 7d an hour, which brought them up, closer than ever before, to within 8% of the male rate, and Barbara Castle announced in the House of Commons that she proposed to start negotiations for implementing statutory equal pay, over a period. It was held up by the controversy about her suggested plan to the unions, 'In Place of Strife', but became law before the Labour government fell in June 1970. The Amalgamated

Union of Engineering Workers, which had always been firmly and candidly anti-feminist (from a semi-religious conviction that men were created to be the engineers) nevertheless made a handsome gesture to Mrs Castle,[20] suggesting that the Equal Pay Act would be a lasting benefit to the whole trade-union movement, long after the failure of 'In Place of Strife' had ceased to matter.

The Act was accepted without much excitement among interested parties at first, mainly because its final effects would not be felt for five years, which would give employers time to think where the extra money was to come from. The expense was likely to be considerable, since the Department of Employment figures for the end of 1972 showed that women's average earnings were little more than half of men's. The T.U.C. conference on Equal Pay in 1973 thought that 'employers are now ... willing to accept the principle of equal pay and their obligation to implement it' even if they did not really understand which categories of women workers it would benefit. But according to a special *Sunday Times*[21] investigation they realised it only too well and were making under-cover plans for dodging and cheese-paring. Some firms put their faith in introducing new job gradings, segregating female employees and keeping the unskilled rate as low as possible. Some re-graded white-collar jobs into three layers, the lowest one predominantly women, the middle one mixed and the upper one predominantly for men. In the clerical areas of engineering firms they stopped recruiting men into particular establishments, so that there should be no male salary by which to measure. An old industrial custom was to pay the man who cleaned the men's lavatories the basic labouring rate and the woman who cleaned the ladies' lavatories the women's unskilled rate. Since it was difficult to make a good case for the two jobs not being identical or comparable, one industrial relations adviser suggested that they should sack both sets of cleaners and bring in a firm of outside contractors untroubled by this traditional differential, to look after the whole thing.

Other firms arranged to let themselves down lightly by having jobs 'evaluated' and then re-graded, so that the ones in which women were predominant should be minimum-rate.[22] And one company, employing 26,000 of whom 70% were women, circulated a list of 'discrimination factors' suitable for use in depressing women's rates and keeping male employees sweet by providing 'an acceptable differential between the take-home pay of men and women'. These were 'Long Service, Merit, Attendance Bonus, Willingness to work overtime'. In all of these except 'merit' – which is, in any case largely in the eye of the beholder – women automatically made a lower score than men. Their working years are shorter; their attendance (like that of all semi-skilled and unskilled workers of either sex) is less good than that of skilled personnel; and married women workers are prevented from doing overtime by having the evening ear-marked for their domestic rôle.

But while the sabotaging of equal pay by thrifty employers might come as no surprise, the minor sub-plotting of male trade-union brothers was disillusioning, particularly after the recent drive to get women into the unions. The T.U.C.

conference had laid down as its main conclusions that: 'If equal pay is not properly implemented, further progress will depend, to a great extent, on the willingness of women to join their unions in greater numbers than has hitherto been the case. It is no accident that the areas in which equal pay has operated for some years, in the public sector, are areas where trade-union organisation among women is most strong.' But the Office of Manpower Economics reported, on the contrary, that 'One in ten managements of companies were said to have claimed that the introduction of equal pay has been blocked by the attitudes of male trade unionists, and in some cases it was said that the men had resisted pay changes which would have narrowed the differentials between themselves and female employees and had successfully demanded the same pay increase.' Besides that, 'We found no clear association between the level of union membership in companies and the extent to which they had progressed towards equal pay.'[23]

CHAPTER NINE

WOMEN ALONE
1970 Onwards

1. *The Polygamous Society*

By the beginning of the Seventies, a new kind of polygamy had been accepted in Britain. Its main problem was that no plans had been made for persons practising it to be able to afford it, since the economy had always been geared to monogamy.

The machinery of polygamy was divorce, separation, single motherhood and unofficial unions. In all these variations the male was still held responsible for the support of the woman with whom he had sexual intercourse, at least until some other man took over the responsibility.

Divorce was now easier than it ever had been. The Divorce Reform Act of 1969, which came into operation on January 1, 1971, established that there was only one ground for divorce, the 'irretrievable breakdown' of the marriage; and this was incorporated into the Matrimonial Causes Act of 1973, which came into force on January 1, 1974.

It was all that Lord Gorell and Sir Alan Herbert had ever

dreamed of, and more. It cut through the hypocrisies of the 'double standard' for men and women, and through the ludicrous, holier-than-thou pretence that divorce was a punishment for adultery. It admitted that the vast majority of people who got divorced did so because they wanted to, probably in order to try marriage again with someone else.

This honesty made the routine of divorce considerably less sordid that it had been before. But the reasons given for people wanting to part from their previous partner remained the same as they always were. It was true that the petitioner now only had to prove that the marriage was no longer working. But the proofs of this non-working were familiar. They were that the respondent had committed adultery and the petitioner therefore found it impossible to live with the respondent any more, or that the petitioner could not be expected to live with the respondent because of unreasonable behaviour; or that they had deserted or parted or lived apart for two or maybe five years. 'Unreasonable behaviour' meant cruelty or sodomy or bestiality or unreasonable sexual demands, much what the Gorell Commission had recommended as grounds for divorce in 1909.

There was now no struggle to wrest one's freedom from a marriage out of a grudging law-court or from an unwilling partner. A couple who had lived apart for two years, who had no children and who both wanted a divorce could get it by sending for the forms and filing them at the court. Even the person who wanted a divorce while the marriage partner definitely did not could get it, by leaving home for five years.

The Finer Committee, which was called in later to make some recommendations about the consequences of the increasingly liberal attitude towards sex relationships, pointed out that the speed with which the new reforms had been accepted showed that 'the Act was one of those measures which commended itself to the general conscience long before it had succeeded in gaining the Statute Book'. The new feminists of the 'Women's Lib' movement were pleased with it, visualising its benefits chiefly in terms of an abused wife escaping from her male-chauvinist pig, like the 'Battered Wives' whom they made their concern, rescuing them and providing a refuge. The Church of England was uneasy about deserted wives left with a family to bring up; and Lady Summerskill called the provisions for divorcing a wife against her will the 'Casanova's Charter',[1] pointing out that its main usefulness would be to the middle-aged husband who wanted to marry his secretary.

The number of middle-aged men changing their partners for younger ones had been steadily increasing since the mid-Fifties. Many were middle-class and at the peak of their career. They remarried twice as often as their divorced wives of the same age-group did, and as the Registrar-General pointed out with a hint of disapproval for the mathematical irregularity rather than the moral, 'are likely to seek their partners for remarriage among spinsters, thus depriving some bachelors of spinster marriage partners'.[2] Very often it was the middle-aged man's young secretary who took the original wife's place, instead of finding her mate from among her own age-group, trading her youth for more money and a better position than she could achieve any other way. This is a very old type of marriage bargain, but the tradition has always been that parents persuaded a girl to be practical and make the best of it, against her will. But in the Seventies, it was the young woman who made the choice, although there was no shortage of available men of her own generation. She took over the discarded wife's place, in her husband's social round. This was accepted without criticism by the business friends and acquaintances who up till now had entertained and been entertained by her predecessor. On the contrary, it was more usual for them to admire the husband's enterprise and virility in making the change at his age.

The former wife thus lost her position, her former income and her social life. She might also find that her share of the joint security previously assured for their old age was also taken away from her and given to the newcomer. As the Finer Report pointed out, if her husband's pension is in the national scheme, 'the married woman who separates from her husband . . . remains entitled to claim a retirement pension on her husband's insurance. . . . A divorced woman, however, loses some of these rights, although she is able to make use of her husband's contribution record for the period until the date of her divorce in the calculation of her retirement pension.' But if he was in an occupational scheme, 'one of the consequences of divorce can be that a woman loses her prospective right to a widow's pension . . . in the event of her ex-husband's death'. And since a middle-aged, middle-class widow of to-day is not likely to be insured under the state scheme herself (though her successor may well be) she will be left unprovided-for when her ex-husband dies. The Finer Committee admitted despairingly that they could not at present see any solution to this particular problem.

The other problem which afflicted both the old wife and the new had been foretold by Lord Justice Hodson, in his *Memorandum* to the Royal Commission of 1955.

It is only in comparatively recent times that it has been a common thing for people to remarry who have not the means to keep more than one wife; and the odd situation has now come on us in which a man of very large means who pays surtax is able to have several wives and deduct the maintenance from his income and be very little worse off than he was; whereas a man in the position of a working man who pays neither surtax nor any considerable amount of income tax finds it quite impossible to comply with the law which still in this country enables divorced wives or wives who have obtained a divorce to obtain maintenance from their husbands who have to provide for a number of wives in excess of one.

One of the safeguards of the reformed divorce law was that the wife who was not supporting herself independently was 'entitled, following the loss of co-habitation, to be maintained at a standard of living no less than her husband's'.[3] But this, of course, was not what it used to be when his money only had to support one household instead of two. Second wives, who had therefore to live more frugally than their contemporaries who were first wives, because they had to share what their common husband could make with a predecessor, were liable to become obsessed by the drain of alimony. 'I resent every penny of it; I work so she can stay at home and sleep.' 'I still wash and dry my week's dirty clothes at the Launderette. His first wife has the washing-machine and a spin-drier and a dishwasher too.' 'When I got a rise in salary, Fred's kids reported the news to Fred's ex. So she phoned him and said, "Since Janet must be earning a lot more you can afford to pay me a lot more."'[4]

These difficulties were usually confined to later-life changes of partner. Since the duty to maintain the ex-wife ceased upon her remarriage, the younger and more attractive she was the better for the husband and his new wife. Men who were under thirty only had to keep both wives for an average of under a year.[5] Husbands under 45 whose divorced wives were under 35 averaged four years of it and after that the older the old wife was the longer he was condemned to maintain her. The middle and upper class got the worst of it, because of their habits of later divorce.

The young husband of a young wife with a job of her own came out of the divorce-court no poorer than when he went in, because the courts felt that 'in the case of a divorcing or separating young couple, married only for a short time, without children, and each engaged in, or capable of gainful occupation, the marriage certificate is not to be regarded as a passport to a substantial maintenance order'.[6]

2. *Fatherless Families*
The people who really lost out, as a result of the new freedom to swap partners, were the children of the odd-woman-out, the one who got left (as the Old Maid used to, back in pre-1914 days) without a supporting male.

According to the 1971 census estimate, there were some

400,000 of them: 'lone mothers, immediately responsible for 720,000 children whose fathers were alive but not living with the family'. Each of these lone mothers had a legally responsible supporter, and if he had been able and willing to subscribe what the law had laid down that he should pay, she would probably have been able to manage on it; although she was never nearly as well off as the wife, mistress or widow of a man without any commitments to another woman. In the polygamous society, such men were becoming rarer, but they were a very good proposition, because they were able to offer an intact income. In fact it was becoming important for a woman to find a man who had not any previous affairs of the kind, in the same way that men used to think it was important to acquire a physical virgin.

But the main difficulty of the lone mother was not that the scheduled amount was too small, but that she could not get it. The chairman of the Greenlaw Committee for assisting fatherless families told the Finer Committee that 'The difficulties and miseries experienced by many mothers in obtaining monies to which they are morally and legally entitled is nothing short of a national scandal.'[7]

The largest group of lone mothers (190,000) consisted of women who were still legally married, but not living with their husbands.[8] A fluctuating number got official 'maintenance' from their husbands as the result of a separation order in the magistrates' court, which was the poor man's highly unsatisfactory substitute for divorce. Another 120,000 lone mothers were divorced, and the same number widowed, and the smallest group was 90,000 unmarried mothers.

The widows were in general better off than the rest. For one thing their income from their supporting male was higher because theirs was not shared with another female dependent. Through National Insurance, private insurances and occupational pensions allowing for a widow, she usually got at least more than a subsistence allowance. And because her status as a woman alone was quite definite, it was made a little easier for her by such benefits as the six-months' allowance after the husband's death, and the chance to claim unemployment or sickness benefit, and a certain indulgence towards her supplementing her statutory benefits by working, whereas other women on their own were liable to be penalised for it. Also, widows, like divorcees, do have possessions, a home and furniture, where others may not. But above all, the widow's income was a certain one, since her supporting male could neither disappear, fail to pay up or get a new woman.

However, as Margaret Wynne found, in her study of *Fatherless Families*, they were worse off at every level of society than the complete one.

Fatherless children face greater risks in many directions . . . It is shown that fatherless families are more likely to break down completely . . . fatherless children are more likely to be underprotected and under-supervised . . . more likely to be homeless . . . to live in inadequate accommodation or to have repeated changes of home . . . the loss of a father increases the risk that a child, particularly a boy, will become a delinquent by a factor of approximately two . . .[9]

As a child-care worker described the fatherless household: 'You can see the whole thing before you look, everything has gone on the children. Mum is half fed, half clothed and half herself, and the whole house is threadbare from top to bottom and they have never had a holiday or any margin for a bit of fun.'

Dennis Marsden, in his survey of unsupported mothers, found that:

Mothers were going short of food, and although the children of school age usually had school meals, their diets were likely to suffer at weekends and during the school holidays. For clothing, mothers relied largely and children also to a large extent, on gifts from the family . . . the children were going to academically inferior schools, and children's lack of success was partly due to being marked off from their schoolmates in many small ways through lack of money. . . . Mothers found themselves unable to keep up with the rising demands of schools, whose requests for money from the home were geared to average levels of living in society. One mother said she dreaded her children going back to school after Christmas because their schoolfellows would ask what they got; and what treats they had been given. . . . Ours are always saying, 'Why can't we go to a party?'[10]

In fact, as far as the children of a mother who lacks a supporting male are concerned, life is much the same as it was for the widow's son, Philip Inman, in the days before the suffragettes had broken a single window in the cause of sex equality and when social security for all was no more than a gleam in Beatrice Webb's eye:

We always knew, and it seemed as if we had always known, the struggle my mother was having to bring us up. We accepted the fact that life for us was harder than for other families. . . . Another boy invited me to go to his home on November the fifth, as they were having fireworks. I went, full of blissful anticipation, but I had not realised that I was to be only a looker-on. The boy's father kept on giving him a succession of fireworks to set off. There were squibs, catherine wheels, roman candles, rockets. There was not one for me. I went home, crying bitterly. Why should I have no fireworks? Why should other boys have pleasures so often while we had none at all?'[11]

Dennis Marsden found that over half of his fatherless families were living in overcrowded accommodation, and 40% of them without the four standard amenities checked in a census (hot and cold water tap, W.C. and fixed bath). Half the mothers never ate breakfast and a sixth of them had no mid-day meal either. The ones living at this level were mostly entitled by court order to an income from a living male supporter. But, as a survey made by Bedford College found, 'There is a large gap between the amounts the court orders the defendants to pay and what the orders actually produce for the wives and children; 39% of all the orders in the Bedford College sample were found to be in arrears. Moreover, the larger the order, the more likely it is to be in arrears.'[12]

This was mainly the problem of the old wife (or for that matter, the old mistress) whom the husband was still supposed to be supporting because, if he simply could not afford to support both of his women, the one on the spot would obviously score. As the Finer Report said,

> When a man is put in such a dilemma, the solution he will lean towards is tolerably clear. He will feed, clothe and house those with whom he is living, knowing that the State will provide for the others. It is the almost inescapable consequence of the principles on which the supplementary benefits scheme is founded that wherever there is not enough money for the husband to support two women, it is the one with whom he is not living who had to resort to the Supplementary Benefits Commission.[13]

Supplementary Benefit took the place of the old National Assistance, as money distributed by the state to those who had not enough to live on. Sixty-eight per cent of those receiving it were women. They included single women not eligible for full National Insurance benefits, unsupported mothers, wives of men claiming supplementary benefit, prisoners' wives, divorced and separated women, widows and women pensioners.

It was less frustrating to apply for Supplementary Benefit than to go on appealing to the man who had left you. As the Finer Committee pointed out, 'One might say of these women that their rights as citizens are much more valuable to them than their rights as dependents.' In 1970, the taxpayer provided some £9.25 million for women who had been discarded by men, of which the Commission recovered about £8.40 million from the 'liable relatives'. But even if all the 'liable' men had dutifully paid up for their previous mates, the liability of the taxpayer would still have been three-quarters of the original amounts, because courts only ordered the man to pay quite modest sums, since they knew very well it was no use ordering more, because his wage, even if it was a good one, was geared to the cost of one family, not two. Therefore, in 1974, half of all fatherless families, other than widows' families, depended on supplementary benefit, less than a third on the mother's earnings, and only one in eight on maintenance payments.

One of the disagreeable features of living on Supplementary Benefit was that, because its original purpose was to provide temporary relief, the Commission officials lived in a continual state of hope that the man who should have been supporting the women and children would turn up again and resume doing so. Failing him, they hoped for some new man to take a fancy to the lone mother. They simply felt that in a society where the sexes were evenly divided – with a slight preponderance of males at the woman-fancying age – there should be enough male breadwinners to go round. They were not looking for Casanovas so much as for scroungers. They believed with Shakespeare that every Jack should have his Jill, but in a social system which still assumes a male breadwinner, he should support her while she is his, otherwise a fluctuating number are getting a woman free, at the taxpayer's expense.

For this reason they were always anxious to know whether a lone woman living on Supplementary Benefit had acquired any kind of a male protector, because it could turn out that he was the missing Jack in this case. He might have a deserted wife living on Supplementary Benefit in another part of the town and now have unfairly acquired a mistress living on Supplementary Benefit as well.

The motives of the Supplementary Benefit officials, against whom Claimants' Unions and the Child Poverty Action Group launched a fierce campaign, were therefore not inspired by old-fashioned sexual morality or chastity or even monogamy; but simply by the principle that individuals should not take more than their share of public service amenities. However, from the receiving end it was just as uncomfortable for the lone mothers whose private life was spied upon as if it had been inspired by the most archaic puritan ethic.

The investigation officer's guide, the Supplementary Benefits Handbook for 1971, explained the rules:

The question that has to be decided ... is whether or not an unmarried couple are in fact living together as man and wife, or, in the language of the Act, cohabiting. ... There is no simple answer. The decision has to be reached after weighing a combination of facts; e.g. Is there a common home? Is there a pooled household fund? Do the couple have children? What are the regular sleeping arrangements? Does the woman use the man's name and are the couple acknowledged as man and wife? ... The answer to any one question is not necessarily conclusive by itself ... and it should be emphasised that the decision depends solely on whether it appears that the couple are living as man and wife in the full sense of the term, not on any moral considerations or on whether a man and woman have slept together on occasions.

To find out whether a man was 'living in the same household' officers were to watch the benefit claimant's house, 'about the time the man is expected to leave (usually in the morning); to watch again that evening and the following morning; if the man is seen to leave or enter on any of these occasions' – the officer is to 'interview the woman' with a view to getting her benefit cut off. The system combined the humiliation of the Means Test of the Thirties with the voyeurism of the days of the King's Proctor and the Common Informer, when private detectives could make a living by ascertaining whether it was the divorcer who was committing adultery, when it was supposed to be the would-be divorcee who was. Just as A. P. Herbert's 'Mr Rigby' always 'put his eye to the keyhole as a matter of form',[14] when on spying duty, so his successor, some thirty-five years after the Herbert Act, 'was discovered kneeling and peering through the letterbox'[15] of a Supplementary Benefit's claimant's home. When asked what he was doing, he replied that he was collecting the census form.

3. *Unrationed Sex*

By the time the Pill was made available to all, on the N.H.S., sexual intercourse was already unrationed. There were wife-swapping parties in the suburbs and young farmers and their wives entertained others by running blue films on their home projector. In the cities, early-evening parties were for finding someone with whom one could go home to spend the rest of the evening in sportive sex. Variations became so tolerated by public opinion that a London group of blackmailers completely failed to ruin a public man by the old and tried and hitherto infallible recipe of disclosing that he was fond of sex for three.

A new female archetype was now presented by the media and the advertising industry, the over-lusting female, whom men cannot satisfy. *Cosmopolitan*, a magazine which specialised in her needs, devoted serious articles to such problems as that of the well-off career-girl, who has all the sexual intercourse she chooses, with strangers, and always enjoys it, but finds it no longer brings her the excitement it once did. Then there is the dilemma of the woman who has gone to a hotel to have intercourse with a likeable stranger who has a heart attack in the middle of it. The practical solution suggested is to dress and go home, telling the hotel staff on the way out that the gentleman in number seven seems to be having a coronary. The weakness of this plan is that if she had stayed by his side it might have turned the scale between life and death and the moral of the story is that 'a woman having sex with an overweight man with a high-tension job and a smoking habit should be prepared – orgasm is a major stress phenomenon'.[16]

A thrice-married woman attacks the dogma that there is any virtue in a lasting marriage.

Why does it not occur to them (the long-married couple) that divorce or break-up can mean that a couple has an altogether higher aspiration for marriage, a higher standard of love than those, like John and his wife, who slog on . . . ? Do they never imagine the

UNRATIONED SEX

pleasure of not being taken for granted, the joys of revealing new aspects of yourself to a new person? I often think that all the traditional gloom of the menopause would simply vanish if the woman were loved, admired, invigorated by a new man.[17]

Long-married couples may well 'develop twisted ties of hatred that are contagious. Their children catch the sickness and grow up to seek neurotic rather than loving relationships.'

The magazine is just as brisk and bossy as the old-fashioned health-and-beauty ones used to be about self-improvement, but its concern is with the duty of having a proper orgasm. That poor-spirited creature the 'non-orgasmic woman' is really nothing but a slacker, because if she only embarked on a determined course of self-help and worked to conquer her sexual inadequacy, she might improve quite considerably. ('If your love-making is only so-so, try these simple and sensual techniques.')[18]

Sex should be started early. A named and qualified doctor and psychiatrist discusses a letter about a sixteen-year-old girl who is having regular intercourse with her boy.

In some circles, a girl who waited until the ripe age of sixteen before sleeping with a boy-friend would be thought backward and retarded. In other, more 'respectable' circles, she would be regarded as either a victim or an incipient nymphomaniac. Naturally . . . teachers, clergy, sociologists and others who earnestly warn against engaging in sex activities too early claim that it stunts physical growth, blunts the intellect and moral fibre and renders a girl less fit for marriage.

On the other hand some researchers maintain on the basis of investigations that early sex experience helps a woman to be fulfilled and orgasmic later in maturity....[19]

There was a determined effort by schoolgirls' magazines to catch and keep younger readers by being the first to introduce sexy features. Suggestions for 'Going back to School with a Smile' in a comic aimed at the comprehensive schoolgirl are, 'Send an anonymous love-letter to one of the boys in your class,' 'Think of that gorgeous sixth-former you've had your eye on for ages – and work out ways to get him to notice you.' 'Leave the house a bit earlier than usual so that you can bump into that super-looking paperboy.'[20]

Earnestly radical young teachers, who believed that by spreading sex revolution among their pupils they were hastening the revolution of the proletariat, pressed the facts about sex on to them as early as possible. *The Little Red School-Book* (which includes advice for girls who have not reached puberty) gives instructions for Masturbation, Orgasm, Intercourse and Petting, and Contraceptives. ('There ought to be one or more contraceptive machines in every school. If your school refuses to instal one, get together with some friends and start your own contraceptive shop.')[21] The capitalist-society magazines, on the other hand, advise spending one's pocket money on make-up. 'We thought it was about time we showed you how to really make the most of your face by using all that female cunning ... playing up your best points and playing down the worst ...'[22] Trendy schoolgirls' fashions were for ankle-length skirts and shoes with soles so thick and heels so high that they could only hobble, like girls with bound feet in pre-revolution China; at an age when their grandmothers had worn short skirts, aertex blouses and underwear, and flat sandals, on the principle that the main business of childhood is to play.

4. Women's Lib

The new feminism, Women's Lib, had started in the United States. Its original begetter was Betty Friedan, whose book, *The Feminine Mystique*, shocked the American public by its heresies on the sacred subject of sex. That was in 1963. Ten years later, her theories seemed perfectly reasonable and in fact obvious, which was a measure of the speed at which they spread.

'It has been popular, in recent years, to laugh at feminism as one of history's dirty jokes, to pity, sniggering, those old-fashioned feminists who fought for women's rights to higher education, careers, the vote. They were neurotic victims of penis envy, it is said now.'[23] Betty Friedan's crusade was to liberate women from the tyranny of having to be sexually attractive or else be despised, and from having to be the 'happy housewife' of the suburbs. Both, she pointed out, were rôles forced on women in order that the commercial interests of the consumer society might prosper; and both prevented women from being educated as fully as they might be and from using their abilities to lead the kind of life they would have chosen. The violence of the reaction to her book came from American husbands and from trade.

The pattern of the movement was different from that of

women's emancipation in Britain, because in the States it followed the Civil Rights campaign and based its tactics on that. Many of the pioneers of Women's Lib had been part of Civil Rights groups, and used those techniques to get the new feminism going – for instance, 'consciousness-raising', which was a system of group confession comparing notes about one's sense of resentment and injustice which had been used to help black people get a sense of identity and shared struggle. White suburban wives and college girls now met and sat in a circle on the floor, confessing to their humiliation when men wolf-whistled them in the street and their permanently remembered resentment when their brothers were put before them in childhood.

This consciousness-raising was designed to give them the spirit to rebel against the way women were treated in American society and most of all within the American system of marriage. Some of the various groups (for instance, 'The Feminists') believed that marriage and the nuclear family would have to be scrapped; others, (such as the 'Pussycat League') thought it capable of being reformed.

The movement first emerged in Britain a year after the Ford sewing-machinists' strike as a spin-off from a short-lived women's committee which had been formed to support the campaign for equal pay. Its members were mainly young and university-educated, and not sure whether they – as a Women's Lib group – ought to get involved in an industrial dispute of this kind – 'whether we should encourage women to go out to work in a capitalist system as this insured that they were doubly exploited; whether we should enrol women in bureaucratic, male-dominated unions, which could only disillusion them'. Also, they feared that 'being middle-class, without any experience of working-class life and conditions of work they had no credentials for getting involved – they would be accused of being patronising'.[24]

Although the idea of the movement quickly caught on, and its name became part of the language overnight, it was not taken very seriously by the older feminist organisations, though most of them were careful not to 'knock' it. It did not spread, gaining a mass of mixed supporters within months, as it had in the United States. This was partly because the standard requirements for sex equality – such as equal education, jobs, opportunities and legal rights – were already being looked after by home-grown organisations, such as the National Council for Civil Liberties, the National Council of Women, the T.U.C. Women's Congress, the Birth Control Campaign, the Child Poverty Action Group; and in addition all three political parties were overtaken by the panic which had overtaken their predecessors when Women's Suffrage was conceded; that female voters might support the party which offered most Women's Rights (a totally unfounded fear, on the evidence) and had appointed committees to decide on how discrimination was to be ended by Act of Parliament. Besides this, the principle of emotional hostility towards men, as a duty, seemed curiously out of date, sixty years after the suffragettes. It belonged to the beginning of the struggle for sex equality, when it had been necessary to work up a head of steam to start the sex war. But by the Seventies, the sex war was over and the details of the peace treaty were being worked out, and it was altogether too late to resurrect the old battle slogans.

Although anti-discrimination bills had just failed to get through Parliament half a dozen times, both political parties were committed to passing such a bill, and there was not, in fact, much difference in their versions of what was needed. But just as Women's Suffrage had required the Sex Disqualification (Removal) Act to complete it, so the granting of Equal Pay needed also the granting of Equal Opportunity, or an act making sex discrimination unlawful. The project was helped by a recent precedent: the Race Relations Acts of 1965 and 1968. Through them, the public knew how an anti-discrimination law worked and had resigned themselves to it as a tiresome but probably necessary part of everyday life. It did not seem absurd to them, therefore, to have similar regulations about women, as it would have seemed earlier.

The results of sex discrimination were that the women were generally poorer than men, the way black people were poorer than white, and that because they were, they had less status and less freedom, in such fields as buying a house, practising a profession, getting promoted to top jobs in their own line, and making themselves felt in trade unions. Equal pay for equal work was not going to solve this; because the chain of sex poverty started with the second-best jobs belonging to women by long custom. (As Willie Hamilton said, introducing his anti-discrimination Bill in 1973, 'On the death of my wife I became ... economically in a better position. If I had died instead, my wife's standard of living would have dropped catastrophically. She would have had to sell house and car and go back to nursing, probably not earning more than £20 a week, with no widow's pension for being under 50 years old.')[25]

The custom of leaving the second-best jobs to women was still rationalised by their having a shorter working life. Early in the twentieth century, most of them had only worked between school and marriage. Now they had a gap while their children were little, and when they returned to work it was not necessarily to the same field, but in any case almost always at a lower level than when they had left. This pattern affected everything, from training for a job or career to getting a retirement pension. It started the discrimination process while the victim was still a little schoolgirl by directing her towards subjects which were more useful in second-rank jobs than top-rank ones; more English Literature than Physics, more Domestic Science than Technology. (And this, as Women's Lib pointed out, dated back further still, to the time when the under-school-age girl was told to play with her Christmas present, which was a doll's house rather than with her brother's, which was a toy railway and in fact much more interesting because it was dynamic and moved on its own.)

The White Paper on Equality for Women, of September 1974, proposed to end this chain-reaction by legislation. The anti-discrimination law was to start at school. Girls were to be offered Maths, Physics and Engineering on the same terms as boys and boys were to be offered Domestic Science. (After all, as a Labour party study-group had sensibly pointed out, some of them would have to set up home on their own since there were not enough wives to go round.)[26] Employment agencies, training organisations, employers and professional associations were forbidden to discriminate on the grounds of sex, and so were housing bodies, hotels, banks and firms offering facilities for entertainment, recreation, refreshment or travel. Allowable exceptions were when a person's sex could be proved to be a 'genuine occupational qualification' for the job. These included, rather strangely, some midwives and some clergy, but not others.)

This legislation, however patchy, did put an official seal on women's emancipation. It was a clear undertaking, by the establishment, to accept the principle of sex equality. From now on, it was only a question of having law-suits about definitions and arguing about the small print.

But actually incorporating the principles of non-discrimination into everyday life was like trying to conduct a Seventies' life-style in a nineteenth-century house. It does not fit modern habits. You have to go all the way to the basement to make your cup of instant coffee and the only way to the bathroom is through someone's bedroom. The original plan of living, for which the house was designed, confronts you at every step. British society had been built, since the Industrial Revolution, on the basis of the supporting male breadwinner. It was as difficult to adapt that pattern to equal pay and equal opportunity as it had been to adapt it to sexual freedom for all.

For instance, if women were now to have equal opportunities in industry, they would have to have equal status in the trade unions. Although their membership of the unions continued to rise (one-third of all women employees and 21 % of trade-union membership in 1973) only 25 of the 1,400 paid trade-union officials were women, and there were only two women on the 39-seat T.U.C. General Council. The reason was that women tend to have a poor record of attendance at union meetings, largely because these are traditionally held after work, when women have to go home to see to the children and get the supper. It is firmly established in British domestic life that the meal is ready for the returning breadwinner and that the wife gets it, and the custom still holds, even if she is also a breadwinner.

This was the point at which the arrival of the Women's Lib missionaries with their gospel of rebelling against the institution of marriage made a difference. Its principles had been widely circulated, because the media found the subject irresistible, and it was now an obligatory joke, at every social level, to ask genially if the wife had joined Women's Lib when a meal was not ready as expected. But it was the wife whom they really needed to convert because (unless she was young, middle-class and radical) she was – and is – basically unwilling to disclaim responsibility for the housework, partly from the expert's irritable conviction that no one does the job properly except oneself; partly guilt about going out to work at all, but mostly because she enjoys the rôle; being the unchallenged mistress of the house, whose return is eagerly awaited because then food and warmth and order will be forthcoming. Sitting in a union meeting, listening to aphorisms about the social and economic value of serving the conveyor-belt, is not an irresistible alternative.

It is also going to take a long time for the Women's Lib girls to convince her that her willingness to look after her own children, instead of agitating for twenty-four-hour nurseries, has got to be conquered if women are to be set free.

The housewife-mother is a backward, conservative force . . . her work is private and because it is private and for no other reason it is unsupervised. . . . For every process of production that involves combined social forces and co-operation (enforced or voluntary) also requires superintendence and direction. . . . There is no inherent reason why the biological and social mother should coincide. . . . Observers of collective methods of child-rearing in the kibbutzim in Israel note that the child who is reared by a trained nurse. . . . does not suffer the backwash of typical parental anxieties and thus may positively gain by the system.[27]

This demand for women to change their colour, like chameleons, to fit the background of their period was one of the penalties of the speed at which their emancipation had been accomplished. Major changes in their state had taken place within the span of each generation, so that every twentieth-century mother, in turn, was amazed at the difference between her daughter's life and her own.

A woman born at the turn of the century could have lived through two periods when it was her moral duty to devote herself, obsessively, to her children; three when it was her duty to society to neglect them; two when it was right to be seductively 'feminine' and three when it was a pressing social obligation to be the reverse; three separate periods in which

WOMEN'S LIB

she was a bad wife, mother and citizen for wanting to go out and earn her own living, and three others when she was an even worse wife, mother and citizen for not being eager to do so.

PUBLISHER'S NOTE: *A Woman's Place* was written for the general reader. For this reason, the author did not think it necessary to provide page references.

REFERENCES

Chapter 1: A Man's World

1. Rudyard Kipling, 'Mandalay', *Barrack-Room Ballads* (National Observer). Methuen, 1892.
2. *Annual Report on Sea-Fisheries*, 1913.
3. Clemence Dane, *Broome Stages*. Heinemann, 1931.
4. *Royal Commission on Population*, 1949.
5. *Ibid.*
6. E. M. Delafield, *Thank Heaven Fasting*. Macmillan, 1932.
7. *Royal Commission on Population*, 1949.
8. Stephen Hobhouse, *Margaret Hobhouse and Her Family*. Stanhope Press, 1934.
9. Kitty Muggeridge and Ruth Adam, *Beatrice Webb: A Life*. Secker & Warburg, 1967.
10. *Census*, 1911.
11. George Gissing, *The Odd Women*. Thomas Nelson & Sons, 1893.
12. A. L. Bowley, *Division of the Product of Industry*, 1919.
13. *Women in the Trade Union Movement*. T.U.C. Publication, 1955.
14. *Report of the War Cabinet on Women in Industry*, 1919.
15. *The Woman's Book*. Edited by Florence Jack. T. C. & E. Jack, 1911.
16. Asher Tropp, *The Schoolteachers: Growth of the Teaching Profession in England and Wales, from 1800 to the Present Day*. Heinemann, 1957.
17. Brian Abel-Smith, *A History of the Nursing Profession*. Heinemann, 1960.
18. *Ibid.*
19. Ray Strachey, *Millicent Garrett Fawcett*. John Murray, 1931.
20. George Dangerfield, *The Strange Death of Liberal England*. MacGibbon, 1935.
21. Frances Perrot, *Reporter*. Hutchinson, 1938.
22. Annie Kenney, *Memories of a Militant*. Edward Arnold, 1924.

REFERENCES

23 Christabel Pankhurst, *Unshackled*. Hutchinson, 1959.
24 *The Suffragette*, 25 April 1913.
25 *Ibid.*

Chapter 2: When the Boys Were Far Away

1 Ray Strachey, *Millicent Garrett Fawcett*.
2 *Ibid.*
3 David Mitchell, *The Fighting Pankhursts*. Cape, 1967.
4 Leslie Baily's *B.B.C. Scrapbooks, 1896–1914*. Allen & Unwin, 1966.
5 *Ibid.*
6 Gilbert Murray, *How Can War Ever Be Right?* Pamphlet in the series, *Why We Are At War*. Central Committee for National Patriotic Organisations, 1914.
7 Rupert Brooke, 'Peace', *1914 and Other Poems*. Sidgwick & Jackson, 1915.
8 Herbert Asquith, 'The Volunteer', *Poems of Today*. Sidgwick & Jackson, 1915.
9 Thomas Hardy, 'Men Who March Away' (Song of the Soldiers). *The Times*, 9 Sept. 1914.
10 Andrews and Hobbs, *Economic Effects of the War Upon Women and Children in Great Britain*. For the Carnegie Trust, New York, 1918.
11 *Ibid.*
12 *New Statesman*, 31 July 1964.
13 David Mitchell, *Women on the Warpath. The Story of the Women of the First World War*. Cape, 1966.
14 Mrs C. S. Peel, *How We Lived Then, 1914–1918*. Bodley Head, 1929.
15 Rose Macaulay, 'Many Sisters to Many Brothers', *Poems of Today*. Sidgwick & Jackson, 1915.
16 *Daily Mail*, 31 Aug. 1914.
17 *The Times*, 28 Aug. 1914.
18 *Home Notes*, 12 Sept. 1914.
19 *Daily Mirror*, 29 Aug. 1914.
20 *Daily Herald*, 19 Dec. 1914.
21 Frances Stevenson, *A Diary*. Edited by A. J. P. Taylor. Hutchinson, 1971.
22 Beatrice Webb, *Diaries 1912–1924*. Longmans Green, 1952.
23 David Lloyd George, *War Memoirs*, Vol. 1. Nicholson & Watson, 1933.
24 *Ibid.*
25 *Forward*, 1 Jan. 1918.
26 Naomi Laughnan, *Munitions Work for Women Warworkers*. Pamphlet, 1917.

REFERENCES

27 Lloyd George, *War Memoirs*.
28 Helena May Swanwick, *I Have Been Young*. Gollancz, 1935.
29 Beatrice Webb, *The Wages of Men and Women. Should They Be Equal?* Minority Report, Fabian Society, 1919.
30 *Home Office Report on Substitution*, 24.
31 *The Times*, 5 March 1917.
32 Lloyd George, *War Memoirs*.
33 *Investigation Into Weight-Lifting*. Professor Cathcart, for the Royal Institution, 1915.
34 *Health of Munition Workers*. Working Committee on Employment of Women. Cmnd. 8185.
35 *Woman Welfare Supervisor*. Cmnd. 9065.
36 Lloyd George, *War Memoirs*.
37 Gervase Huxley, *Lady Denman, O.B.E., 1884–1954*. Chatto & Windus, 1961.
38 Lloyd George, *War Memoirs*.
39 Ray Strachey, *Millicent Garrett Fawcett*.
40 Lady Diana Cooper, *The Rainbow Comes and Goes*. Hart-Davis, 1958.
41 *Nursing Times*, 10 April 1915.
42 *British Journal of Nursing*, 2 Oct. 1915.
43 Vera Brittain, *Testament of Youth. An Autobiographical Study of the Years 1900–1925*. Gollancz, 1933.
44 *Daily Mail*, 17 April 1916.
45 R. H. Gretton, *Modern History of the English People, 1880–1922*. Martin Secker, 1929.
46 Sheila Kaye-Smith, *Little England*. Cassell, 1917.
47 Warren Chetham-Strode, *Sometimes Even Now*. Embassy Theatre, London, May 1933.
48 Mary Agnes Hamilton, *Our Freedom And Its Results*. Edited by Ray Strachey. Hogarth Press, 1936.
49 Ronald McNeill, *Morning Post*, 17 April 1915.
50 Helen Blackburne, *National Council for the Unmarried Mother and Her Child*. Report, 1967.
51 *Ibid*.
52 *Registrar-General's Report*, 1916.
53 *Our First Year's Work*. N.C.U.M.C. Report, 1919.
54 *Twenty Years and After*. N.C.U.M.C., 1946.
55 Memo. of the Women's Advisory Committee to the Ministry of Reconstruction, 9 Dec. 1918.

REFERENCES

Chapter 3: The Boys Come Home

1. Ray Strachey, *Millicent Garrett Fawcett*.
2. *Hansard*, 28 March 1916.
3. *Millicent Garrett Fawcett*.
4. Millicent Garrett Fawcett, *The Women's Victory and After*. Sidgwick & Jackson, 1920.
5. *Women on the Warpath*.
6. Beatrice Webb, *Diaries*. 12 Dec. 1918.
7. Pamela Brookes, *Women At Westminster*. Peter Davies, 1967.
8. Beatrice Webb, *Diaries*. 12 Dec. 1918.
9. Annie Kenney, *Memories of a Militant*.
10. *The Times*, 12 Dec. 1918.
11. *Star*, 16 Oct. 1918.
12. *Women on the Warpath*.
13. Esther Roper, *Prison Letters of Constance Markievicz*. Longmans Green, 1934.
14. David Mitchell, *Women on the Warpath*.
15. Maurice Collis, *Nancy Astor: An Informal Biography*. Faber & Faber, 1960.
16. David Mitchell, *Women on the Warpath*.
17. Elsie M. Lang, 'The War and Afterwards', *British Women in the Twentieth Century*. Werner Laurie, 1929.
18. *Daily News*, 15 Feb. 1919.
19. Mary Agnes Hamilton, *Our Freedom*.
20. *Daily News*, 29 Nov. 1919.
21. *The Lady*, Jan. 1920.
22. *The Times Educational Supplement*, 14 March 1918.
23. Brian Abel-Smith, *A History of the Nursing Profession*.
24. House of Lords Debate, 27 June 1919.
25. Philip Gibbs, *Pageant of the Years*. Hutchinson, 1928.
26. W. Somerset Maugham, *For Services Rendered*. Globe Theatre, Nov. 1932.
27. *The Times*, 28 May 1920.
28. *The Lady*, 4 March 1920.
29. *The Times*, 12 Aug. 1920.

Chapter 4: The Sex Revolution

1. *Registrar-General's Report*, 1930.
2. Rudyard Kipling, 'The Road to Endor' *The Years Between*. Methuen, 1919.

REFERENCES

3 Stephen Hobhouse, *Margaret Hobhouse*.
4 Vera Brittain, *Testament of Youth*.
5 'Repression of War Experiences', *War Poems of Siegfried Sassoon*. Heinemann, 1919.
6 Emile Delaveny, *D. H. Lawrence: The Man and His Work*. Heinemann, 1972.
7 Maude Royden, *The Making of Women*. Symposium, edited by Victor Gollancz. Allen & Unwin, 1917.
8 Noël Coward, 'He Never Did That To Me', *Collected Sketches and Lyrics*. Hutchinson, 1924.
9 'Mild Oats.' *Ibid*.
10 Dodie Smith, *Autumn Crocus*. Lyric Theatre, London, April 1931.
11 Aldous Huxley, *Antic Hay*. Chatto & Windus, 1923.
12 *Registrar-General's Reports*, 1920–1930.
13 Nigel Nicolson, *Portrait of a Marriage*. Weidenfeld & Nicolson, 1973.
14 Rosamund Lehmann, *Dusty Answer*. Chatto & Windus, 1927.
15 Radclyffe Hall, *The Well of Loneliness*. Cape, 1928.
16 E. M. Delafield, *Challenge to Clarissa*. Macmillan, 1931.
17 James Laver, *A Concise History of Costume*. Thames & Hudson, 1969.
18 D. H. Lawrence, *A Propos of Lady Chatterley's Lover*. Heinemann, 1928.
19 Mary Agnes Hamilton, *Our Freedom*.
20 *Good Housekeeping Magazine*, March 1924.
21 *Royal Commission on Population Report*, 1949.
22 Hilda Martindale, *Women Servants of the State. A history of Women in the Civil Service*. Allen & Unwin, 1938.
23 *Ibid*.
24 *Ibid*.
25 *The Times*, 12 Aug. 1920.
26 *Nursing Times*, 30 Oct. 1920.
27 Brian Abel-Smith, *A History of the Nursing Profession*.
28 Mary Agnes Hamilton, *Our Freedom*.
29 *The Times Educational Supplement*, 30 Sept. 1922.
30 *Ibid*.
31 *Ibid*.
32 Arthur Marwick. *The Deluge*. Bodley Head, 1965.
33 Bernard Shaw, *The Apple-Cart*. Malvern, 1929.
34 Leah Manning, *A Life for Education. An Autobiography*. Gollancz, 1970.
35 Margaret Bondfield, *The Labour Woman*, 15 Nov. 1947.
36 K. Muggeridge and R. Adam, *Beatrice Webb: A Life*.
37 *Ibid*.

REFERENCES

38 *Manchester Guardian*, 23 March 1929.
39 Elizabeth Grey, *Winged Victory. The Story of Amy Johnson*. Constable, 1966.
40 *Ibid.*
41 Bernard Shaw, *Saint Joan*. New Theatre, 1924.

Chapter 5: Depression

1 Leah Manning, *A Life for Education.*
2 David L. Somervell, *The Reign of King George V*. Faber & Faber, 1935.
3 C. L. Mowat, *Britain Between the Wars: 1918–1940*. Methuen, 1955.
4 Walter Greenwood, *Love On The Dole*. Cape, 1932.
5 Mrs Pallas, *Time To Spare*. B.B.C. Talks Series, 1934.
6 C. L. Mowat, *Britain Between the Wars.*
7 Colin Cross, 'The Forging of the North', *Observer Magazine*, 6 Feb. 1966.
8 Mrs Pallas, *Time To Spare.*
9 Mary Agnes Hamilton, *Our Freedom.*
10 Walter Greenwood, *Love On The Dole.*
11 Mrs Pallas, *Time To Spare.*
12 J. B. Priestley, *Angel Pavement*. Heinemann, 1930.
13 Unemployed Women in Lancashire. Plight of the Old. *Manchester Guardian*, 8 June 1937.
14 Equal Pay Commission, 1944.
15 Beatrice Webb, *Women In Industry*. Wages of Men and Women, Fabian Society.
16 *Royal Commission on Population*, 1949.
17 Mary Agnes Hamilton, *Our Freedom.*
18 *The Times*, 2 Feb. 1935.
19 *Ibid.* (advertisement), 2 Feb. 1935.
20 Mrs Pallas, *Time To Spare.*
21 *Women's Leader*, 2 Jan. 1931.
22 John Reith, *Into the Wind*. Hodder & Stoughton, 1949.
23 Asa Briggs, *Golden Age of Wireless*. Oxford University Press, 1965.
24 J. S. Lambert, *Ariel and All His Quality*. Gollancz, 1940.
25 *Daily Telegraph*, 31 Dec. 1931.
26 Asa Briggs, *Golden Age of Wireless.*
27 *Manchester Guardian*, 30 June 1931.
28 Political and Economic Planning, *Women in Top Jobs*. Allen & Unwin, 1971.
29 Sir Frank Tillyard and F. N. Ball, *Unemployment Insurance in Great Britain 1911–1948*. Thames Bank Publishing Co., 1949.

REFERENCES

30 Political and Economic Planning, *Report on the British Press*, 1938.
31 *News Chronicle*, 7 June 1937.
32 *Ibid.*, 1 July 1937.
33 Harold Herd, *March of Journalism. Story of the British Press from 1622 to the Present Day*. Allen & Unwin, 1952.
34 *Woman and Beauty*, Jan. 1936.
35 James Laver, *Concise History of Costume*.
36 *Royal Commission on Population*, 1949.
37 *Ibid.*
38 *News Chronicle*, 15 June 1937.
39 *Ibid.*, 29 June 1937.
40 *Film Pictorial*, 30 Sept. 1933.
41 A. J. P. Taylor, *English History 1914–1945*. Oxford University Press, 1965.
42 *News Chronicle*, 2 June 1937.
43 N. Branson and M. Heinemann, *Britain in the Thirties*. Weidenfeld & Nicolson, 1971.
44 A. J. P. Taylor, *English History 1914–1945*.
45 Malcolm Muggeridge, *The Thirties*. Hamish Hamilton, 1940.
46 *Royal Commission on Population*.
47 A. J. P. Taylor, *English History 1914–1945*.

Chapter 6: Women in Uniform

1 *The Times*, 4 Sept. 1939.
2 Richard Titmuss, *Problems of Social Policy. History of the Second World War*. H.M.S.O., 1950.
3 *Ibid.*
4 *The Times*, 11 Sept. 1939.
5 *Public Health*, Nov. 1939. No. 2, Vol. LIII.
6 *Ministry of Health Circular*, 1907. 7 Nov. 1939.
7 Richard Titmuss, *Problems of Social Policy*.
8 Letter from the Treasury to the Ministry of Health, 8 Aug. 1939.
9 Richard Titmuss, *Problems of Social Policy*.
10 *Registrar-General's Report*, 1960.
11 Elaine Burton, *What of the Women?* Frank Muller, 1941.
12 E. M. Delafield, *The Provincial Lady in Wartime*. Macmillan, 1940.
13 *The Times*, 7 Sept. 1939.
14 E. S. Turner, *Phoney War on the Home Front*. Michael Joseph, 1961.
15 Vera Douie, *Daughters of Britain. An Account of the Work of British Women during the 2nd World War*. Ronald, 1950.

REFERENCES

16 Norman Longmate, *How We Lived Then: The History of Everyday Life in the Second World War*. Hutchinson, 1971.
17 House of Commons Debate, 2 Dec. 1941. *Hansard*.
18 Allan Bullock, *The Life and Times of Ernest Bevin*, Vol. I. Heinemann, 1960.
19 *Women in the Trade Union Movement*, T.U.C., 1955.
20 *Mass-Observation*.
21 *The Times*, 13 Dec. 1941.
22 Richard Titmuss, *Problems of Social Policy*.
23 *Mass-Observation*.
24 Mary Lee Settle, *All the Brave Promises*. Heinemann, 1966.
25 *Manchester Guardian*, 4 Dec. 1941.
26 Vera Douie, *Daughters of Britain*.
27 *Report of the Royal Commission on Equal Pay*, 1944.
28 *Ibid*.
29 William Beveridge, *Power and Influence*. Hodder & Stoughton, 1953.
30 Richard Titmuss, *Problems of Social Policy*.
31 Angus Calder, *The People's War*. Cape, 1969.
32 Virginia Wimperis, *The Unmarried Mother and Her Child*. Allen & Unwin, 1961.
33 *Registrar-General's Report*, 1961.
34 Angus Calder, *The People's War*.
35 Richard Titmuss, *Problems of Social Policy*.

Chapter 7: Wives and Mothers Again

1 *Registrar-General's Report*, 1961.
2 *Daily Herald*, 22 Feb. 1948.
3 *Reynolds News*, 25 March 1948.
4 Alan Bullock, *The Life and Times of Ernest Bevin*.
5 *Report of T.U.C. Conference*. 1946.
6 Margaret Mead, in the *American Journal of Orthopsychiatry*, July 1954.
7 Myrdal and Klein, *Women's Two Roles*. Routledge & Kegan Paul, 1956.
8 *Registrar-General's Report*, 1961.
9 Virginia Wimperis, *The Unmarried Mother and Her Child*.
10 *Royal Commission on Marriage and Divorce*, 1955.
11 *Ibid*.
12 Ann Shearer, *The Marriage Menders. Marriage and Divorce*. Edited by Christopher Macy. Pemberton Publishing Co., 1969.
13 J. H. Wallis. *Marriage Observed*. Routledge, 1970.
14 *Ibid*.

REFERENCES

15 *Ibid.*
16 Conservative Party Conference, Oct. 1954.
17 Pearl Jephcott, with Nancy Seear and John H. Smith, *Married Women Working*. Allen & Unwin, 1962.
18 *Ibid.*
19 Myrdal and Klein, *Women's Two Roles.*
20 *Married Women Working.*
21 *Daily Telegraph*, 13 Aug. 1953.
22 *The Times*, 15 April 1957.
23 Anthea Holme and Simon Yudkin, *Working Mothers and Their Children.* Michael Joseph, 1963.
24 *Ibid.*

Chapter 8: Emancipation

1 John Montgomery, *The Fifties*. Allen & Unwin, 1965.
2 W. Somerset Maugham, *The Breadwinner*. Vaudeville Theatre, 1930.
3 Peter Laurie, *Teenage Revolution*. Anthony Blond, 1965.
4 *Ibid.*
5 *Registrar-General's Report*, 1967.
6 *Ibid.*
7 *The Sunday Times*, 10 Dec. 1961.
8 *Ibid.*
9 *Finer Report on One-Parent Families*, 1974.
10 *Registrar-General's Report*, 1961.
11 *Finer Report*, Vol. I.
12 Chaucer, *The Clerk's Tale*, 1387.
13 *Women and Abortion*. Evidence to the Lane Commission, 1971.
14 *Finer Report.*
15 *Observer*, 21 Oct. 1962.
16 *Equality for Women*, Cmnd. 5724.
17 *Census*, 1961.
18 Brian Abel-Smith, A *History of the Nursing Profession.*
19 *Cosmopolitan*, March 1974.
20 *A.U.E.W. Journal*, August 1970.
21 Lewis Chester and Sarah Preston, *The Sunday Times*, 3 Feb. 1973.
22 *Ibid.*
23 T.U.C. Conference. *Office of Manpower Economics Report*, 18 Jan. 1973.

REFERENCES

Chapter 9: Women Alone

1 *Putting Asunder. Divorce Law for Contemporary Society.* S.P.C.K., 1966.
2 *Registrar-General's Report*, 1967.
3 Anna Coote and Tess Gill, *Women's Rights*. Penguin Special, 1974.
4 'How to Succeed as a Second Wife', *Over 21*, August 1972.
5 *Finer Report*, Vol. I.
6 *Ibid.*
7 *Ibid.*
8 *Finer Report*, Vol. II.
9 Margaret Wynn, *Fatherless Families*. Michael Joseph, 1964.
10 Dennis Marsden, *Mothers Alone*. Allen Lane, 1969.
11 Philip Inman, *No Going Back*. Williams & Norgate, 1952.
12 *Finer Report*, Vol. I.
13 *Ibid.*
14 A. P. Herbert, *Holy Deadlock*. Methuen, 1934.
15 Ruth Lister, *As Man and Wife? A Study of the Cohabitation Rule*. Child Poverty Action Group, 1972.
16 *Cosmopolitan*, March 1974.
17 *Ibid.*, Sept. 1974.
18 *Ibid.*
19 *Ibid.*
20 *Melanie*, 31 Aug. 1974.
21 Hans Retizels, *Little Red School-Book*. Forlag A/S, Copenhagen, 1971.
22 *Pink*, 31 Aug. 1974.
23 Betty Friedan, *Feminine Mystique*. Penguin Books, 1965.
24 Leonora Lloyd, *Women Workers in Britain*. Socialist Women Publications, 1972.
25 *Guardian*, 14 Feb. 1973.
26 *Discrimination Against Women*. Opposition Green Paper. Labour Party, 1973.
27 Juliet Mitchell, *Women's Estate*. Pelican Original, 1971.

INDEX

Abortion Act (1967), 268–70
Abrams, Mark, 259
Adoption Act (1926), 135
Agricultural Organisation Society, 65–6
Allen of Hurtwood, Lady, 224, 243
Amalgamated Engineering Union (A.E.U.), 178, 203, 206, 215, 230, 233, 278–9
Amalgamated Society of Engineers, 58
Ann Veronica, (Wells), 13, 14, 18, 179
Anomalies Regulations, 176–7
Answers to Correspondents, 51
Antic Hay (Huxley), 128
Apple-Cart, The (Shaw), 91–2, 149–50
Asquith, Herbert (Earl of Oxford and Asquith), 33–5, 38–9, 44, 53, 54, 83–4
Astor, Nancy, Lady, 90–3, 148–9
Atholl, Duchess of, 149, 150
A.T.S., 213
Autumn Crocus (Dodie Smith), 124–5
Ayrton-Gould, Barbara, 231

Back to Methuselah (Shaw), 118
Bacon, Alice, 231
Baldwin, Stanley, 191

Balfour, Lord, 52–3
Barnes, Sir George, 112
Barrie, James, 13, 18, 52, 116
'Bartimeus', 4–5
Beardmore, William, 60
Bennett, Arnold, 53, 130
Berkeley, Dr Comyns, 140–1
Besant, Annie, 10
Beveridge Report (1942), 220
Bevin, Ernest, 203–7, 232
Bill of Divorcement, A (Dane), 15
Bolton, Mrs Frances B., 223
Bondfield, Margaret, 87, 150–2
Bowlby, Dr John, 235–7, 256
Braddock, Bessie, 229
Bradlaugh, Charles, 10
British Broadcasting Corporation, 172–6
British Expeditionary Force: (1914), 48–9; (1939), 204
British Journal of Nursing, 70
Brittain, Vera, 26–7, 70–3, 116
Brooke, Rupert, 44
Burnham Committee on Teachers' Pay, 104, 141
Burton, Elaine, 201
Butler, Josephine, 78
Butler, R. A., 235, 253

INDEX

Cambridge University, 144
Candida (Shaw), 13
Caravanners, The (Russell), 13
Carmichael, Molly, 181
Castle, Barbara, 231, 277–9
Cathcart, Edward P., 63
Catholic Marriage Advisory Council, 248
Central Committee on Women's Training and Employment, 96, 99–100
Charles, Dr Enid, 184
Child Care and the Growth of Love (Bowlby), 236
Children Act (1948), 199, 240, 242
Children's Department, 240–2
Church of England, 78, 272, 284
Churchill, Winston, 35, 86, 95, 203–4, 208, 221
Civil Service, 136–7, 140, 175
Collis, Maurice, 92
Cooper, Lady Diana, 69–70
Cosmopolitan, 296
Coward, Noël, 4, 122, 123, 188
Crawford, Joan, 187
Cross, Colin, 161
Curtis Committee on Care of Children, 225, 240–1
Curzon, Lord, 84–5

Daily Herald, 51
Daily Mail, 54, 88
Daily Mirror, 51
Daily Telegraph, 174
Dane, Clemence, 6, 15, 190
Darkened Rooms (Gibbs), 116
Datchelor (Mary) School, 145, 274
Dawson of Penn, Lord, 126, 186–7
Deaconesses, Order of, 139
Decline and Fall (Waugh), 118

Delafield, E. M., 8, 131–2, 182–4
Diary of a Provincial Lady (Delafield), 182–3, 201
Divorce Reform Act (1969), 282
Don Juan in Hell (Shaw), 247
Dufferin and Ava, Marquis of, 108
Dusty Answer (Lehmann), 129–30

East London Federation of Working Women, 39
Education, Ministry of, 252
Education Act (1944), 214–5, 235, 273
Education of Girls, The (Newsom), 235
Edward VIII, 188
Ellis, H. Havelock, 118, 119, 120, 130, 250
Emergency Powers (Defence) Act (1941), 203
Engineer, 63
Equal Pay, Royal Commission on (1944), 215–9
Equal Pay Act (1970), 277–81
Equality for Women, White Paper on (1974), 303–4
Evening Standard, 91

Fairbanks, Douglas, Jr., 187–8
Family Allowances, 153, 220, 233–4
Family Welfare Association, 248
Fatherless Families (Wynne), 289–90
Fawcett, Millicent, 32, 41, 68, 84, 88
Feminine Mystique, The (Friedan), 299
Feminist Movement, The (Snowden), 16
Finer Committee and Report (1974), 82, 284, 286, 288, 292

INDEX

Fisher, H. A. L., 102
Fitzgerald, Admiral Penrose, 50
For Services Rendered (Maugham), 106
Ford's of Dagenham, 278, 300
French, Lord, 53
Freud, Sigmund, 118–9
Friedan, Betty, 299
Fugitive, The (Galsworthy), 19

Galsworthy, John, 14, 19
Garvin, J. L., 83
Gates, Reginald, 125
General Nursing Council, 107
Getting Married (Shaw), 14
Gibbs, Philip, 116
Gissing, George, 12, 18
Golding, Louis, 117–8
Good Housekeeping, 134
Gorell Commission on Divorce (1909), 14–15, 189, 282–3
Greenlaw Committee on Fatherless Families, 288
Greenwood, Walter, 159–60

Haig, Lord, 111
Haldane, Lord, 53
Hall, Radclyffe, 130–1
Hamilton, Mary Agnes, 149, 153, 175
Hamilton, Willie, 302–3
Handbook of Employment, 56
Hardie, Keir, 34, 38, 39
Hardy, Thomas, 15, 27, 45
Health, Ministry of, 198–200, 252
Hearts of Oak Friendly Society, 11
Herbert, A. P., 189–90, 272, 282–3, 295
Herbison, Margaret, 231

Hill, Sir Leonard, 185
Hobhouse, Maggie, 115
Hodson, Lord Justice, 286
Holland, Sidney, 30
Holme, Anthea, 256
Holy Deadlock (Herbert), 189–90
Home Notes, 51
Horrocks, Sir Brian, 43
Hubback, Judith, 234
Hull, E. M., 118
Huxley, Aldous, 128

'In Place of Strife', 278–9
In Which We Serve (film), 4
Inglis, Elsie, 47
Inman, Philip, 290–1
Inns of Court, 105

Jephcott, Pearl, 254
Jewson, Dorothy, 152
Joan of Arc, 155
Johnson, Amy, 154–5
Jude the Obscure (Hardy), 27
Justice (Galsworthy), 14

Kaye-Smith, Sheila, 75
Kenney, Annie, 33, 35, 87
King, Truby, 237
Kipling, Rudyard, 2, 44, 115
Kitchener, Lord, 48–9, 50, 52–4
Klein, Vera, 238, 255

Labour and National Security, Ministry of, 203–6
Lady, The, 45, 46, 111–2
Lady Chatterley's Lover (Lawrence), 121, 132–3, 271
Lancet, 196
Lancet Commission, 141
Lansbury, George, 34, 38, 39, 191

INDEX

Lawrence, D. H., 121, 132–3, 271
Lawrence, Susan, 94, 149–52
League of Nations, 192
Lee, Jennie, 153
Legal Aid and Advice Act (1949), 245
Lehmann, Rosamund, 129–30
Listener, The, 174
Little Red School-Book, 298
Living London (Woolmer), 22
Lloyd George, David, 38, 46, 52, 54–5, 57–60, 63–5, 67, 77, 84, 86–8, 167
London Society (later Service) for Women's Suffrage, 42, 56
Long, Walter, 68
Loughlin, Dame Anne, 216
Love on the Dole (Greenwood), 159–60

Macarthur, Mary, 20–1, 60, 86–7, 94, 98, 150, 152
Macaulay, Rose, 47–8
McCracken, Esther, 222
McGowan, Cathy, 258
Malthusian League, 127
Man and Superman (Shaw), 13
Man in the Making, A ('Bartimeus'), 4–5
Manchester Guardian, 153, 165, 174
Manchester Sunday Chronicle, 27
Manning, Leah, 150, 157
Manpower Economics, Office of, 281
'Many Sisters to Many Brothers' (Macaulay), 47–8
Markievicz, Countess, 89–90
Marriage and Divorce, Royal Commission on (1951), 246–8

Marriage Guidance Council, 248–51
Married Love (Stopes), 126
Married Women's Property Acts, 8–9
Marsden, Dennis, 290–1
Mass-Observation, 209–10, 250, 254–5
Maternal Deprivation and Mental Health (Bowlby), 236
Matheson, Hilda, 174
Matrimonial Causes Act: (1923), 128 ; (1937–'Herbert Act'), 15, 190, 247, 272; (1973), 282–3
Maugham, W. Somerset, 106, 111, 258
Mead, Margaret, 237–8
Means Test, 158–9
Methodist Church, 271
Middle Temple, Inns of Court, 105
Mild Oats (Coward), 123–4
Moral Welfare Homes, 64, 78, 80
Muggeridge, Malcolm, 193
Munitions of War (Amendment) Bill (1915), 58
Murray, Gilbert, 44
Myra, 10
Myrdal, Alva, 238, 255

Nash, Mrs Vaughan, 82
National Association of Schoolmasters, 216
National Birthday Trust Fund, 161
National Council for the Unmarried Mother and her Child, 82–4
National Council of Women, 256
National Federation of Women Workers, 20, 60, 150, 152
National Health Service, 220

INDEX

National League for Opposing Women's Suffrage, 35
National Service (No. 2) Act (1941), 205
National Union of General and Municipal Workers (N.U.G.M.W.), 203, 206,
National Union of Teachers, 28–9
National Union of Women Teachers, 28–9
National Union of Women's Suffrage Societies, 32
Nettlefold, Miss L. F., 216
Neuve-Chapelle, battle of (1915), 31, 52–3, 76
'New Look', 227–8
New Statesman, 43
New York Tribune, 42
News Chronicle, 178–9, 186
Newsom, John, 235, 274
Nicolson, Harold, 129
No Medals (McCracken), 222
Northcliffe, Lord, 56, 83, 87–8
Nurses' Registration Act (1919), 31
Nursing, College of, 107
Nursery Nurse training colleges, 170
Nursing Times, 70

O'Neill, Dennis, 243
Old Lady Shows Her Medals, The (Barrie), 52
Other Side, The (Vachell), 115
Oxford University, 144, 191

Pankhurst, Christabel, 32–4, 38–40, 42, 87–8
Pankhurst, Emmeline, 32–4, 38–40, 77

Pankhurst, Sylvia, 32, 39, 43, 85, 88, 91
Parliament (Qualification of Women) Act (1910), 86, 91, 136, 139
Peace Ballot, 190–2
Peace Pledge Union, 191
Philipson, Mabel, 149
Pill, the, 263–4
Pine, Sister C. E., 77
Poor Law Act (1930), 241
Population, Royal Commission on (1949), 184–5, 234
Poverty and the Welfare State (Rowntree and Layers), 252
Priestley, J. B., 43, 163
Prince of Wales Fund for the Relief of the Unemployed, 4
Psychology of Sex, The (Ellis), 118
Punch, 12–13, 69
Putting Asunder, 272

Quakers, 271–2

Race Relations Acts (1965 and 1968), 302
Rathbone, Eleanor, 153, 220, 233
Ravensdale, Lord, 196
Reconstruction Committee, 80, 82, 94
Reeves, Amber, 14
Registration for Employment Order (1941), 205
Reith, Lord, 173
Rhondda, Lady, 97–8, 183
Ridealgh, Mabel, 228
Roe, Humphrey, 126
Royal British Nurses Association, 107

INDEX

Royden, Dr Maude, 121–2, 202
Russell, Lord, 31
Russell, Elizabeth, Countess, 13

Sackville-West, Vita, 129
Sassoon, Siegfried, 117
School Friend, The, 146–7
Schoolgirls' Own, The, 146–7
Settle, Mary Lee, 210–12
Sex Disqualification (Removal) Act (1919), 29, 105, 136, 139, 302
Shaw, Bernard, 10, 13, 14, 53, 91–2, 118, 149, 155–6, 230, 247
Sheik, The (Hull), 118, 121
Sheppard, Dick, 191
Short v. Poole Corporation, 140
Snowden, Ethel, 16, 20–1, 87, 172–3
Somerville, Mary, 173, 175
Sometimes Even Now (Chetham-Strode), 76
'Song of the Soldiers' (Hardy), 45
Stanley, Sir Arthur, 107
Stark v. Stark and Hitchins, 13–14
Stevenson, Frances, 52–3, 77, 92–3
Stopes, Marie, 125–7
Store of Ladies (Golding), 117
Strachey, Ray, 32, 40, 88, 98
Suffragette, The, 40, 42
Summerskill, Dr Edith, 208, 231, 284
Sunday Express, 130
Sunday Times, 279
Supplementary Benefits Commission, 292–5
Swanwick, Helena, 60

Terrington, Lady, 149
Testament of Youth (Brittain), 26–7, 70–72

Thank Heaven Fasting (Delafield), 8
Times, The, 46, 62, 91, 169–70, 194–5, 196, 201, 209
Times Educational Supplement, The, 26, 102–3, 144
To See Ourselves (Delafield), 183–4
Towards a Quaker View of Sex, 271–2
Transport and General Workers' Union (T.G.W.), 203, 206
Trefusis, Violet, 129
T.U.C. conference on Equal Pay (1973), 279–81
T.U.C. General Council, 305
Twelve-Pound Look, The (Barrie), 18
Twilight of Parenthood, The (Charles), 184

Unemployment Assistance Board, 158
Unemployment Insurance Fund, 158

Vachell, H. A., 115
V.A.D.s (Voluntary Aid Detachments), 68–72, 107
Vaughan, Dr Janet, 216
Venereal Diseases, Commission on, 80
Vile Bodies (Waugh), 128
'Volunteer, The' (Asquith), 44

W.A.A.F., 210–12
Wages of Men and Women, The: Should They Be Equal? (Webb), 109–10
Wallis, J. H., 249
War Committee on Women in Industry, 94
Ward, Mrs Humphrey, 32, 84
Waugh, Evelyn, 118, 128
Weatherhead, Dr Leslie, 261

INDEX

Webb, Beatrice, 9–10, 32, 53, 61, 86, 109–10, 115, 151, 166, 220
Webb, Sidney, 10, 220
Well of Loneliness, The (Hall), 130–1
Well-Remembered Voice, A (Barrie), 116
Wells, H. G., 13, 14, 18
What Every Woman Knows (Barrie), 13
Where the Rainbow Ends (Mills and Ramsay), 3–4
White, Eirene, 272
Whose Children?, 224
Wife's Handbook, 10
Wilbaut, Mrs, 16
Wilkinson, Ellen, 92, 152–3
Wintringham, Mrs, 148–9
Wise Parenthood (Stopes), 126
Wives Who Went to College (Hubback), 234
Woman and Beauty, 181
Woman's Book, The, 17, 20, 23
Woman's Dreadnought, The, 43
Women's Employment Federation, 201
Women's Industrial League, 97
Women's Institutes, 65–6
Women's Leader, The, 172
Women's League of Health and Beauty, 182
'Women's Lib', 269, 284, 299–307
Women's Social and Political Union, 33–40
Women's Suffrage Act (1918), 29
Woolmer, D. L., 22
Working Mothers and Their Children (Yudkin and Holme), 256
Working Women and the Suffrage (Wilbaut), 16
Wynne, Margaret, 289–90

Yudkin, Simon, 256

AFTERWORD

In 1975, when *A Woman's Place* was first published, no matter what the difference in class or wealth or education, the majority of women shared a common experience: they were treated by the male Establishment as second class citizens. On the threshold of the twenty-first century, for one group in particular, that is no more. In the year 2000, many a young twenty-something, child-free, professional female will say she is living in the era of post-feminism. What that means for her, is that the battle of the sexes is over. Equality has been won. She may earn more than her male colleagues; she expects promotion as her due; she may tell you that she rarely, if ever, encounters sexism; she is treated as one of the boys. She sleeps with whom she chooses; she behaves exactly as the lads do - and heeds no murmur of disapproval. She has choice on a scale unknown to her mother and grandmother before her. She is having the time of her life. The difficulty is that she believes it will always be that way.

The only problem with some younger women, said the American feminist Gloria Steinam, speaking in the Eighties, is that they have yet to realise there is a problem. Survey after

AFTERWORD

survey on the state of British women reveals contradictory and conflicting evidence not least because of society's continuing contrary expectations of how a modern woman should behave. At the beginning of the twenty-first century, for women in their thirties and older, the most striking template is more likely to be exhaustion rather than emancipation. Many females blame feminism because they now face what American sociologist Arlie Hochschild labelled in 1987, The Double Shift. They carry the burden of both home and work: a strange kind of Liberation. Yet, they also continue to have faith in their right to have a life outside the house no matter how tough the challenge. In one recent survey, only 12% of parents expressed a wish to be at home full time.

Twenty-five years after Ruth Adam wrote her book almost each and every woman, no matter her initial optimism, will reach a point when she realises that as long as she squeezes her needs into the male mould that has prevailed for decades, equality of sorts is hers. She is allowed to join the system – but not to change it. And radical change is still what is desperately required. Without it, a woman finds herself instantly handicapped by her gender when, for example, in work, she moves from being childless to becoming a mother, or when a less qualified male colleague is promoted over her head not because she has children but because she might; or when she finds herself a divorcee with a young family reliant on benefits.

In some ways, the divorcee, for instance, is more pressured now than in 1975. In the year 2000 emancipation may have freed a woman from a rotten relationship but it has also delivered her into a society in which, still, the value of caring is infinitely lower than the appreciation of productivity in the labour market. In 1975, she would have been deemed a good mother for staying at home, however impoverished. A quarter of a century later, in the same circumstances, she is deemed as bad because the New Labour government interprets duty as primarily the duty to enter paid work. Yet, if she does take up employment, she opens herself to fresh criticism on a different front. This time she will be blamed if her children's academic standards flag – as if fathers have no culpability. So how does she decide whom to satisfy? Traditional expectations? Modern political demands? Or her own instincts – no matter that this may mean life on the breadline?

Alongside these conundrums, over the past couple of decades, the differences between women have been glossed over but they remain as marked as ever. Less than half a million females pay tax at the top rate – yet it is their style of life and standard of living, their aspirations which flood the media and create the myth that women, all women, have never had it so good. According to research conducted on behalf of the the government's women's unit, over 45% of women have under £100 a week individual income compared with 20% of men. Worst hit of all, of course, are lone mothers, who now number a million (this represents 20% of all parents, a massive increase from 8% in 1971). They care for three million children, the majority of whom live in or close to poverty because benefits are set too low – around a

AFTERWORD

miserable £120 a week in the year 2000 for a mother and two children.

Twenty-five years ago, as Ruth Adam records, the nuclear family – father in paid work; mother the home-maker – was already splintering. Matrimony has since dropped to its lowest rate since the early 1940s while, if present trends continue, four in ten marriages will end in divorce (although the rate of divorce has begun to plateau); cohabitation is widespread bringing with it an even higher rate of break-up. One in three births take place outside of marriage. The pessimist's view is that women have become too selfish to allow marriage to survive. And they have paid a price.

Britain has 3.8m women in their thirties – a quarter of whom are single or divorced. The Old Maid has transformed into the *seule femme*, also known as Bridget Jones or the waif-like man-obsessed TV lawyer, Ally McBeal. I do not think there is an answer, she says of her fruitless attempts to have it all, just anxiety and conflict. Except that surveys indicate that for many twenty-first century spinsters, a man at any price is no longer the only aim of life; happily, it offers other interests too.

In contrast, an optimist reads the last thirty years as a period of transition. Marriage has moved from an institution in which women often contributed far more than they received, to a relationship negotiated between two people, living as a team. We are marrying later (at around 28) and having our first child at around 30, which means we bring more maturity and experience to the endeavour. Simultaneously, the fragility of marriage has helped girls with

AFTERWORD

aspirations to realise that self-sufficiency is not just the badge of the sisterhood, it is every woman's vital tool if she is to survive the vicissitudes of modern life. Marriage, today, is based on romance with realism.

Over the past three decades insecurity in relationships has been matched by insecurity in work. In the Seventies and Eighties the massive slump in traditional industries such as mining, manufacturing and shipbuilding meant that the pressure increased on wives to earn, not for pin money but to keep the family afloat. At the same time, companies began to realise that by undervaluing female talent, they were overlooking the potential of half the population; while those women and their children who had reaped the benefit of the Sixties educational reforms were – and still are – hungry to do better.

The proportion of young women achieving two or more A levels or their equivalent has doubled since the mid-70s to 25%, and nearly three-quarters of young women aged 16 in 1997/8 are in full-time education. For several years, women have made up half or more of the student intake for the major professions. Each of these tributaries of change have wound their way into a single fast flowing river which has created society's single most significant catalyst – the influx of women, particularly mothers, into the labour market.

In 1973 only 27% of mothers with a child under five worked. By 1998, the figure had risen to 75% among the highly qualified and 55% of those with few or no qualifications. Women now make up 68% of the workforce (11.4m) but half are part-time (compared with 8% of men). Ironically, employment – a test bed for equality – has delivered the most damning evidence yet that even in the twenty-first century, Britain is a man's world to which women are invited – and are duly penalised. This is particularly demonstrated in three vital areas – in the (lack of) cash in women's pockets; in the dearth of career opportunities; and in the absence of appropriate child care.

According to research conducted by the London School of Economics published in 2000, a woman who chooses not to have children and competes equally with men will still earn £100,000 less over a lifetime. A mother pays a female forfeit of a quarter of a million pounds. In 1975 the top 10% female earners received 59.7% of their male colleagues salaries. By 1999, that had crawled up to 62.7%. Part-time women earn only 60% of the full time male rate; full time women are given 80%. So, in 2000, non-manual men earn £525 per week, women £346; while in the higher echelons male administrators are paid £16.78 an hour and women receive £12.19. Identical job, different genders.

If women do not earn adequately, they suffer in old age. Female incomes in retirement are half those of men; only one in three part-timers has an occupational pension. The new stakeholder pension for those earning between £9,000 and £20,000 will permit a woman to continue to pay into her pension, tax free, even when she has time out from work, for instance, to have a child. What is also required is government help with these contributions, and a far tougher Equal Pay Act.

Women are not just penalised financially. In 1999,

AFTERWORD

Whitehall announced it wanted to raise the percentage of women in top positions from 7% to 20% in five years. Talented women have become stuck in middle management unable to break the glass ceiling, or they have melted away in spite of measures such as job shares and career breaks. The same pattern repeats itself in other sectors too. For instance, in 1998, women comprised only 3.6% of directors and 18% of executives. Is it simply that they are unable to hack it? Each time a star female announces she is leaving the competitive field, the media celebrates. In 1997 Brenda Barnes left her $2m a year job as head of Pepsi Cola's North American division. I am not leaving because my children need more of me, she explained, I am leaving because I need more of them. She and other women have been rebelling against the rampant workaholism which is so much bound up in masculine identity: the insistence that the emotional needs of the family should have low priority and the traditional definition of success should be one entirely identified with achievements in the public arena.

Junior women also remove themselves from the fray because they have a radically different way of operating – one which fails to please the male gatekeepers, who promote according to different criteria. Professor Beverly Alimo-Metcalfe, who specialises in the study of leadership, points out the differences between the traditional masculine model (often adopted by women) – isolated, authoritarian, poor consultation, little delegation – and the transformational female style, (increasingly part of American management techniques) – more collaborative, team-orientated, seeks advice, desists from pulling rank, praises rather than intimidates. Put one with the other and the male will fail to rate the woman while the latter thinks he is a bull-shitter. But, since he is the boss, she leaves.

Childcare or, more precisely, the assumption that childcare is women's business, is, of course, the weakest rung in women's ladder of opportunity. In the Eighties, when the Conservatives ruled under Margaret Thatcher, childcare, clouded in ambivalence about whether mothers should work at all, was treated as a private problem for the individual parent to solve. New Labour, elected in 1997, is the first government to treat it as a public concern. It is committed to ensuring there is affordable, accessible, high quality childcare for all those who require it, placing the issue at the centre of its economic strategy; a position taken by many other European countries years ago.

A National Childcare Strategy is under way alongside the reworking of taxes and benefits to give lower income families more financial support, including help with childcare costs. (Childcare – at between £100-£300 a week – makes paupers of us all, even the middle classes, who receive no help.) Investment has also been promised for training and provision and inspection. Still, two major difficulties remain: the sheer scale of the undertaking and New Labour's reluctance to pressure employers to do more.

Elsewhere in the EU, child care is a tripartite effort – parents, government and employers. Here, only 5% of employers contribute to childcare costs; 5% offer a workplace nursery and 2% offer reserved nursery places. In addition, half of all childcare staff are untrained; turnover is high and pay (because mainly women are hired) is desperately low. Again, the value of caring needs to be raised. (In Norway, for instance, the goal is to attract more men into the profession, increasing wages as well as changing the image of caring as a women-only domain.)

The danger in the twenty-first century is that choice will be narrowed rather than widened. Ironically, exactly like the traditional male breadwinner in the decades before, more and more women will be propelled into full time paid work against their own judgment when the network of paid childcare is poor or nonexistent – and some mothers (or fathers) would prefer, for a particular period in a child's upbringing, to remain at home.

The promise of feminism, said the American commentator Barbara Ehrenreich in the Eighties, is that there might be a future in which no adult person is either a dependent creature or an overburdened breadwinner. Ironically, for several years, one of the greatest sources of support for this increased flexibility has come from fathers – at least in their rhetoric if not their actions. One not untypical survey, for instance, indicated that almost a quarter of fathers would like to work less even if it damaged their careers (compared with 18% of women). According to research conducted by Professor Charlie Lewis of Lancaster University in the late Nineties, the father who is least happy is the one who works full time and is also striving to have more involvement with his children. He is mirroring the experience of his over-employed wife.

AFTERWORD

Margaret Hodge, a Government Minister, has said that Work-Life issues are a concern whose time has come. Still, a system designed sixty years ago around the idea of the male breadwinner and the wife at home is proving resistant to change. This is partly because employers are reluctant to accept that family friendly policies are also good for profits; unions no longer have the clout to drive change and although New Labour has promised action in areas such as paid parental leave, career structures for part-timers and improved maternity and paternity benefits – it has yet properly to deliver. In addition, still too many fathers (and an increasing number of mothers) insist on being the last man in the office.

Early in 2000 a women's magazine conducted a survey of 5,000 women: 77% believed career stress damaged their health; 80% said full time working emotionally damaged their children; and only 23% were happy with their career. A survey conducted by the University of Bristol indicated that, after having a child, 17% of working mothers move to part-time work, while 19% give up altogether within two years of returning to employment, worn out by the effort of trying to fit a woman's extra commitments (including supporting elderly relatives) into a man's world.

In May 2000 a MORI poll was published at the same time as Leo Blair was born, the fourth child of the Prime Minister and his wife, Cherie Booth. It indicated that 75% do not believe women have sufficient access to affordable child care. Cherie Booth has pronounced herself a defender of the right to family life. At the same time, New Labour needs to hold on to its women voters if it is to win power for a second term – so

AFTERWORD

perhaps, twenty-five years hence, the system may have finally been given its belated overhaul. In the meantime, as in the past, women are having to seek their own solutions.

One in four women is opting not to have a child – whether this is because of infertility or genuine choice or because they believe motherhood is incompatible with a career is unclear. A growing minority are delaying childbirth until their late thirties and forties. As a result, one in eighty women is now seeking IVF treatment, a gruelling and punishing route to pregnancy with a low rate of success. Reproductive control, permitted by the arrival of The Pill and other forms of contraception, has begun to reveal a hidden price. Women's experience of pregnancy, however, has been hugely varied.

Britain, for instance, has the highest rate of teenage pregnancy in the western world, apart from the USA. Babies are born to girls who have no qualifications, little self-esteem and who welcome premature motherhood because at least it means they matter to someone – but they become parents on almost no income and with little prospect of improving their situation in later life. Several government initiatives are now targeting the problem but the old adage remains true: aspiration is the best contraception.

The female experience of employment since the Seventies has given what the feminist academic, Lynne Segal, calls the genetic fundamentalists a rich source of propaganda. They treat it as proof that the woman's natural place is in the home. Furthermore, they argue that the current alleged crisis in masculinity has been triggered precisely because women have feminised men into domesticity and manoeuvred them out of their rightful roles as undisputed head of the family, chief hunter and sexual predator. Men are doing worse, they say, because women are performing better.

As proof, the finger is pointed at concerns such as boys' poorer academic results, the crime rate of young men and their higher incidence of suicide. Feminism is blamed but modern capitalism is a far more likely culprit. As academics such as Richard Sennett have pointed out in *The Corrosion of Character*, the system now expects the average man to work even harder and change jobs up to a dozen times; it values the young (and cheaper) over the old; it has no use for the unskilled and it shows no pity when it prematurely discards men who live for their work. In the Fifties, women were forced or opted to find alternative roles to that of the full-time mother. Half a century later, it is men who are facing the challenge of redefining masculinity so that it means more than the wage the man earns and a stoic refusal to show emotion.

Such is the continuing force of anti-feminist polemic, however, some women do blame themselves for what they see as the plight of British men. Sue Tibballs, for her pamphlet, *The Sexual Renaissance: Making Sense of Sex Difference in a New Era*, discovered from market research that women's guilt means that they repudiate feminism all the more speedily. Even so, she says, they are united in seeing themselves as outsiders in a persistent male culture resistant to their skills, contributions and needs.

In spite of the disavowal of feminism since the Seventies

AFTERWORD

many women have worked together, forging links with women in the Third World too, at times helped by male allies, to make both their own unique mark (for instance, in 1980, against the presence of American cruise missiles at Greenham Common); as well as launching significant challenges to the Establishment's prejudices, practices, laws and customs. As a result, what were once feminist goals have now become mainstream practice. To offer only a few examples – the increasing recognition by the police and the courts of the seriousness of domestic violence and of rape, sexual harassment and child abuse; the ordination of Anglican women priests; the acknowledgement that women of colour and lesbians have different as well as overlapping goals in the fight for equality; and the arrival of 101 Labour women MPs in the House of Commons after the 1997 General Election.

This last achievement was only made possible as a result of the campaign by female activists for women only parliamentary candidates lists, subsequently declared illegal. (In spite of the arrival of the patronisingly labelled Blair's Babes, the face of politics at Westminster and in government remains unmodernised and almost entirely male. Furthermore, the number of Labour women MPs is likely to decline at the next election without further positive discrimination.) Women make up 18% of the total number of MPs at Westminster but they are are much more strongly represented in the Scottish Parliament (37%) and the Welsh Assembly (40%).

In the Seventies some feminists argued that women were inherently nicer, more compassionate, an altogether higher quality of human being than men; female virtue was pitched against masculine evil. This argument has been undermined by the behaviour of some of the few women who have tasted power. Other feminists insisted women were the same as men – only denied an opportunity to fulfil their destiny. At the beginning of a new century the focus has shifted again to a recognition of the differences between men and women, as well as their similarities.

What has prevailed in the UK for the past twenty-five years is the idea of formal equality, treating the genders identically. What is growing in popularity is the concept of substantive equality, already adopted in Canada. What does that mean in practice? In Britain, under the 1975 Sex Discrimination Act, individuals are protected from discrimination in employment, education and advertising. A tribunal decides if the case is justified and awards compensation. In contrast, the aim of the Canadian courts is not to blame and punish the individual perpetrator of discrimination but to remedy the situation.

Canadian National Railways, for instance, gave only 1% of blue collar jobs to women. The court ordered changes to recruitment policy and the introduction of a quota system (illegal here). It argued that a critical mass of women was essential to provide a significant chance for the self-correction of the system. A Charter of Rights and Freedoms, established in 1982, incorporated this concept of substantive equality. Two decades later, one precedent after another has been set with fear of litigation speeding the process of change throughout the system. In Britain, we too need a bill of rights, a stronger Sex Discrimination Act and a fresh definition of equality. We need a catalyst. . . .

AFTERWORD

At the beginning of a new century, modern capitalism and feminism have unconsciously united to subvert the traditional stereotypes while demanding much greater flexibility in work and home. We have both house husbands and women who are the sole breadwinner. A woman may move through many phases in one life time from career woman to full time mother to part-time worker to becoming her own boss. Such transitions should be available to men too without either male or female paying a massive penalty in terms of the progress of their careers or the loss of financial security in old age. As part of that change, the importance of the role of caring for others has to be recognised, and properly valued.

Gender too is no longer so rigidly defined – women drink, smoke and fight while real men spend more on perfumery for themselves than ever before and footballers unabashedly wear a sarong. Some modern feminists now argue that women's (and men's) possibilities for happiness, and their development as human beings, are linked to society's reshaping. It is a dynamic process which requires a constant struggle to find the balance between collective co-operation, personal fulfilment, care for others and competitive individualism.

The struggle goes on.

Yvonne Roberts
London, 2000

If you have enjoyed this Persephone Book why not telephone or write to us for details of our other titles, in print and forthcoming?

PERSEPHONE BOOKS LTD
28 Great Sutton Street
London EC1V 0DS

Telephone: 020 7253 5454
Fax: 020 7253 5656
sales@persephonebooks.co.uk
www.persephonebooks.co.uk

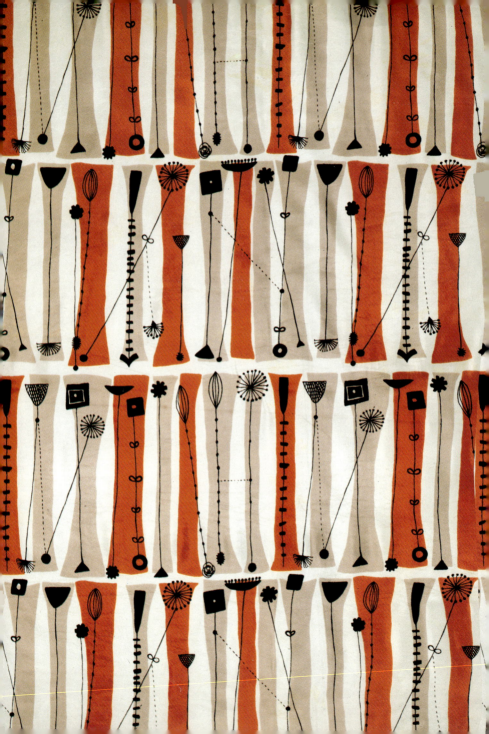